A HISTORY *of the* WORLD *in* 6 GLASSES

A HISTORY of the WORLD

in 6 GLASSES

TOM STANDAGE

ANCHOR CANADA

LIBRARY AND ARCHIVES CANADA CATALOGUING IN PUBLICATION

Standage, Tom
A history of the world in 6 glasses / Tom Standage.

Includes bibliographical references and index.
ISBN-13: 978-0-385-66087-7
ISBN-10: 0-385-66087-1

1. Beverages—History. 2. Alcoholic beverages—History.
3. Tea—History. 4. Coffee—History. 5. Cola drinks—History.
I. Title.

GT2880.S73 2006   394.1'2   C2006-901541-4

Art credits: Page 11, the University of Pennsylvania Museum; the original object is in
the Iraq Museum (IM # 25048). Pages 12 and 34, created by the author. Pages 33, 36,
and 45, © copyright the Trustees of The British Museum. Pages 63 (engraving based on
bust in the Uffizi Gallery, Florence), 189 (engraving after Sir Peter Lely), and 227,
(engraving by W. Holl after a picture by Gilbert Stewart), the Mary Evans Picture
Library. Pages 122 and 125, North Wind Picture Archives. Pages 237, 243, and 254,
courtesy of The Coca-Cola Company. Page 259, Vice President Nixon in Russia and
Poland 1959 (photos); Series 1959 U.S.S.R. Trip Photographs;
Pre-Presidential Papers of Richard M. Nixon; courtesy of the
National Archives—Pacific Region (Laguna Niguel).

Book design: Chris Welch
Printed and bound in Canada

Published in Canada by
Anchor Canada, a division of
Random House of Canada Limited

Visit Random House of Canada Limited's website: www.randomhouse.ca

TRANS   10   9   8   7   6   5   4   3   2

To my parents

Contents

Contents

Coffee in the Age of Reason

Tea and the British Empire

Coca-Cola and the Rise of America

Introduction

Vital Fluids

There is no history of mankind, there are only many histories of all kinds of aspects of human life.—*Karl Popper, philosopher of science (1902–94)*

T HIRST IS DEADLIER than hunger. Deprived of food, you might survive for a few weeks, but deprived of liquid refreshment, you would be lucky to last more than a few days. Only breathing matters more. Tens of thousands of years ago, early humans foraging in small bands had to remain near rivers, springs, and lakes to ensure an adequate supply of freshwater, since storing or carrying it was impractical. The availability of water constrained and guided humankind's progress. Drinks have continued to shape human history ever since.

Only in the past ten thousand years or so have other beverages emerged to challenge the preeminence of water. These drinks do not occur naturally in any quantity but must be made deliberately. As well as offering safer alternatives to contaminated, disease-ridden water supplies in human settlements, these new beverages have taken on a variety of roles. Many of them have been used as currencies, in religious rites, as political symbols, or as sources of philosophical and artistic inspiration. Some have served to highlight the power and status of the elite, and others to subjugate or appease the downtrodden. Drinks have been used to celebrate births, commemorate deaths, and forge and strengthen social bonds; to seal business transactions and treaties; to sharpen the senses or dull the mind; to convey lifesaving medicines and deadly poisons.

As the tides of history have ebbed and flowed, different drinks have come to prominence in different times, places, and cultures, from stone-age villages to ancient Greek dining rooms or Enlightenment coffeehouses. Each one became popular when it met a particular need or aligned with a historical trend; in some cases, it then went on to influence the course of history in unexpected ways. Just as archaeologists divide history into different periods based on the use of different materials—the stone age, the bronze age, the iron age, and so on—it is also possible to divide world history into periods dominated by different drinks. Six beverages in particular—beer, wine, spirits, coffee, tea, and cola—chart the flow of world history. Three contain alcohol, and three contain caffeine, but what they all have in common is that each one was the defining drink during a pivotal historical period, from antiquity to the present day.

The event that set humankind on the path toward modernity was the adoption of farming, beginning with the domestication of cereal grains, which first took place in the Near East around ten thousand years ago and was accompanied by the appearance of a rudimentary form of beer. The first civilizations arose around five thousand years later in Mesopotamia and Egypt, two parallel cultures founded on a surplus of cereal grains produced by organized agriculture on a massive scale. This freed a small fraction of the population from the need to work in the fields and made possible the emergence of specialist priests, administrators, scribes, and craftsmen. Not only did beer nourish the inhabitants of the first cities and the authors of the first written documents, but their wages and rations were paid in bread and beer, as cereal grains were the basis of the economy.

The flourishing culture that developed within the city-states of ancient Greece in the first millennium BCE spawned advances in philosophy, politics, science, and literature that still underpin modern Western thought. Wine was the lifeblood of this Mediterranean civilization, and the basis of vast seaborne trade that helped to spread Greek ideas far and wide. Politics, poetry, and philosophy were discussed at formal drinking parties, or *symposia,* in which the participants drank from a shared bowl of diluted wine. The spread of wine drinking continued under the Romans, the structure of whose hierarchical society was reflected in a minutely calibrated pecking order of wines and wine styles. Two of the world's major religions issued opposing verdicts on the drink: The Christian ritual of the Eucharist has wine at its center, but following the collapse of the Roman Empire and the rise of Islam, wine was banned in the very region of its birth.

The rebirth of Western thought a millennium after the fall of

Rome was sparked by the rediscovery of Greek and Roman knowledge, much of which had been safeguarded and extended by scholars in the Arab world. At the same time, European explorers, driven by the desire to circumvent the Arab monopoly on trade with the East, sailed west to the Americas and east to India and China. Global sea routes were established, and European nations vied with one another to carve up the globe. During this Age of Exploration a new range of beverages came to the fore, made possible by distillation, an alchemical process known in the ancient world but much improved by Arab scholars. Distilled drinks provided alcohol in a compact, durable form ideal for sea transport. Such drinks as brandy, rum, and whiskey were used as currency to buy slaves and became particularly popular in the North American colonies, where they became so politically contentious that they played a key role in the establishment of the United States.

Hard on the heels of this geographic expansion came its intellectual counterpart, as Western thinkers looked beyond long-held beliefs inherited from the Greeks and devised new scientific, political, and economic theories. The dominant drink of this Age of Reason was coffee, a mysterious and fashionable beverage introduced to Europe from the Middle East. The establishments that sprung up to serve coffee had a markedly different character from taverns that sold alcoholic drinks, and became centers of commercial, political, and intellectual exchange. Coffee promoted clarity of thought, making it the ideal drink for scientists, businessmen, and philosophers. Coffeehouse discussions led to the establishment of scientific societies, the founding of newspapers, the establishment of financial institutions, and provided fertile ground for revolutionary thought, particularly in France.

In some European nations, and particularly in Britain, coffee was challenged by tea imported from China. Its popularity in Europe helped to open lucrative trade routes with the East and underpinned imperialism and industrialization on an unprecedented scale, enabling Britain to become the first global superpower. Once tea had established itself as Britain's national drink, the desire to maintain the tea supply had far-reaching effects on British foreign policy, contributing to the independence of the United States, the undermining of China's ancient civilization, and the establishment of tea production in India on an industrial scale.

Although artificially carbonated beverages originated in Europe in the late eighteenth century, the soft drink came into its own with the invention of Coca-Cola one hundred years later. Originally devised as a medicinal pick-me-up by an Atlanta pharmacist, it became America's national drink, an emblem of the vibrant consumer capitalism that helped to transform the United States into a superpower. Traveling alongside American servicemen as they fought wars around the world during the twentieth century, Coca-Cola went on to become the world's most widely known and distributed product and is now an icon of the controversial march toward a single global marketplace.

Drinks have had a closer connection to the flow of history than is generally acknowledged, and a greater influence on its course. Understanding the ramifications of who drank what, and why, and where they got it from, requires the traversal of many disparate and otherwise unrelated fields: the histories of agriculture, philosophy, religion, medicine, technology, and commerce. The six beverages highlighted in this book demonstrate the complex interplay of different civilizations and the interconnectedness of world cultures. They survive in our homes today as living reminders of bygone eras, fluid testaments to the forces that shaped the modern world. Uncover their origins, and you may never look at your favorite drink in quite the same way again.

BEER *in* MESOPOTAMIA *and* EGYPT

1

A Stone-Age Brew

Fermentation and civilization are inseparable.
—*John Ciardi, American poet (1916–86)*

A Pint of Prehistory

THE HUMANS WHO migrated out of Africa starting around 50,000 years ago traveled in small nomadic bands, perhaps thirty strong, and lived in caves, huts, or skin tents. They hunted game, caught fish and shellfish, and gathered edible plants, moving from one temporary camp to another to exploit seasonal food supplies. Their tools included bows and arrows, fishhooks, and needles. But then, starting around 12,000 years ago, a remarkable shift occurred. Humans in the Near East abandoned the old hunter-gatherer lifestyle of the Paleolithic period (old stone age) and began to take up farming instead, settling down in villages which eventually grew to become the world's first cities. They also developed many new technologies, including pottery, wheeled vehicles, and writing.

9

Beer in Mesopotamia and Egypt

Ever since the emergence of "anatomically modern" humans, or *Homo sapiens sapiens*, in Africa around 150,000 years ago, water had been humankind's basic drink. A fluid of primordial importance, it makes up two-thirds of the human body, and no life on Earth can exist without it. But with the switch from the hunter-gatherer lifestyle to a more settled way of life, humans came to rely on a new beverage derived from barley and wheat, the cereal grains that were the first plants to be deliberately cultivated. This drink became central to social, religious, and economic life and was the staple beverage of the earliest civilizations. It was the drink that first helped humanity along the path to the modern world: beer.

Exactly when the first beer was brewed is not known. There was almost certainly no beer before 10,000 BCE, but it was widespread in the Near East by 4000 BCE, when it appears in a pictogram from Mesopotamia, a region that corresponds to modern-day Iraq, depicting two figures drinking beer through reed straws from a large pottery jar. (Ancient beer had grains, chaff, and other debris floating on its surface, so a straw was necessary to avoid swallowing them.)

Since the first examples of writing date from around 3400 BCE, the earliest written documents can shed no direct light on beer's origins. What is clear, however, is that the rise of beer was closely associated with the domestication of the cereal grains from which it is made and the adoption of farming. It came into existence during a turbulent period in human history that witnessed the switch from a nomadic to a settled lifestyle, followed by a sudden increase in social complexity manifested most strikingly in the emergence of cities. Beer is a liquid relic from human

A pictogram from a seal found at Tepe Gawra in Mesopotamia dating from around 4000 BCE. It shows two figures drinking beer through straws from a large pottery jar.

prehistory, and its origins are closely intertwined with the origins of civilization itself.

The Discovery of Beer

Beer was not invented but discovered. Its discovery was inevitable once the gathering of wild grains became widespread after the end of the last ice age, around 10,000 BCE, in a region known as the Fertile Crescent. This area stretches from modern-day Egypt, up the Mediterranean coast to the southeast corner of Turkey, and then down again to the border between Iraq and Iran. It is so named because of a happy accident of geography. When the ice age ended, the uplands of the region provided an ideal environment for wild sheep, goats, cattle, and pigs—and, in some areas, for dense stands of wild wheat and barley. This meant the Fertile Crescent provided unusually rich pickings for

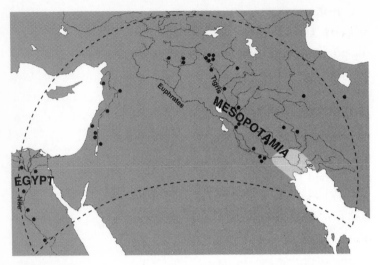

The Fertile Crescent, a region of the Near East where humans first took up farming and established large-scale settlements (shown here as black dots)

roving bands of human hunter-gatherers. They not only hunted animals and gathered edible plants but collected the abundant cereal grains growing wild in the region.

Such grains provided an unexciting but reliable source of food. Although unsuitable for consumption when raw, they can be made edible by roughly pounding or crushing them and then soaking them in water. Initially, they were probably just mixed into soup. A variety of ingredients such as fish, nuts, and berries would have been mixed with water in a plastered or bitumen-lined basket. Stones, heated in a fire, were then dropped in, using a forked stick. Grains contain tiny granules of starch, and when placed in hot water they absorb moisture and then burst, releasing the starch into the soup and thickening it considerably.

Cereal grains, it was soon discovered, had another unusual property: Unlike other foodstuffs, they could be stored for consumption months or even years later, if kept dry and safe. When no other foodstuffs were available to make soup, they could be used on their own to make either a thick porridge or a thin broth or gruel. This discovery led to the development of tools and techniques to collect, process, and store grain. It involved quite a lot of effort but provided a way to guard against the possibility of future food shortages. Throughout the Fertile Crescent there is archaeological evidence from around 10,000 BCE of flint-bladed sickles for harvesting cereal grains, woven baskets for carrying them, stone hearths for drying them, underground pits for storing them, and grindstones for processing them.

Although hunter-gatherers had previously led semisettled rather than entirely nomadic lives, moving between a number of temporary or seasonal shelters, the ability to store cereal grains began to encourage people to stay in one place. An experiment carried out in the 1960s shows why. An archaeologist used a flint-bladed sickle to see how efficiently a prehistoric family could have harvested wild grains, which still grow in some parts of Turkey. In one hour he gathered more than two pounds of grain, which suggested that a family that worked eight-hour days for three weeks would have been able to gather enough to provide each family member with a pound of grain a day for a year. But this would have meant staying near the stands of wild cereals to ensure the family did not miss the most suitable time to harvest them. And having gathered a large quantity of grain, they would be reluctant to leave it unguarded.

The result was the first permanent settlements, such as those established on the eastern coast of the Mediterranean from around 10,000 BCE. They consisted of simple, round huts with roofs supported by wooden posts and floors sunk up to a yard into the ground. These huts usually had a hearth and a floor paved with stones and were four or five yards in diameter. A typical village consisted of around fifty huts, supporting a community of two hundred or three hundred people. Although the residents of such villages continued to hunt wild animals such as gazelles, deer, and boar, skeletal evidence suggests that they subsisted on a mainly plant-based diet of acorns, lentils, chickpeas, and cereals, which at this stage were still gathered in the wild, rather than cultivated deliberately.

Cereal grains, which started off as relatively unimportant foodstuffs, took on greater significance following the discovery that they had two more unusual properties. The first was that grain soaked in water, so that it starts to sprout, tastes sweet. It was difficult to make storage pits perfectly watertight, so this property would have become apparent as soon as humans first began to store grain. The cause of this sweetness is now understood: Moistened grain produces diastase enzymes, which convert starch within the grain into maltose sugar, or malt. (This process occurs in all cereal grains, but barley produces by far the most diastase enzymes and hence the most maltose sugar.) At a time when few other sources of sugar were available, the sweetness of this "malted" grain would have been highly valued, prompting the development of deliberate malting techniques, in which the grain was first soaked and then dried.

The second discovery was even more momentous. Gruel that was left sitting around for a couple of days underwent a mysterious transformation, particularly if it had been made with malted grain: It became slightly fizzy and pleasantly intoxicating, as the action of wild yeasts from the air fermented the sugar in the gruel into alcohol. The gruel, in short, turned into beer.

Even so, beer was not necessarily the first form of alcohol to pass human lips. At the time of beer's discovery, alcohol from the accidental fermentation of fruit juice (to make wine) or water and honey (to make mead) would have occurred naturally in small quantities as people tried to store fruit or honey. But fruit is seasonal and perishes easily, wild honey was only available in limited quantities, and neither wine nor mead could be stored for very long without pottery, which did not emerge until around 6000 BCE. Beer, on the other hand, could be made from cereal crops, which were abundant and could be easily stored, allowing beer to be made reliably, and in quantity, when needed. Long before pottery was available, it could have been brewed in pitch-lined baskets, leather bags or animal stomachs, hollowed-out trees, large shells, or stone vessels. Shells were used for cooking as recently as the nineteenth century in the Amazon basin, and Sahti, a traditional beer made in Finland, is still brewed in hollowed-out trees today.

Once the crucial discovery of beer had been made, its quality was improved through trial and error. The more malted grain there is in the original gruel, for example, and the longer it is left to ferment, the stronger the beer. More malt means more sugar, and a longer fermentation means more of the sugar is turned into alcohol. Thoroughly cooking the gruel also contributes to the beer's strength. The malting process converts only around 15 percent of the starch found in barley grains into sugar, but when malted barley is mixed with water and brought to the boil, other starch-converting enzymes, which become active at higher temperatures, turn more of the starch into sugar, so there is more sugar for the yeast to transform into alcohol.

Ancient brewers also noticed that using the same container repeatedly for brewing produced more reliable results. Later historical records from Egypt and Mesopotamia show that brewers always carried their own "mash tubs" around with them, and one Mesopotamian myth refers to "containers which make the beer good." Repeated use of the same mash tub promoted successful fermentation because yeast cultures took up residence in the container's cracks and crevices, so that there was no need to rely on the more capricious wild yeast. Finally, adding berries, honey, spices, herbs, and other flavorings to the gruel altered the taste of the resulting beer in various ways. Over the next few thousand years, people discovered how to make a variety of beers of different strengths and flavors for different occasions.

Later Egyptian records mention at least seventeen kinds of beer, some of them referred to in poetic terms that sound, to modern ears, almost like advertising slogans: Different beers were known as "the beautiful and good," "the heavenly," "the joy-bringer," "the addition to the meal," "the plentiful," "the fermented." Beers used in religious ceremonies also had special names. Similarly, early written references to beer from Mesopotamia, in the third millennium BCE, list over twenty different kinds, including fresh beer, dark beer, fresh-dark beer, strong beer, red-brown beer, light beer, and pressed beer. Red-brown beer was a dark beer made using extra malt, while pressed beer was a weaker, more watery brew that contained less grain. Mesopotamian brewers could also control the taste and color of their beer by adding different amounts of *bappir*, or beer-bread. To make *bappir*, sprouted barley was shaped into lumps, like small loaves, which were baked twice to produce a dark-brown, crunchy, unleavened bread that could be stored for years before being crumbled into the brewer's vat. Records indicate that *bappir* was kept in government storehouses and was only eaten during food shortages; it was not so much a foodstuff as a convenient way to store the raw material for making beer.

The Mesopotamian use of bread in brewing has led to much debate among archaeologists, some of whom have suggested that bread must therefore be an offshoot of beer making, while others have argued that bread came first and was subsequently used as an ingredient in beer. It seems most likely, however, that both bread and beer were derived from gruel. A thick gruel could be baked in the sun or on a hot stone to make flatbread; a thin gruel could be left to ferment into beer. The two were different sides of the same coin: Bread was solid beer, and beer was liquid bread.

Under the Influence of Beer?

Since writing had not been invented at the time, there are no written records to attest to the social and ritual importance of beer in the Fertile Crescent during the new stone age, or Neolithic period, between 9000 BCE and 4000 BCE. But much can be inferred from later records of the way beer was used by the first literate civilizations, the Sumerians of Mesopotamia and the ancient Egyptians. Indeed, so enduring are the cultural traditions associated with beer that some of them survive to this day.

From the start, it seems that beer had an important function as a social drink. Sumerian depictions of beer from the third millennium BCE generally show two people drinking through straws from a shared vessel. By the Sumerian period, however, it was possible to filter the grains, chaff, and other debris from beer, and the advent of pottery meant it could just as easily have been served in individual cups. That beer drinkers are, nonetheless, so widely depicted using straws suggests that it was a ritual that persisted even when straws were no longer necessary.

The most likely explanation for this preference is that, unlike food, beverages can genuinely be shared. When several people drink beer from the same vessel, they are all consuming the same liquid; when cutting up a piece of meat, in contrast, some parts are usually deemed to be more desirable than others. As a result, sharing a drink with someone is a universal symbol of hospitality and friendship. It signals that the person offering the drink can be trusted, by demonstrating that it is not poisoned or otherwise unsuitable for consumption. The earliest beer, brewed in a primitive vessel in an era that predated the use of individual cups, would have to have been shared. Although it is no longer customary to offer visitors a straw through which to drink from a communal vat of beer, today tea or coffee may be offered from a shared pot, or a glass of wine or spirits from a shared bottle. And when drinking alcohol in a social setting, the clinking of glasses symbolically reunites the glasses into a single vessel of shared liquid. These are traditions with very ancient origins.

Just as ancient is the notion that drinks, and alcoholic drinks in particular, have supernatural properties. To Neolithic drinkers, beer's ability to intoxicate and induce a state of altered consciousness seemed magical. So, too, did the mysterious process of fermentation, which transformed ordinary gruel into beer. The obvious conclusion was that beer was a gift from the gods; accordingly, many cultures have myths that explain how the gods invented beer and then showed humankind how to make it. The Egyptians, for example, believed that beer was accidentally discovered by Osiris, the god of agriculture and king of the afterlife. One day he prepared a mixture of water and sprouted grain, but forgot about it and left it in the sun. He later returned to find the gruel had fermented, decided to drink it, and was so pleased with the result that he passed his knowledge on to humankind. (This tale seems to tally closely with the way beer was probably discovered in the stone age.) Other beer-drinking cultures tell similar stories.

Since beer was a gift from the gods, it was also the logical thing to present as a religious offering. Beer was certainly used in religious ceremonies, agricultural fertility rites, and funerals by the Sumerians and the Egyptians, so it seems likely that its religious use goes back farther still. Indeed, the religious significance of beer seems to be common to every beer-drinking culture, whether in the Americas, Africa, or Eurasia. The Incas offered their beer, called *chicha,* to the rising sun in a golden cup, and poured it on the ground or spat out their first mouthful as an offering to the gods of the Earth; the Aztecs offered their beer, called pulque, to Mayahuel, the goddess of fertility. In China, beers made from millet and rice were used in funerals and other ceremonies. The practice of raising a glass to wish someone good health, a happy marriage, or a safe passage into the after-life, or to celebrate the successful completion of a project, is the modern echo of the ancient idea that alcohol has the power to invoke supernatural forces.

Beer and Farming, the Seeds of Modernity

Some anthropologists have even suggested that beer might have played a central role in the adoption of agriculture, one of the turning points of human history. Farming paved the way for the emergence of civilization by creating food surpluses, freeing some members of society from the need to produce food and enabling them to specialize in particular activities and crafts, and so setting humanity on the path to the modern world. This happened first in the Fertile Crescent, starting around 9000 BCE, as people began cultivating barley and wheat deliberately, rather than sim-ply gathering wild grains for consumption and storage.

Of course, the switch from hunting and gathering to farming was a gradual transition over a few thousand years, as deliber-ately cultivated crops played an increasingly significant dietary role. Yet in the grand scheme of human history, it happened in an eyeblink. Humans had been hunter-gatherers ever since humankind diverged from the apes, around seven million years earlier; then they suddenly took up farming. Exactly why the switch to farming occurred, and occurred when it did, is still hotly debated, and there are dozens of theories. Perhaps the amount of food available to hunter-gatherers in the Fertile Cres-cent diminished, for example, either because of climatic changes, or because some species died out or were hunted to extinction.

Another possibility is that a more sedentary (but still hunter-gatherer) lifestyle increased human fertility, allowing the population to grow and creating demand for new sources of food. Or perhaps once beer had been discovered, and its consumption had become socially and ritually important, there was a greater desire to ensure the availability of grain by deliberate farming, rather than relying on wild grains. Farming was, according to this view, adopted partly in order to maintain the supply of beer.

Tempting though it is to attribute the adoption of agriculture entirely to beer, it seems most likely that beer drinking was just one of many factors that helped to tip the balance away from hunting and gathering and toward farming and a sedentary lifestyle based on small settlements. Once this transition had begun, a ratchet effect took hold: The more farming was relied on as a means of food production by a particular community, and the more its population grew, the harder it was to go back to the old nomadic lifestyle based on hunting and gathering.

Beer drinking would also have assisted the transition to farming in a more subtle way. Because long-term storage of beer was difficult, and complete fermentation takes up to a week, most beer would have been drunk much sooner, while still fermenting. Such a beer would have had a relatively low alcohol content by modern standards but would have been rich in suspended yeast, which dramatically improved its protein and vitamin content. The high level of vitamin B, in particular, would have compensated for the decline in the consumption of meat, the usual source of that vitamin, as hunting gave way to farming.

Furthermore, since it was made using boiled water, beer was safer to drink than water, which quickly becomes contaminated with human waste in even the smallest settlements. Although the link between contaminated water and ill health was not understood until modern times, humans quickly learned to be wary of unfamiliar water supplies, and to drink where possible from clear-running streams away from human settlements. (Hunter-gatherers did not have to worry about contaminated water supplies, since they lived in small, mobile bands and left their human waste behind when they moved on.) In other words, beer helped to make up for the decline in food quality as people took up farming, provided a safe form of liquid nourishment, and gave groups of beer-drinking farmers a comparative nutritional advantage over non-beer drinkers.

Farming spread throughout the Fertile Crescent between 7000 BCE and 5000 BCE, as an increasing number of plants and animals (starting with sheep and goats) were domesticated, and new irrigation techniques made farming possible on the hot, dry lowlands of Mesopotamia and in the Nile Valley of Egypt. A typical farming village of the period consisted of huts built from clay and reed mats, and perhaps some rather grander houses built of sun-dried mud bricks. Beyond the village would have been fields where cereals, dates, and other crops were cultivated, with a few sheep and oxen tethered or penned nearby. Wild fowl, fish, and game, when available, supplemented the villagers' diet. It was a very different lifestyle from the hunting and gathering of just a few thousand years earlier. And the transition toward an even more complex society had begun. Settlements from this period often had a storehouse where valuable items were kept, including sacred objects and stores of surplus food. These storehouses were definitely communal, since they were far larger than would have been needed by any single family.

Keeping surplus food in the storehouse was one way to ward off future food shortages; ritual and religious activity, in which the gods were called upon to ensure a good harvest, was another. As these two activities became intertwined, deposits of surplus food came to be seen as offerings to the gods, and the storehouses became temples. To ensure all villagers were pulling their weight, contributions to the common storehouse were recorded using small clay tokens, found throughout the Fertile Crescent from as early as 8000 BCE. Such contributions were justified as religious offerings by administrator-priests who lived off the surplus food and directed communal activities, such as the construction of buildings and the maintenance of irrigation systems. Thus were sown the seeds of accountancy, writing, and bureaucracy.

The idea that beer provided some of the impetus for this dramatic shift in the nature of human activity, after millions of years of hunting and gathering, remains controversial. But the best evidence for the importance of beer in prehistoric times is its extraordinary significance to the people of the first great civilizations. For although the origins of this ancient drink inevitably remain shrouded in mystery and conjecture, there is no question that the daily lives of Egyptians and Mesopotamians, young and old, rich and poor, were steeped in beer.

2

Civilized Beer

Pleasure—it is beer. Discomfort—it is an expedition.
—*Mesopotamian proverb, c. 2000 BCE*

The mouth of a perfectly contented man is filled with beer.
—*Egyptian proverb, c. 2200 BCE*

The Urban Revolution

THE WORLD'S FIRST cities arose in Mesopotamia, "the land between the streams," the name given to the area between the Tigris and Euphrates rivers that roughly corresponds to modern Iraq. Most of the inhabitants of these cities were farmers, who lived within the city walls and walked out to tend their fields each morning. Administrators and craftsmen who did not work in the fields were the earliest humans to live entirely urban lives. Wheeled vehicles trundled through the matrix of city streets; people bought and sold goods in bustling marketplaces. Religious ceremonies and public holidays passed by in a reassuringly regular cycle. Even the proverbs of the time have a familiar world-weariness, as this example shows: "He who possesses much silver may be happy; he who possesses much barley may be happy; but he who has nothing at all can sleep."

Exactly why people chose to live in large cities rather than small villages remains unclear. It was probably the result of several overlapping factors: People may have wanted to be near important religious or trading centers, for example, and in the case of Mesopotamia, security may have been a significant motivation. The lack of natural boundaries—Mesopotamia is essentially a large open plain—meant the area was subject to repeated invasions and attacks. From around 4300 BCE villages began to band together, forming ever-larger towns and eventually cities, each of which sat at the center of its own system of fields and irrigation channels. By 3000 BCE the city of Uruk, the largest of its day, had a population of around fifty thousand and was surrounded by a circle of fields ten miles in radius. By 2000 BCE almost the entire population in southern Mesopotamia was living in a few dozen large city-states, including Uruk, Ur, Lagash, Eridu, and Nippur. Thereafter Egypt took the lead, and its cities, such as Memphis and Thebes, grew to become the ancient world's largest.

These two earliest examples of *civilization*—a word that simply means "living in cities"—were different in many ways. Political unification enabled Egyptian culture to endure almost unchanged for nearly three thousand years, for example, while Mesopotamia was the scene of constant political and military upheaval. But in one vital respect they were similar: Both cultures were made possible by an agricultural surplus, in particular an excess of grain. This surplus not only freed a small elite of administrators and craftsmen from the need to produce their own food but also funded vast public works such as canals, temples, and pyramids. As well as being the logical medium of exchange, grain was the basis of the national diet in both Egypt and Mesopotamia. It was a sort of edible money, and it was consumed in both solid and liquid forms, as bread and beer.

The Drink of the Civilized Man

The recorded history of beer, and indeed of everything else, begins in Sumer, a region in southern Mesopotamia where writing first began to emerge around 3400 BCE. That beer drinking was seen as a hallmark of civilization by the Mesopotamians is particularly apparent in a passage from the *Epic of Gilgamesh*, the world's first great literary work. Gilgamesh was a Sumerian king who ruled around 2700 BCE, and whose life story was subsequently embroidered into an elaborate myth by the Sumerians and their regional successors, the Akkadians and Babylonians. The story tells of Gilgamesh's adventures with his friend Enkidu, who starts off as a wild man running naked in the wilderness but is introduced to the ways of civilization by a young woman. She takes Enkidu to a shepherds' village, the first rung on the ladder toward the high culture of the city, where

> *They placed food in front of him,*
> *they placed beer in front of him;*
> *Enkidu knew nothing about eating bread for food,*
> *and of drinking beer he had not been taught.*
> *The young woman spoke to Enkidu, saying:*

"Eat the food, Enkidu, it is the way one lives.
Drink the beer, as is the custom of the land."
Enkidu ate the food until he was sated,
He drank the beer—seven jugs!—and became expansive
and sang with joy.
He was elated and his face glowed.
He splashed his shaggy body with water,
and rubbed himself with oil, and turned into a human.

Enkidu's primitive nature is demonstrated by his lack of familiarity with bread and beer; but once he has consumed them, and then washed himself, he too becomes a human and is then ready to go to Uruk, the city ruled by Gilgamesh. The Mesopotamians regarded the consumption of bread and beer as one of the things that distinguished them from savages and made them fully human. Interestingly, this belief seems to echo beer's association with a settled, orderly lifestyle, rather than the haphazard existence of hunter-gatherers in prehistoric times.

The possibility of drunkenness seems to have done nothing to undermine the equation of beer drinking with civilization. Most references to drunkenness in Mesopotamian literature are playful and humorous: Enkidu's initiation as a human, indeed, involved getting drunk and singing. Similarly, Sumerian myths depict the gods as very fallible, human characters who enjoy eating and drinking, and often drink too much. Their capricious behavior was blamed for the precarious and unpredictable nature of Sumerian life, in which harvests could fail and marauding armies could appear on the horizon at any moment. Sumerian religious ceremonies involved laying out a meal on a table in the temple before a divine image, followed by a banquet at which the consumption of food and drink by the priests and worshipers invoked the presence of the gods and the spirits of the dead.

Beer was just as important in ancient Egyptian culture, where references to it go back almost as far. It is mentioned in documents from the third dynasty, which began in 2650 BCE, and several varieties of beer are mentioned in "Pyramid Texts," the funerary texts found inscribed in pyramids from the end of the fifth dynasty, around 2350 BCE. (The Egyptians developed their own form of writing shortly after the Sumerians, to record both mundane transactions and kingly exploits, but whether it was an independent development or inspired by Sumerian writing remains unclear.) One survey of Egyptian literature found that beer, the Egyptian word for which was *hekt*, was mentioned more times than any other foodstuff. As in Mesopotamia, beer was thought to have ancient and mythological origins, and it appears in prayers, myths, and legends.

One Egyptian tale even credits beer with saving humankind from destruction. Ra, the sun god, learned that humankind was plotting against him, and dispatched the goddess Hathor to exact punishment. But such was her ferocity that Ra feared there would soon be nobody left to worship him, and he took pity on humankind. He prepared a vast amount of beer—seven thousand jars of it, in some versions of the story—dyed it red to resemble blood, and spread it over the fields, where it shone like a vast mirror. Hathor paused to admire her reflection and then stooped to drink some of the mixture. She became intoxicated, fell asleep, and forgot about her bloody mission. Humankind was saved, and Hathor became the goddess of beer and brewing. Versions of this story have been found inscribed in the tombs of Egyptian kings, including Tutankhamen, Seti I, and Ramses the Great.

In contrast to the Mesopotamians' relaxed attitude toward intoxication, however, a strong disapproval of drunkenness was expressed in the practice texts copied out by apprentice scribes in Egypt, many of which have survived in large quantities in rubbish mounds. One passage admonishes young scribes: "Beer, it scareth men from thee, it sendeth thy soul to perdition. Thou art like a broken steering-oar in a ship, that is obedient on neither side." Another example, from a collection of advice called "The Wisdom of Ani," gives a similar warning: "Take not upon thyself to drink a jug of beer. Thou speakest, and an unintelligible utterance issueth from thy mouth." Such scribal training texts, however, are unrepresentative of Egyptian values in general. They disapprove of almost everything except endless studying in order to pursue a career as a scribe. Other texts have titles such as "Do Not Be a Soldier, Priest or Baker," "Do Not Be a Husbandman," and "Do Not Be a Charioteer."

Mesopotamians and Egyptians alike saw beer as an ancient, god-given drink that underpinned their existence, formed part of their cultural and religious identity, and had great social importance. "To make a beer hall" and "to sit in the beer hall" were popular Egyptian expressions that meant "to have a good time" or "to carouse," while the Sumerian expression a "pouring of beer" referred to a banquet or celebratory feast, and formal visits by the king to high officials' homes to receive tribute were recorded as "when the king drank beer at the house of so-and-so." In both cultures, beer was a staple foodstuff without which no meal was complete. It was consumed by everyone, rich and poor, men and women, adults and children, from the top of the social pyramid to the bottom. It was truly the defining drink of these first great civilizations.

The Origins of Writing

The earliest written documents are Sumerian wage lists and tax receipts, in which the symbol for beer, a clay vessel with diagonal linear markings drawn inside it, is one of the most common words, along with the symbols for grain, textiles, and livestock. That is because writing was originally invented to record the collection and distribution of grain, beer, bread, and other goods. It arose as a natural extension of the Neolithic custom of using tokens to account for contributions to a communal storehouse. Indeed, Sumerian society was a logical continuation of Neolithic social structures but on a far larger scale, the culmination of thousands of years of increasing economic and cultural complexity. Just as the chieftain of a Neolithic village collected surplus food, the priests of the Sumerian cities collected surplus barley, wheat, sheep, and textiles. Officially, these goods were offerings to the gods, but in practice they were compulsory taxes that were consumed by the temple bureaucracy or traded for other goods and services. The priests could, for example, pay for the maintenance of irrigation systems and the construction of public buildings by handing out rations of bread and beer.

This elaborate system gave the temple direct control over much of the economy. Whether this resulted in a redistributive nirvana—a form of ancient socialism in which the state provided for everyone—or an exploitative regime of near-slavery is difficult to say. But it seems to have arisen in response to the unpredictable nature of the Mesopotamian environment. There was little rain, and the flooding of the Tigris and Euphrates was erratic. So agriculture depended on the use of carefully maintained communal irrigation systems and, the Sumerians believed, on making the appropriate offerings to the local gods. Both these tasks were handled by the priesthood, and as villages grew into towns and then cities, more and more power was concentrated into their hands. The simple storehouses of the Neolithic period became elaborate temples, or ziggurats, built on raised, stepped platforms. Numerous rival city-states arose, each with its own resident god, and each ruled by an elite priesthood who maintained the agricultural economy and lived off the surplus it produced. Carvings depict them wearing beards, long kilts, and round headdresses, and drinking beer from large pots through long straws.

For all this to work, the priests and their subjects needed to be able to record what they had taken in and paid out. Tax receipts were initially kept in the form of tokens within clay "envelopes"—hollow shells of clay, called *bullae*, with several tokens rattling around inside. Tokens of different shapes were used to represent standard amounts of grain, textiles, or individual cattle. When goods were presented at the temple, the corresponding tokens were placed in a clay envelope, and the tax collector and taxpayer would both impress the envelope's wet clay with their personal signature seals to signify that the envelope's contents accurately reflected the tax paid. The envelope was then stored in the temple archive.

It soon became clear, however, that an easier way to achieve the same result was to use a tablet of wet clay, and to press the tokens into it to make different-shaped impressions signifying barley, cattle, and so on. The signature seals could then be applied to this tablet, which was baked in the sun to make the impressions permanent. Tokens were no longer needed; their impressions would do instead. Gradually, tokens were abandoned altogether in favor of pictograms scratched into the clay, derived from the shapes of the tokens or of the objects they represented. Some pictograms thus came to stand as direct representations of physical goods, while other combinations of indentations stood for abstract concepts such as numbers.

The oldest written documents, dating from around 3400 BCE from the city of Uruk, are small, flat tablets of clay that fit comfortably into the palm of one hand. They are commonly divided into columns and then subdivided into rectangles by straight lines. Each compartment contains a group of symbols, some made by pressing tokens into the clay, and others scratched using a stylus. Although these symbols are read from left to right and top to bottom, in all other respects this early script is utterly unlike modern writing and can only be read by specialists. But look closely, and the pictogram for beer—a jar on its side, with diagonal linear markings inside it—is easy to spot. It appears in wage lists, in administrative documents, and in word lists written by scribes in training, which include dozens of brewing terms. Many tablets consist of lists of names, next to each of which is the indication "beer and bread for one day"—a standard wage issued by the temple.

A modern analysis of Mesopotamian ration texts found that

the standard issue of bread, beer, dates, and onions, sometimes supplemented with meat or fish and with additional vegetables such as chickpeas, lentils, turnips, and beans, provided a nutritious and balanced diet. Dates provided vitamin A, beer provided vitamin B, onions provided vitamin C, and the ration as a whole provided 3,500 to 4,000 calories, in line with modern recommendations for adult consumption. This suggests that state rations were not just occasional handouts, but were the primary source of food for many people.

An early cuneiform tablet, dating from around 3200 BCE, recording the allocation of beer

Having started out as a means of recording tax receipts and ration payments, writing soon evolved into a more flexible, expressive, and abstract medium. By around 3000 BCE some symbols had come to stand for particular sounds. At the same time, pictograms made up of deep, wedge-shaped impressions took over from those composed of shallow scratches. This made writing faster but reduced the pictographic quality of the symbols, so that writing began to look more abstract. The end result was the first general-purpose form of writing, based on wedge-shaped, or "cuneiform," indentations made in clay tablets using reeds. It is the ancestor of modern Western alphabets, which are descended from it via the Ugaritic and Phoenician alphabets devised during the second millennium BCE.

Compared with early pictograms, the cuneiform symbol for beer is barely recognizable as a jar shape. But it can be seen, for example, on tablets that tell the story of Enki, the cunning and wily god of agriculture, as he prepares a feast for his father, Enlil. The description of the brewing process is, admittedly, somewhat cryptic. But the steps are recognizable, which means that the world's oldest written recipe is for beer.

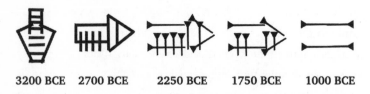

| 3200 BCE | 2700 BCE | 2250 BCE | 1750 BCE | 1000 BCE |

The evolution of the written symbol for beer in cuneiform. Over the years the depiction of the beer jar gradually became more abstract.

Liquid Wealth and Health

In Egypt, as in Mesopotamia, taxes in the form of grain and other goods were presented at the temple and were then redistributed to fund public works. This meant that in both civilizations barley and wheat, and their processed solid and liquid forms, bread and beer, became more than just staple foodstuffs; they were convenient and widespread forms of payment and currency. In Mesopotamia, cuneiform records indicate that the lowest-ranking members of the Sumerian temple workforce were issued a *sila* of beer a day—roughly equivalent to a liter, or two American pints—as part of their ration. Junior officials were given two *sila*, higher officials and ladies of the court three *sila*, and the highest officials five *sila*. Large numbers of identically sized bevel-rimmed bowls found at Sumerian sites seem to have been used as standard units of measurement. Senior officials were given more beer not because they drank more; having drunk their fill, they had some left over to tip messengers and scribes and pay other workers. Liquids, being easily divisible, make ideal currencies.

Later documents from the reign of Sargon, one of a series of kings from the neighboring region of Akkad who united and ruled Sumer's rival city-states from around 2350 BCE, refer to beer as part of the "bride price" (a wedding payment made by the groom's family to the bride's family). Other records indicate that beer was given as payment to women and children for doing a few days' work at the temple: Women received two *sila* and children one *sila*. Similarly, documents show that refugee women and children, who may have been slaves or prisoners of war, were issued monthly beer rations of twenty *sila* for women and ten *sila* for children. Soldiers,

The impression of a cylinder seal depicting a banquet scene, including seated figures drinking beer from a large jar through straws

policemen, and scribes also received special payments of beer on particular occasions, as did messengers as a form of bonus payment. One document from 2035 BCE is a list of provisions paid out to official messengers in the city of Umma. Various amounts of "excellent" beer, "ordinary" beer, garlic, cooking oil, and spices were issued to messengers whose names included Shu-Dumuzi, Nur-Ishtar, Esur-ili, Ur-Ningirsu, and Bazimu. By this time, the Sumerian state employed three hundred thousand people, all of whom received monthly rations of barley and annual rations of wool, or the equivalent amount of other goods: bread or beer instead of barley, and fabric or garments instead of wool. And every transaction was noted down methodically on indestructible cuneiform tablets by Mesopotamian accountants.

What is without doubt the most spectacular example of the use of beer as a form of payment can be seen on Egypt's Giza plateau.

Civilized Beer

The workers who built the pyramids were paid in beer, according to records found at a nearby town where the construction workers ate and slept. The records indicate that at the time of the pyramids' construction, around 2500 BCE, the standard ration for a laborer was three or four loaves of bread and two jugs containing about four liters (eight American pints) of beer. Managers and officials received larger quantities of both. No wonder that, according to some ancient graffiti, one team of workers on the third Giza pyramid, built for King Menkaure, styled themselves the "Drunkards of Menkaure." Written records of payments to the construction workers show that the pyramids were built by state employees, rather than by an army of slaves, as was once thought. One theory is that the pyramids were built by farmers during the flood season, when their fields were under water. The state collected grain as tribute and then redistributed it as payment; the building work instilled a sense of national unity, demonstrated the wealth and power of the state, and provided a justification for taxation.

The use of bread and beer as wages or currency meant that they became synonymous with prosperity and well-being. The ancient Egyptians identified them so closely with the necessities of life that the phrase "bread and beer" meant sustenance in general; their combined hieroglyphs formed the symbol for food. The phrase "bread and beer" was also used as an everyday greeting, much like wishing someone good luck or good health. One Egyptian inscription urges women to supply their schoolboy sons with two jars of beer and three small loaves of bread daily to ensure their healthy development. Similarly, "bread and beer" was used by Mesopotamians to mean "food and drink," and one Sumerian word for banquet literally means "the place of beer and bread."

Beer also had a more direct link to health, for both the Mesopotamians and Egyptians used it medicinally. A cuneiform tablet from the Sumerian city of Nippur, dated to around 2100 BCE, contains a pharmacopoeia, or list of medical recipes, based on beer. It is the oldest surviving record of the use of alcohol in medicine. In Egypt, beer's use as a mild sedative was recognized, and it was also the basis for several medicinal concoctions of herbs and spices. Beer was, of course, less likely to be contaminated than water, being made with boiled water, and also had the advantage that some ingredients dissolve more easily in it. "The Ebers Papyrus," an Egyptian medical text that dates from around 1550 BCE but is evidently based on far older documents, contains hundreds of recipes for herbal remedies, many of which involve beer. Half an onion mixed with frothy beer was said to cure constipation, for example, while powdered olives mixed with beer cured indigestion; a mixture of saffron and beer massaged into a woman's abdomen was prescribed for labor pains.

The Egyptians also believed that their well-being in the afterlife depended on having an adequate supply of bread and beer. The standard funerary offering consisted of bread, beer, oxen, geese, cloth, and natron, a purification agent. In some Egyptian funeral texts the deceased is promised "beer that would not turn sour"—signaling both a desire to be able to pursue beer drinking eternally and the difficulty of storing beer. Scenes and models of brewing and baking have been found in Egyptian tombs, along with jars of beer (long since evaporated) and beer-making equipment. Special sieves for beer making were found in the tomb of Tutankhamen, who died around 1335 BCE.

Ordinary citizens who were laid to rest in simple shallow graves were also buried with small jars of beer.

A Drink from the Dawn of Civilization

Beer permeated the lives of Egyptians and Mesopotamians from the cradle to the grave. Their enthusiasm for it was almost inevitable because the emergence of complex societies, the need to keep written records, and the popularity of beer all followed from the surplus of grain. Since the Fertile Crescent had the best climatic conditions for grain cultivation, that was where farming began, where the earliest civilizations arose, where writing first emerged, and where beer was most abundant.

Although neither Mesopotamian nor Egyptian beer contained hops, which only became a standard ingredient in medieval times, both the beverage and some of its related customs would still be recognizable to beer drinkers today, thousands of years later. While beer is no longer used as a form of payment, and people no longer greet each other with the expression "bread and beer," in much of the world it is still considered the staple drink of the working man. Toasting someone's health before drinking beer is a remnant of the ancient belief in beer's magical properties. And beer's association with friendly, unpretentious social interaction remains unchanged; it is a beverage that is meant to be shared. Whether in stone-age villages, Mesopotamian banqueting halls, or modern pubs and bars, beer has brought people together since the dawn of civilization.

WINE *in*

GREECE

and ROME

3

The Delight of Wine

Quickly, bring me a beaker of wine, so that I may wet
my mind and say something clever.—*Aristophanes, Greek*
comic poet (c. 450–385 BCE)

A Great Feast

ONE OF THE greatest feasts in history was given by
King Ashurnasirpal II of Assyria, around 870 BCE, to
mark the inauguration of his new capital at Nimrud.
At the center of the new city was a large palace, built on a
raised mud-brick platform in the traditional Mesopotamian
manner. Its seven magnificent halls had ornate wood-and-bronze
doors and were roofed with cedar, cypress, and juniper wood.
Elaborate murals celebrated the king's military exploits in foreign lands. The palace was surrounded by canals and waterfalls,
and by orchards and gardens filled with both local plants and
those gathered during the king's far-flung military campaigns:
date palms, cedars, cypresses, olive, plum, and fig trees, and
grapevines, all of which "vied with each other in fragrance,"

according to a contemporary cuneiform inscription. Ashurnasirpal populated his new capital with people from throughout his empire, which covered much of northern Mesopotamia. With these cosmopolitan populations of plants and people, the capital represented the king's empire in microcosm. Once construction was completed, Ashurnasirpal staged an enormous banquet to celebrate.

The feasting went on for ten days. The official record attests that the celebration was attended by 69,574 people: 47,074 men and women from across the empire, 16,000 of the new inhabitants of Nimrud, 5,000 foreign dignitaries from other states, and 1,500 palace officials. The aim was to demonstrate the king's power and wealth, both to his own people and to foreign representatives. The attendees were collectively served 1,000 fattened cattle, 1,000 calves, 10,000 sheep, 15,000 lambs, 1,000 spring lambs, 500 gazelles, 1,000 ducks, 1,000 geese, 20,000 doves, 12,000 other small birds, 10,000 fish, 10,000 jerboa (a kind of small rodent), and 10,000 eggs. There were not many vegetables: a mere 1,000 crates were provided. But even allowing for some kingly exaggeration, it was clearly a feast on an epic scale. The king boasted of his guests that "[he] did them due honors and sent them back, healthy and happy, to their own countries."

Yet what was most impressive, and most significant, was the king's choice of drink. Despite his Mesopotamian heritage, Ashurnasirpal did not give pride of place at his feast to the Mesopotamians' usual beverage. Carved stone reliefs at the palace do not show him sipping beer through a straw; instead, he is depicted elegantly balancing a shallow bowl, probably made of

Ashurnasirpal II seated in state, holding a shallow wine bowl. Attendants on either side hold flyswatters to keep flies away from the king and his wine.

gold, on the tips of the fingers of his right hand, so that it is level with his face. This bowl contained wine.

Beer had not been banished: Ashurnasirpal served ten thousand jars of it at his feast. But he also served ten thousand skins of wine—an equal quantity, but a far more impressive display of wealth. Previously, wine had only been available in Mesopotamia in very small quantities, since it had to be imported from the mountainous, wine-growing lands to the northeast. The cost of transporting wine down from the mountains to the plains made it at least ten times more expensive than beer, so it was regarded as an exotic foreign drink in Mesopotamian culture. Accordingly, only the elite could afford to drink it, and its main use was religious; its scarcity and high price made it worthy for consumption by the gods, when it was available. Most people never tasted it at all.

So Ashurnasirpal's ability to make wine and beer available to his seventy thousand guests in equal abundance was a vivid illustration of his wealth. Serving wine from distant regions within his empire also underlined the extent of his power. More impressive still was the fact that some of the wine had come from the vines in his own garden. These vines were intertwined with trees, as was customary at the time, and were irrigated with an elaborate system of canals. Ashurnasirpal was not only fabulously rich, but his wealth literally grew on trees. The dedication of the new city was formally marked with a ritual offering to the gods of this local wine.

Subsequent banquet scenes from Nimrud show people drinking wine from shallow bowls, seated on wooden couches and flanked by attendants, some of whom hold jugs of wine, while others hold fans, or perhaps flyswatters to keep insects away from the precious liquid. Sometimes large storage vessels are also depicted, from which the attendants refill their serving jugs.

Under the Assyrians, wine drinking developed into an increasingly elaborate and formal social ritual. An obelisk from around 825 BCE shows Ashurnasirpal's son, Shalmaneser III, standing beneath a parasol. He holds a wine bowl in his right hand, his left hand rests on the hilt of his sword, and a supplicant kneels at his feet. Thanks to this kind of propaganda, wine and its associated drinking paraphernalia became emblems of power, prosperity, and privilege.

"The Excellent 'Beer' of the Mountains"

Wine was newly fashionable, but it was anything but new. As with beer, its origins are lost in prehistory: its invention, or discovery, was so ancient that it is recorded only indirectly, in myth and legend. But archaeological evidence suggests that wine was first produced during the Neolithic period, between 9000 and 4000 BCE, in the Zagros Mountains in the region that roughly corresponds to modern Armenia and northern Iran. The convergence of three factors made wine production in this area possible: the presence of the wild Eurasian grape vine, *Vitis vinifera sylvestris*, the availability of cereal crops to provide year-round food reserves for wine-making communities, and, around 6000 BCE, the invention of pottery, instrumental for making, storing, and serving wine.

Wine consists simply of the fermented juice of crushed grapes. Natural yeasts, present on the grape skins, convert the sugars in the juice into alcohol. Attempts to store grapes or grape juice for long periods in pottery vessels would therefore have resulted in wine. The earliest physical evidence for it, in the form of reddish residue inside a pottery jar, comes from Hajji Firuz Tepe, a Neolithic village in the Zagros Mountains. The jar has been dated to 5400 BCE. Wine's probable origin in this region is reflected in the biblical story of Noah, who is said to have planted the first vineyard on the slopes of nearby Mount Ararat after being delivered from the flood.

From this birthplace, knowledge of wine making spread west to Greece and Anatolia (modern-day Turkey), and south through the Levant (modern-day Syria, Lebanon, and Israel) to Egypt. In around 3150 BCE one of Egypt's earliest rulers, King Scorpion I, was buried with seven hundred jars of wine, imported at great expense from the southern Levant, a significant wine-producing area at the time. Once the pharaohs acquired a taste for wine, they established their own vineyards in the Nile Delta, and limited domestic production was under way by 3000 BCE. As in Mesopotamia, however, consumption was restricted to the elite, since the climate was unsuitable for large-scale production. Wine-making scenes appear in tomb paintings, but these give a disproportionate impression of its prevalence in Egyptian society, for only the wine-drinking rich could afford lavish tombs. The masses drank beer.

A similar situation prevailed in the eastern Mediterranean, where vines were being cultivated by 2500 BCE on Crete, and possibly in mainland Greece too. That the vine was introduced, rather than having always been present, was acknowledged in later Greek myths, according to which the gods drank nectar (presumably mead), and wine was introduced later for human consumption. Grapevines were grown alongside olives, wheat, and barley and were often intertwined with olive or fig trees. In the Mycenaean and Minoan cultures of the second millennium BCE, on the Greek mainland and on Crete, respectively, wine remained an elite drink, however. It is not listed in ration tablets for slave workers or lower-ranking religious officials. Access to wine was a mark of status.

The reigns of Ashurnasirpal and his son, Shalmaneser,

therefore marked a turning point. Wine came to be seen as a social as well as a religious beverage and started to become increasingly fashionable throughout the Near East and the eastern Mediterranean. And its availability grew in two senses. First, wine production increased, as did the volume of wine being traded by sea, making wine available over a larger geographic area. The establishment of ever-larger states and empires boosted the availability of wine, for the fewer borders there were to cross, the fewer taxes and tolls there were to pay, and the cheaper it was to transport wine over long distances. The luckiest rulers, like the Assyrian kings, had empires that encompassed wine-making regions. Second, as volumes grew and prices fell, wine became accessible to a broader segment of society. The growing availability of wine is evident in the records that list the tribute presented to the Assyrian court. During the reigns of Ashurnasirpal and Shalmaneser, wine began to be mentioned as a desirable tribute offering, along with gold, silver, horses, cattle, and other valuable items. But two centuries later it had vanished from the tribute lists, because it had become so widespread, at least in Assyria, that it was no longer deemed expensive or exotic enough for use as an offering.

Cuneiform tablets from Nimrud dating from around 785 BCE show that by that time wine rations were being provided to as many as six thousand people in the Assyrian royal household. Ten men were allocated one *qa* of wine per day to share between them; this amount is thought to have been about one liter, so each man would have received roughly one modern glass of wine per day. Skilled workers got more, with one *qa* being divided between six of them. But everyone in the household, from the highest officials to the lowliest shepherd boys and assistant cooks, was granted a ration.

As the enthusiasm for wine spread south into Mesopotamia, where local production was impractical, the wine trade along the Euphrates and Tigris rivers expanded. Given its heavy and perishable nature, wine was difficult to transport over land. Long-distance trade was done over water, using rafts or boats made of wood and reeds. The Greek historian Herodotus, who visited the region around 430 BCE, described the boats used to carry goods by river to Babylon and noted that "their chief freight is wine." Herodotus explained that once they had arrived downstream and had been unloaded, the boats were nearly worthless, given the difficulty of transporting them back upstream. Instead, they were broken up and sold, though typically only for a tenth of their original value. This cost was reflected in the high price of the wine.

So though wine became more fashionable in Mesopotamian society, it never became widely affordable outside wine-producing areas. The prohibitive cost for most people is shown by the boast made by Nabonidus, the last ruler of the Neo-Babylonian Empire before it fell to the Persians in 539 BCE. Nabonidus bragged that wine, which he referred to as "the excellent 'beer' of the mountains, of which my country has none," had become so abundant during his reign that an imported jar containing eighteen *sila* (about eighteen liters, or twenty-four modern wine bottles) could be had for one shekel of silver. At the time, one shekel of silver per month was regarded as the minimum wage, so wine could only have become an everyday drink among the very rich. For everyone else, a substitute drink became popular instead: date-palm wine, an alcoholic drink made from fermented date syrup. Date palms were widely cultivated in southern Mesopotamia, so the resulting "wine" was just a little more expensive than beer. During the first millennium BCE, even the beer-loving Mesopotamians turned their backs on beer, which was dethroned as the most cultured and civilized of drinks, and the age of wine began.

The Cradle of Western Thought

The origins of contemporary Western thought can be traced back to the golden age of ancient Greece in the sixth and fifth centuries BCE, when Greek thinkers laid the foundations for modern Western politics, philosophy, science, and law. Their novel approach was to pursue rational inquiry through adversarial discussion: The best way to evaluate one set of ideas, they decided, was by testing it against another set of ideas. In the political sphere, the result was democracy, in which supporters of rival policies vied for rhetorical supremacy; in philosophy, it led to reasoned arguments and dialogues about the nature of the world; in science, it prompted the construction of competing theories to try to explain natural phenomena; in the field of law, the result was the adversarial legal system. (Another form of institutionalized competition that the Greeks particularly loved was athletics.) This approach underpins the modern Western way of life, in which politics, commerce, science, and law are all rooted in orderly competition.

The idea of the distinction between Western and Eastern worlds is also Greek in origin. Ancient Greece was not a unified nation but a loose collection of city-states, settlements, and colonies whose allegiances and rivalries shifted constantly. But as early as the eighth century BCE, a distinction was being made between the Greek-speaking peoples and foreigners, who were known as *barbaroi* because their language sounded like incomprehensible babbling to Greek ears. Chief among these barbarians were the Persians to the east, whose vast empire encompassed Mesopotamia, Syria, Egypt, and Asia Minor (modern Turkey). At first the leading Greek city-states, Athens and Sparta, united to fend off the Persians, but Persia later backed both Sparta and Athens in turn as they fought each other. Eventually, Alexander the Great united the Greeks and defeated Persia in the fourth century BCE. The Greeks defined themselves in opposition to the Persians, believing themselves to be fundamentally different from (and indeed superior to) Asian peoples.

Enthusiasm for civilized competition and Greece's presumed superiority over foreigners were apparent in the Greek love of wine. It was drunk at formal drinking parties, or *symposia*, which were venues for playful but adversarial discussion in which drinkers would try to outdo each other in wit, poetry, or rhetoric. The formal, intellectual atmosphere of the *symposion* also reminded the Greeks how civilized they were, in contrast to the barbarians, who either drank lowly, unsophisticated beer or—even worse—drank wine but failed to do so in a manner that met with Greek approval.

In the words of Thucydides, a Greek writer of the fifth century BCE who was one of the ancient world's greatest historians, "the peoples of the Mediterranean began to emerge from barbarism when they learnt to cultivate the olive and the vine." According to one legend, Dionysus, the god of wine, fled to Greece to escape beer-loving Mesopotamia. A more kindly but still rather patronizing Greek tradition relates that Dionysus created beer for the benefit of people in countries where the vine could not be cultivated. In Greece, however, Dionysus had made wine available to everyone, not just the elite. As the playwright Euripides put it in *The Bacchae*: "To rich and poor alike hath he granted the delight of wine, that makes all pain to cease."

Wine was plentiful enough to be widely affordable because the climate and terrain of the Greek islands and mainland were ideal for viticulture. Cultivation of the vine rapidly took hold throughout Greece from the seventh century BCE, starting in Arcadia and Sparta in the Peloponnese Peninsula, and then spreading up toward Attica, the region around Athens. The Greeks were the first to produce wine on a large commercial scale and took a methodical, even scientific approach to viticulture. Greek writing on the subject begins with Hesiod's *Works and Days*, written in the eighth century BCE, which incorporates advice on how and when to prune, harvest, and press grapes. Greek vintners devised improvements to the wine press and adopted the practice of growing vines in neat rows, on trellises and stakes, rather than up trees. This allowed more vines to be packed into a given space, increasing yields and providing easier access for harvesting.

Gradually, grain farming was overtaken by the cultivation of grapevines and olives, and wine production switched from subsistence to industrial farming. Rather than being consumed by the farmer and his dependents, wine was produced specifically as a commercial product. And no wonder; a farmer could earn up to twenty times as much from cultivating vines on his land as he could from growing grain. Wine became one of Greece's main exports and was traded by sea for other commodities. In Attica, the switch from grain production to viticulture was so dramatic that grain had to be imported in order to maintain an adequate supply. Wine was wealth; by the sixth century BCE, the property-owning classes in Athens were categorized according to their vineyard holdings: The lowest class had less than seven acres, and the next three classes up owned around ten, fifteen, and twenty-five acres, respectively.

Wine production was also established on remote Greek islands, including Chios, Thásos, and Lesbos, off the west coast of modern Turkey, whose distinctive wines became highly esteemed. Wine's economic importance was underlined by the appearance of wine-related imagery on Greek coins: Those from Chios portrayed the distinctive profile of its wine jars, and the wine god Dionysus reclining on a donkey was a common motif on both the coins and amphora handles of the Thracian city of Mende. The commercial significance of the wine trade also meant that vineyards became prime targets in the Peloponnesian War between Athens and Sparta and were often trampled and burned. On one occasion, in 424 BCE, Spartan troops arrived just before harvest time at Acanthus, a wine-producing city in Macedonia that was allied with Athens. Fearing for their grapes, and swayed by the oratory of Brasidas, the Spartan leader, the locals held a ballot and decided to switch allegiances. The harvest was then able to continue unaffected.

As wine became more widely available—so widely available

that even the slaves drank it—what mattered was no longer whether or not you drank wine, but what kind it was. For while the availability of wine was more democratic in Greek society than in other cultures, wine could still be used to delineate social distinctions. Greek wine buffs were soon making subtle distinctions between the various homegrown and foreign wines. As individual styles became well known, different wine-producing regions began shipping their wines in distinctively shaped amphorae, so that customers who preferred a particular style could be sure they were getting the real thing. Archestratus, a Greek gourmet who lived in Sicily in the fourth century BCE and is remembered as the author of *Gastronomia*, one of the world's first cookbooks, preferred wine from Lesbos. References in Greek comic plays of the fifth and fourth centuries BCE suggest that the wines of Chios and Thásos were also particularly highly regarded.

After a wine's place of origin, the Greeks were primarily interested in its age, rather than its exact vintage. They made little distinction between one vintage and the next, probably because variations caused by storage and handling far outweighed the differences between vintages. Old wine was a badge of status, and the older it was, the better. Homer's *Odyssey*, written in the eighth century BCE, describes the strong room of the mythical hero Odysseus, "where piled-up gold and bronze was lying and clothing in chests and plenty of good-smelling oil: and in it stood jars of old sweet-tasting wine, with the unmixed divine drink in them, packed in rows against the wall."

For the Greeks, wine drinking was synonymous with civilization and refinement: What kind of wine you drank, and its age, indicated how cultured you were. Wine was preferred over beer, fine wines were preferred over ordinary ones, and older wines over young. What mattered even more than your choice of wine, however, was how you behaved when you drank it, which was even more revealing of your innermost nature. As Aeschylus, a Greek poet, put it in the sixth century BCE: "Bronze is the mirror of the outward form; wine is the mirror of the mind."

How to Drink Like a Greek

What most distinguished the Greek approach to wine from that of other cultures was the Greek practice of mixing wine with water before consumption. The pinnacle of social sophistication was the consumption of the resulting mixture at a private drinking party, or *symposion*. This was an all-male aristocratic ritual that took place in a special "men's room," or *andron*. Its walls were often decorated with drinking-related murals or paraphernalia, and the use of a special room emphasized the separation between everyday life and the *symposion*, during which different rules applied. The *andron* was sometimes the only room in the house with a stone floor, which sloped toward the center to make cleaning easier. Its importance was such that houses were often designed around it.

The men sat on special couches, with a cushion under one arm, a fashion imported from the Near East in the eighth century BCE. Typically, a dozen individuals attended a *symposion*, and certainly no more than thirty. Although women were not allowed to sit with the men, female servers, dancers, and musicians were often present. Food was served first, with little or nothing to drink. Then the tables were cleared away, and the wine was brought out. The Athenian tradition was to pour three libations: one to the gods, one to fallen heroes, particularly one's ancestors, and one to Zeus, the king of the gods. A young woman might play the flute during this ceremony, and a hymn would then be sung. Garlands of flowers or vine leaves were handed out, and in some cases perfume was applied. Then the drinking could begin.

The wine was first mixed with water in a large, urn-shaped bowl called a *krater*. Water from a three-handled vessel, the *hydria*, was always added to wine, rather than the other way around. The amount of water added determined how quickly everyone would become intoxicated. Typical mixing ratios of water to wine seem to have been 2:1, 5:2, 3:1, and 4:1. A mixture of equal parts of water and wine was regarded as "strong wine"; some concentrated wines, which were boiled down before shipping to a half or a third of their original volume, had to be mixed with eight or even twenty times as much water. In hot weather, the wine was cooled by lowering it into a well or mixing it with snow, at least by those who could afford such extravagances. The snow was collected during the winter and kept in underground pits, packed with straw, to keep it from melting.

Drinking even a fine wine without first mixing it with water was considered barbaric by the Greeks, and by the Athenians in particular. Only Dionysus, they believed, could drink unmixed wine without risk. He is often depicted drinking from a special type of vase, the use of which indicates that no water has been added. Mere mortals, in contrast, could only drink wine whose strength had been tempered with water; otherwise they would become extremely violent or even go mad. This

Drinkers at a Greek *symposion*. The seated men drink watered-down wine from shallow wine bowls, while a flutist plays music and a slave fetches more wine from the communal *krater*.

was said by Herodotus to have happened to King Cleomenes of Sparta, who picked up the barbaric habit of drinking unmixed wine from the Scythians, a nomadic people from the region north of the Black Sea. Both they and their neighbors the Thracians were singled out by the Athenian philosopher Plato as being clueless and uncultured in their use of wine: "The Scythians and Thracians, both men and women, drink unmixed wine, which they pour on their garments, and this they think a happy and glorious institution." Macedonians were also notorious for their fondness for unmixed wine. Alexander the Great and his father, Philip II, were both reputed to have been heavy drinkers. Alexander killed his friend Clitus in a drunken brawl, and there is some evidence that heavy wine drinking contributed to his death from a mysterious illness in 323 BCE. But it is difficult to evaluate the trustworthiness of such claims, since the equation of virtue with moderate drinking, and corruption with overindulgence, is so widespread in the ancient sources.

Water made wine safe; but wine also made water safe. As well as being free of pathogens, wine contains natural antibacterial agents that are liberated during the fermentation process. The Greeks were unaware of this, though they were familiar with the dangers of drinking contaminated water; they preferred water from springs and deep wells, or rainwater collected in cisterns. The observation that wounds treated with wine were less likely to become infected than those treated with water (again, because of the lack of pathogens and the presence of antibacterial agents) may also have suggested that wine had the power to clean and purify.

Not drinking wine at all was considered just as bad as drinking it neat. The Greek practice of mixing wine and water was thus a middle ground between barbarians who overindulged and those who did not drink at all. Plutarch, a Greek writer from the later Roman period, put it this way: "The drunkard is insolent and rude. . . . On the other hand, the complete teetotaler is disagreeable and more fit for tending children than for presiding over a drinking party." Neither, the Greeks believed, was able to make proper use of the gift of Dionysus. The Greek ideal was to be somewhere between the two. Ensuring that this was the case was the job of the *symposiarch*, or king of the *symposion*—either the host, or one of the drinking group, chosen by ballot or a roll of dice. Moderation was the key: The *symposiarch*'s aim was to keep the assembled company on the borderline between sobriety and drunkenness, so that they could enjoy the freedom of tongue and release from worry, but without becoming violent like barbarians.

Wine was most frequently drunk from a shallow, two-handled bowl with a short stem called a *cylix*. It was also sometimes served in a larger, deeper vessel called a *cantharos*, or a drinking horn called a *rhyton*. A wine jug, or *oinochoë*, which in some cases resembled a long-handled ladle, was used by servants, under the direction of the *symposiarch*, to transfer wine from the *krater* to the drinking vessels. Once one *krater* had been emptied, another would be prepared.

Drinking vessels were elaborately decorated, often with Dionysian imagery, and they became increasingly ornate. For pottery vessels, the classic form was the "black-figure" technique, in which figures and objects were represented by areas of black paint, with details picked out by incising lines before firing. This technique, pioneered in Corinth in the seventh century BCE, quickly spread to Athens. From the sixth century BCE, it was progressively replaced by the "red-figure" technique, in which figures were depicted by leaving the natural red color of the clay unpainted, and adding details in black. The survival to this day of so much black-figure and red-figure pottery, including drinking vessels, is misleading, however. The rich drank from silver or gold drinking vessels, rather than pottery. But it is the pottery vessels that survive because they were used in burials.

Adherence to the rules and rituals of wine drinking, and the use of the appropriate equipment, furniture, and dress all served to emphasize the drinkers' sophistication. But what actually went on while the wine was being consumed? There is no single answer; the *symposion* was as varied as life itself, a mirror of

Greek society. Sometimes there would be formal entertainment, in the form of hired musicians and dancers. At some *symposia*, the guests themselves would compete to improvise witty songs, poetry, and repartee; sometimes the *symposion* was a formal occasion for the discussion of philosophy or literature, to which young men were admitted for educational purposes.

But not all *symposia* were so serious. Particularly popular was a drinking game called *kottabos*. This involved flicking the last remaining drops of wine from one's cup at a specific target, such as another person, a disk-shaped bronze target, or even a cup floating in a bowl of water, with the aim of sinking it. Such was the craze for *kottabos* that some enthusiasts even built special circular rooms in which to play it. Traditionalists expressed concern that young men were concentrating on improving their *kottabos* rather than javelin throwing, a sport that at least had some practical use in hunting and war.

As one *krater* succeeded another, some *symposia* descended into orgies, and others into violence, as drinkers issued challenges to each other to demonstrate loyalty to their drinking group, or *hetaireia*. The *symposion* was sometimes followed by the *komos*, a form of ritual exhibitionism in which the members of the *hetaireia* would course through the streets in nocturnal revelry to emphasize the strength and unity of their group. The *komos* could be good-natured but could also lead to violence or vandalism, depending on the state of the participants. As a fragment from a play by Euboulos puts it: "For sensible men I prepare only three kraters: one for health, which they drink first, the second for love and pleasure, and the third for sleep. After the third one is drained, wise men go home.

The fourth krater is not mine anymore—it belongs to bad behavior; the fifth is for shouting; the sixth is for rudeness and insults; the seventh is for fights; the eighth is for breaking the furniture; the ninth is for depression; the tenth is for madness and unconsciousness."

At heart, the *symposion* was dedicated to the pursuit of pleasure, whether of the intellectual, social, or sexual variety. It was also an outlet, a way of dealing with unruly passions of all kinds. It encapsulated the best and worst elements of the culture that spawned it. The mixture of water and wine consumed in the *symposion* provided fertile metaphorical ground for Greek philosophers, who likened it to the mixture of the good and bad in human nature, both within an individual and in society at large. The *symposion*, with its rules for preventing a dangerous mixture from getting out of hand, thus became a lens through which Plato and other philosophers viewed Greek society.

The Philosophy of Drinking

Philosophy is the pursuit of wisdom; and where better to discover the truth than at a *symposion*, where wine does away with inhibitions to expose truths, both pleasant and unpleasant? "Wine reveals what is hidden," declared Eratosthenes, a Greek philosopher who lived in the third century BCE. That the *symposion* was thought to be a suitable venue for getting at the truth is emphasized by its repeated use as a literary form, in which several characters debate a particular topic while drinking wine. The most famous example is Plato's *Symposium*, in which the participants, including Plato's depiction of his mentor, Socrates, discuss the subject of love. After an entire night's drinking, everyone has fallen asleep except Socrates, who remains apparently unaffected by the wine he has drunk and sets off on his day's business. Plato depicts him as the ideal drinker: He uses wine in the pursuit of truth but remains in total control of himself and suffers no ill effects. Socrates also appears in a similar work written by another of his pupils. Xenophon's *Symposium*, written around 360 BCE, is another fictional account of an Athenian drinking party where the conversation is rather more sparkling and witty, and the characters rather more human, than in Plato's more serious work. The main subject, once again, is love, and the conversation is fueled by fine Thasian wine.

Such philosophical *symposia* took place more in literary imagination than in real life. But in one respect, at least, wine could be used in everyday life to reveal truth: It could expose the true

The Greek philosopher Plato, who believed that wine provided a good way to test a man's character

nature of those drinking it. While he objected to the hedonistic reality of actual *symposia*, Plato saw no reason why the practice could not, in theory, be put to good use as a test of personality. Speaking through one of the characters in his book *Laws*, Plato argues that drinking with someone at a *symposion* is in fact the simplest, fastest, and most reliable test of someone's character. He portrays Socrates postulating a "fear potion" that induces fear in those who drink it. This imaginary drink can then be used to instill fearlessness and courage, as drinkers gradually increase the dose and learn to conquer their fear. No such potion exists, of course; but Plato (speaking, as Socrates, to a Cretan interlocutor) draws an analogy with wine, which he suggests is ideally suited to instill self-control.

What is better adapted than the festive use of wine, in the first place to test, and in the second place to train the character of a man, if care be taken in the use of it? What is there cheaper, or more innocent? For do but consider which is the greater risk: Would you rather test a man of a morose and savage nature, which is the source of ten thousand acts of injustice, by making bargains with him at a risk to yourself, or by having him as a companion at the festival of Dionysus? Or would you, if you wanted to apply a touchstone to a man who is prone to love, entrust your wife, or your sons, or daughters to him, imperiling your dearest interests in order to have a view of the condition of his soul? . . . I do not believe that either a Cretan, or any other man, will doubt that such a test is a fair test, and safer, cheaper, and speedier than any other.

Similarly, Plato saw drinking as a way to test oneself, by submitting to the passions aroused by drinking: anger, love, pride, ignorance, greed, and cowardice. He even laid down rules for the proper running of a *symposion*, which should ideally enable men to develop resistance to their irrational urges and triumph over their inner demons. Wine, he declared, "was given [to man] as a balm, and in order to implant modesty in the soul, and health and strength in the body."

The *symposion* also lent itself to political analogies. To modern eyes, a gathering at which everyone drank as equals from a shared bowl appears to embody the idea of democracy. The *symposion* was indeed democratic, though not in the modern sense of the word. It was strictly for privileged men; but the same was true, in the Athenian form of democracy, of the right to vote, which was only extended to free men, or around a fifth of the population. Greek democracy relied on slavery. Without slaves to do all the hard work, the men would not have had enough leisure time to participate in politics.

Plato was suspicious of democracy. For one thing, it interfered with the natural order of things. Why should a man obey his father, or a scholar his teacher, if they were technically equals? Placing too much power in the hands of the ordinary people, Plato argued in his book *The Republic*, led inevitably to anarchy—at which point order could only be restored through tyranny. In *The Republic*, he depicted Socrates denouncing proponents of democracy as evil wine pourers who encouraged the thirsty people to overindulge in the "strong wine of freedom." Power, in other words, is like wine and can intoxicate when consumed in large quantities by people who are not used to it.

The result in both cases is chaos. This is one of many allusions in *The Republic* to the *symposion*, nearly all of which are disparaging. (Plato believed, instead, that the ideal society would be run by an elite group of guardians, led by philosopher kings.)

In short, the *symposion* reflected human nature and had both good and bad aspects. But provided the right rules were followed, Plato concluded, the good in the *symposion* could outweigh the bad. Indeed, when he set up his academy, just outside Athens, where he taught philosophy for over forty years and did most of his writing, the *symposion* provided the model for his style of teaching. After each day of lectures and debates, he and his students ate and drank together, one chronicler noted, in order to "enjoy each other's company and chiefly to refresh themselves with learned discussion." Wine was served according to Plato's directions, in moderate quantities to ensure that the chief form of refreshment was intellectual; a contemporary observed that those who dined with Plato felt perfectly well the next day. There were no musicians or dancers, for Plato believed that educated men ought to be capable of entertaining themselves by "speaking and listening in turns in an orderly manner." Today, the same format survives as a framework for academic interchange, in the form of the scholarly seminar, or symposium, where participants speak in turn and discussion and argument, within proscribed limits, are encouraged.

An Amphora of Culture

With its carefully calibrated social divisions, its reputation for unparalleled cultural sophistication, and its encouragement of both hedonism and philosophical inquiry, wine embodied Greek culture. These values went along with Greek wine as it was exported far and wide. The distribution of Greek wine jars, or amphorae, provides archaeological evidence for Greek wine's widespread popularity and the far-reaching influence of Greek customs and values. By the fifth century BCE, Greek wine was being exported as far afield as southern France to the west, Egypt to the south, the Crimean Peninsula to the east, and the Danube region to the north. It was trade on a massive scale; a single wreck found off the southern coast of France contained an astonishing 10,000 amphorae, equivalent to 250,000 liters or 333,000 modern wine bottles. As well as spreading wine itself, Greek traders and colonists spread knowledge of its cultivation, introducing wine making to Sicily, southern Italy, and southern France, though whether viticulture was introduced to Spain and Portugal by the Greeks or the Phoenicians (a seafaring culture based in a region of modern-day Syria and Lebanon) is unclear.

A Celtic grave-mound found in central France, dating from the sixth century BCE, contained the body of a young noblewoman lying on the frame of a wagon, the wheels of which had been removed and laid alongside. Among the valuables found in the tomb was a complete set of imported Greek drinking vessels, including an enormous and elaborately decorated *krater*. Similar vessels have been found in other Celtic graves. Vast amounts of Greek wine and drinking vessels were also exported to Italy, where the Etruscans enthusiastically embraced the custom of the *symposion* to demonstrate their own sophistication.

Greek customs such as wine drinking were regarded as worthy of imitation by other cultures. So the ships that carried Greek wine were carrying Greek civilization, distributing it around the Mediterranean and beyond, one amphora at a time. Wine displaced beer to become the most civilized and sophisticated of drinks—a status it has maintained ever since, thanks to its association with the intellectual achievements of Ancient Greece.

4

The Imperial Vine

Baths, wine and sex ruin our bodies. But what makes life worth living except baths, wine and sex?—*Corpus Inscriptionis VI, 15258*

Rome Versus Greece

BY THE MIDDLE of the second century BCE the Romans, a people from central Italy, had displaced the Greeks as the dominant power in the Mediterranean basin. Yet it was a strange sort of victory, since the Romans, like many other European peoples, liked to show how sophisticated they were by appropriating aspects of Greek culture. They borrowed Greek gods and their associated myths, adopted a modified form of the Greek alphabet, and imitated Greek architecture. The Roman constitution was modeled on Greek lines. Educated Romans studied Greek literature and could speak the language. All of this led some Romans to argue that Rome's supposed victory over Greece was, in reality, a defeat. As fine Greek statues were triumphantly brought into Rome after the sack of the Greek colony of Syracuse in 212 BCE, Cato the Elder, a curmudgeonly Roman who regarded the

Greeks as a bad influence, remarked that "the vanquished have conquered us, not we them." He had a point.

Cato and other skeptics contrasted what they regarded as the weak, unreliable, and self-indulgent nature of the Greeks with the Romans' practical, no-nonsense manner. Although Greek culture had once had many admirable qualities, they argued, it had since degenerated: The Greeks had become entranced by their glorious history and overly fond of wordplay and philosophizing. Yet for all these criticisms, there was no denying the debt the Romans owed to Greek culture. The paradoxical result was that while many Romans were wary of becoming too much like the Greeks, the Romans carried the intellectual and artistic legacy of the Greeks farther than ever before, as their sphere of influence expanded around the Mediterranean and beyond.

Wine offered one way to resolve this paradox, for the cultivation and consumption of wine provided a way to bridge Greek and Roman values. The Romans were proud of their origins and saw themselves as a nation of unpretentious farmers turned soldiers and administrators. After successful campaigns, Roman soldiers were often rewarded with tracts of farmland. The most prestigious crop to grow was the vine; by doing so, Roman gentleman farmers could convince themselves that they were remaining true to their roots, even as they also enjoyed lavish feasts and drinking parties in Greek-style villas.

Cato himself agreed that viticulture provided a way to reconcile the traditional Roman values of frugality and simplicity with Greek sophistication. Cultivating vines was honest and down-to-earth, but the resulting wine was a symbol of civilization. For the Romans, wine therefore embodied both where they had come from and what they had become. The military might of a culture founded by hardworking farmers was symbolized by the Roman centurion's badge of rank: a wooden rod cut from the sapling of a vine.

All Vines Lead to Rome

At the beginning of the second century BCE, Greek wine still dominated the Mediterranean wine trade and was the only product being exported in significant quantities to the Italian peninsula. But the Romans were catching up fast, as wine making spread northward from the former Greek colonies in the south—the region known to the Greeks as "Oenotria," or "the land of the trained vines," which was under Roman rule by this time. The Italian peninsula became the world's foremost wine-producing region around 146 BCE, just as Rome became the leading Mediterranean power with the fall of Carthage in northern Africa and the sack of the Greek city of Corinth.

Just as they assimilated and then distributed so many other aspects of Greek culture, the Romans embraced Greece's finest wines and wine-making techniques. Vines were transplanted from Greek islands, enabling Chian wine, for example, to be grown in Italy. Winemakers began to make imitations of the most popular Greek wines, notably the seawater-flavored wine of Cos, so that Coan became a style rather than a mark of origin. Leading winemakers headed from Greece to Italy, the new center of the trade. By 70 CE, the Roman writer Pliny the Elder estimated that there were eighty wines of note in the Roman world, two-thirds of which were grown in Italy.

Such was the popularity of wine that subsistence farming could not meet demand, and the ideal of the noble farmer was displaced by a more commercial approach, based on large villa estates operated by slaves. Wine production expanded at the expense of grain production, so that Rome became dependent on grain imports from its African colonies. The expansion of the villa estates also displaced the rural population as small farmers sold their property and moved to the city. Rome's population swelled from around one hundred thousand in 300 BCE to around a million by 0 CE, making it the world's most populous metropolis. Meanwhile, as wine production intensified at the heart of the Roman world, consumption spread on its fringes. People adopted wine drinking, along with other Roman customs, wherever Roman rule extended—and beyond. Wealthy Britons put aside beer and mead in favor of wines imported from as far away as the Aegean; Italian wine was shipped as far as the southern Nile and northern India. In the first century, wine production in the Roman provinces of southern Gaul and Spain was stepped up to keep pace with demand, though Italian wines were still regarded as the best.

Wine was shipped from one part of the Mediterranean to another in freighters typically capable of carrying two thousand to three thousand clay amphorae, along with secondary cargoes of slaves, nuts, glassware, perfumes, and other luxury items. Some winemakers shipped their own wine; wrecks have been found in which the name of the winemaker on the amphorae matches the name cast into the anchor. The amphorae in which wine was shipped were generally regarded as disposable, nonre-turnable containers and were usually smashed when they had served their purpose. Thousands of amphora handles, with stamps indicating their place of origin, contents, and other infor-mation, have been found on rubbish heaps in Marseilles, Athens, Alexandria, and other Mediterranean ports, and in Rome itself. Analyzing these stamps makes it possible to map patterns of trade and see the influence of Roman politics on the wine busi-ness. Amphora handles from a 150-foot-high rubbish heap at the Horrea Galbana, a huge warehouse in Rome, are mostly Spanish during the second century CE, following a mysterious decline of Italian production, possibly caused by plague. In the early third century, North African wines start to dominate after the rise to power of Septimius Severus in 193 CE. The merchants of Roman Spain had supported his rival, Albius Clodius, so he encouraged investment in the region around his hometown, Lepcis Magna (modern Tripoli), and favored wines from there instead.

Most of the best wine ended up in Rome itself. Arriving at the port of Ostia, a few miles to the southwest of Rome, a wine ship would be unloaded by a swarm of stevedores, skilled in handling the heavy and unwieldly amphorae across precarious gangplanks. Divers stood ready to rescue any amphorae that fell overboard. Once transferred into smaller vessels, the wine continued its journey up the river Tiber to the city of Rome. It was then manhandled into the dim cellars of wholesale ware-houses and transferred into vast jars sunk into the ground to keep the contents cool. From here it was sold to retailers and transported in smaller amphorae through the city's narrow alleyways on handcarts. Juvenal, a Roman satirist of the early second century CE, gives the following impression of the bustle of Rome's streets:

> *We are blocked*
> *In our hurry by a surging mass before us, while the*
>   *great crowd*
> *Crushes our backs from behind us; an elbow or a stick*
> *Hits you, a beam or a wine-jar smacks you on the head;*
> *My leg is caked in splashing mud, from every side*
> *I'm trampled by shoes, and a soldier spears*
> *My foot with his spiked shoes.*

Having made its way through the chaotic streets, wine was sold by the jug from neighborhood shops, or by the amphora when larger quantities were needed. Roman households sent slaves laden with empty jugs to buy wine, or arranged to have regular supplies delivered; wine vendors wheeled their wares from house to house on carts. Wine from the far provinces of the Roman world then reached the tables, and ultimately the lips, of Rome's citizens.

A Drink for Everyone?

It is not often that choosing one wine over another is a matter of life or death. Yet that is what determined the fate of Marcus Antonius, a Roman politician and a renowned orator. In 87 BCE, he found himself on the wrong side of one of Rome's many interminable power struggles. Gaius Marius, an elderly general, had seized power and was ruthlessly hunting down supporters of his rival, Sulla. Marcus Antonius sought refuge in the house of an associate of far lower social status, hoping that nobody would think of looking for him in such a poor man's house. His host, however, unwittingly gave him away by sending his servant out to buy wine worthy of such a distinguished guest. The servant went to the neighborhood wine shop and, after tasting what was on offer, asked for a far better and more expensive wine than usual. When the vintner asked why, the servant revealed the identity of his master's guest. The vintner went straight to Marius, who dispatched a handful of soldiers to kill Marcus Antonius. Yet having burst into his room, the soldiers could not bring themselves to kill him, such was the power of his oratory. Eventually, their commanding officer, who was waiting outside, went in to see what was happening. Denouncing his men as cowards, he drew his sword and beheaded Marcus Antonius himself.

Like the Greeks before them, the Romans regarded wine as a universal staple. It was drunk by both caesar and slave alike. But the Romans took Greek connoisseurship to new heights. Marcus Antonius's host would not have dreamed of serving him the lesser wine he drank himself. Wine became a symbol of social differentiation, a mark of the wealth and status of the drinker. The disparity between Roman society's richest and poorest members was reflected in the contents of their wine goblets. For wealthy Romans, the ability to recognize and name the finest wines was an important form of conspicuous consumption; it showed that they were rich enough to afford the finest wines and had spent time learning which was which.

The finest wine of all, by universal assent, was Falernian, an

Italian wine grown in the region of Campania. Its name became a byword for luxury and is still remembered today. Falernian had to be made from vines growing in strictly defined regions on the slopes of Mount Falernus, a mountain south of the city of Neapolis (modern Naples). Caucine Falernian was grown on the highest slopes; Faustian Falernian, deemed the best kind, was grown in the middle, on the estate of Faustus, son of the dictator Sulla; and wine grown on the lower slopes was known simply as Falernian. The finest Falernian was a white wine, generally aged for at least ten years and ideally for much longer, until it turned golden in color. The limited production area and the fashion for long aging made Falernian extremely expensive, so it naturally became the wine of the elite. It was even said to have had divine origins: The wandering wine god Bacchus (the Roman version of the Greek god Dionysus) supposedly covered Mount Falernus with vines in gratitude to a noble farmer who, unaware of the god's identity, offered him shelter for the night. Bacchus, the story goes, also turned all the milk in the man's house into wine.

By far the most famous Falernian vintage was that of 121 BCE, known as Opimian Falernian after Opimius, who held the office of consul that year. This wine was drunk by Julius Caesar during the first century BCE, and 160-year-old Opimian was served to the emperor Caligula in 39 CE. Martial, a first-century Roman poet, described Falernian as "immortal," though the Opimian vintage was probably undrinkable by this time. Other high-ranking Roman wines included Caecuban, Surrentine, and Setine, which was popular in summer, mixed with snow brought down from the mountains. Some Roman writers, including Pliny the Elder, denounced the fashion for cold drinks prepared in this way as yet another example of the decadence of the times, complaining that it was unnatural, since it went against the seasons. And while traditionalists called for a return to old-fashioned Roman frugality, others worried that ostentatious spending on food and drink might provoke the wrath of the poor.

Accordingly, numerous "sumptuary laws" were passed to try to restrain the luxurious tastes of Rome's richest citizens. That so many such laws were passed demonstrates that they were rarely obeyed or enforced. One law, passed in 161 BCE, specified the amount that could be spent on food and entertainment on each day of the month; later laws introduced special rules for weddings and funerals, regulated what sorts of meat could or could not be served, and banned certain foods from being served altogether. Other rules stipulated that men could not wear silk garments; that gold vases were only to be used in religious ceremonies; and that dining rooms had to be built with windows facing outward, so officials could check that no rules were being broken. By the time of Julius Caesar, inspectors sometimes loitered in markets or burst into banquets to confiscate banned foodstuffs, and menus had to be submitted for review by state officials.

While the richest Romans drank the finest wines, poorer citizens drank lesser vintages, and so on down the social ladder. So fine was the calibration of wine with status that drinkers at a Roman banquet, or *convivium*, would be served different wines depending on their positions in society. This was just one of the many ways in which the *convivium* differed from its

Greek prototype, the *symposion*. Where the *symposion* was, at least in theory, a forum in which the participants drank as equals from a shared *krater*, pursuing pleasure and perhaps philosophical enlightenment, the *convivium* was an opportunity to emphasize social divisions, not to set them aside in a temporary alcoholic haze.

Like the Greeks, the Romans drank their wine in the "civilized" manner, namely, mixed with water, which was brought into their cities via elaborate aqueducts. Each drinker, however, usually mixed wine and water for himself, and the communal *krater* was, it seems, rarely used. The seating arrangement was less egalitarian than that of the *symposion* too, since some seats were associated with higher status than others. The *convivium* reflected the Roman class system, which was based on the notion of patrons and clients. Client citizens depended on patrons, who in turn depended on patrons of their own, and each patron provided benefits (such as a financial allowance, legal advice, and political influence) to clients in return for specific duties. Clients were expected to accompany their patrons to the Forum each morning, for example; the size of each patron's entourage was a sign of his power. If a patron invited a client to a *convivium*, however, the client would often find himself being served inferior food and wine to those of other guests and might find himself the butt of the other guests' jokes. Pliny the Younger, writing in the late first century CE, described a dinner at which fine wine was served to the host and his friends, second-rate wine to other guests, and third-rate wine to freedmen (former slaves).

These coarser, cheaper wines were often adulterated with

Wine drinkers at an elaborate Roman feast

various additives, either to serve as preservatives or to conceal the fact that they had spoiled. Pitch, which was sometimes used to seal amphorae, was occasionally added to wine as a preservative, as were small quantities of salt or seawater, a practice inherited from the Greeks. Columella, a Roman agricultural writer of the first century CE, claims that when used carefully, such preservatives could be added to wine without affecting its taste. They could even improve it; one of his recipes, for a white wine fermented with seawater and fenugreek, produces a sharp, nutty wine very similar to a modern dry sherry. *Mulsum*, a mixture of wine and honey, emerged as a fashionable aperitif during the reign of Tiberius in the early first century, while *rosatum* was a similar drink flavored with roses. But herbs, honey, and other additives were more commonly added to lesser wines to conceal their imperfections. Some Romans even carried herbs and other flavorings with them while traveling, to improve the taste of bad wine. While modern wine drinkers may turn up their noses at the Greek and Roman use of additives, it is not that different from the modern use of oak as a flavoring agent, often to make otherwise unremarkable wines more palatable.

Below these adulterated wines was *posca*, a drink made by mixing water with wine that had turned sour and vinegarlike. *Posca* was commonly issued to Roman soldiers when better wines were unavailable, for example, during long campaigns. It was, in effect, a form of portable water-purification technology for the Roman army. When a Roman soldier offered Jesus Christ a sponge dipped in wine during his crucifixion, the wine in question would have been *posca*. Finally, at the bottom of the Roman scale of wines was *lora*, the drink normally served to slaves, which hardly qualified as wine at all. It was made by soaking and pressing the skins, seeds, and stalks left over from wine making to produce a thin, weak, and bitter wine. From the legendary Falernian down to lowly *lora*, there was a wine for every rung on the social ladder.

Wine and Medicine

One of the greatest wine tastings in history took place around 170 CE in the imperial cellars in Rome. Here, at the center of the known world, was the finest collection of wines available anywhere, a collection built up by successive emperors for whom cost was no object. Into these cool, damp cellars, pierced with shafts of sunlight, descended Galen, personal physician to the emperor Marcus Aurelius, on a singular mission: to find the best wine in the world.

Galen was born in Pergamon (now Bergama, in modern Turkey), a city in the Greek-speaking eastern part of the Roman Empire. As a youth, he studied medicine in Alexandria and then traveled in Egypt, where he learned about Indian and African remedies. Building on the earlier ideas of Hippocrates, Galen believed that illness was the result of an imbalance of the body's four "humors": blood, phlegm, yellow bile, and black bile. Surplus humors could accumulate in particular parts of the body and were associated with particular temperaments; a buildup of black bile in the spleen, for example, made one melancholic, sleepless, and irritable. The humors could be brought back into balance using techniques such as bloodletting. Different foodstuffs, which were deemed to be hot or cold, wet or dry, could also influence the humors: Cold and wet foods were thought to produce phlegm; hot and dry foods, yellow bile. This systematic approach, promoted by Galen's voluminous writings, was hugely influential and was the basis of Western medicine for more than a thousand years. That it was utter nonsense only became clear in the nineteenth century.

Galen's interest in wine was mainly, though not entirely, professional. As a young doctor he had treated gladiators, using wine to disinfect their wounds, a common practice at the time. Wine, like other foodstuffs, could also be used to regulate the humors. Galen regularly prescribed wine and wine-based remedies for the emperor. Within the framework of the theory of humors, wine was regarded as being hot and dry, so that it promoted yellow bile and reduced phlegm. This meant wine was to be avoided by anyone suffering from a fever (a hot and dry disease) but could be taken as a remedy for a cold (a cold and wet disease). The better the wine, Galen believed, the more medically effective it was; "always try to get the best," he advised in his writings. Since he was treating the emperor, Galen wanted to ensure that he was prescribing the finest possible vintage. Accompanied by a cellarman to open and reseal the amphorae, he duly headed straight for the Falernian.

"Since all that is best from every part of the world finds its way to the great ones of the earth," Galen wrote, "from their excellence must be chosen the very best for the greatest of them all. So, in execution of my duty, I deciphered the vintage marks on the amphorae of every Falernian wine and submitted to my palette every wine over 20 years old. I kept on until I found a wine without a trace of bitterness. An ancient wine which has not lost its sweetness is the best of all." Alas, Galen did not record the year of the Faustian Falernian vintage he eventually deemed most suitable for medical use by the emperor. But having identified it, he insisted that Marcus Aurelius should use that wine, and no other, for medical purposes. This included washing down his daily medicine, a universal antidote designed to protect the emperor against illness generally, and poisoning in particular.

The notion of such an antidote had been pioneered in the first century BCE by Mithradates, the king of Pontus, a region in what is now northern Turkey. He conducted a series of experiments, in which dozens of prisoners were given various deadly poisons, in order to determine the most effective antidote in each case. Eventually, he settled on a mixture of forty-one antidote ingredients, to be taken daily. It tasted disgusting (diced viper's flesh was one ingredient) but meant that Mithradates no longer had to worry about being poisoned. He was eventually overthrown by his son. The story goes that, holed up in a tower, the king tried to kill himself but, ironically, found that no poison had any effect. Finally, he had to ask one of his guards to stab him to death.

Galen extended Mithradates' recipe considerably. His recipe for theriac—a universal antidote to poisons, and a general cure-all—contained seventy-one ingredients, including ground-up lizards, poppy juice, spices, incense, juniper berries, ginger, hemlock seed, raisins, fennel, aniseed, and liquorice. It is hard to imagine that Marcus Aurelius was able to appreciate the taste of Falernian after swallowing such a mixture, but he did as his eminent doctor told him, and washed it down with the world's greatest wine.

Why Christians Drink Wine and Muslims Do Not

Marcus Aurelius died in 180 CE, not from poisoning but from illness. For the last week of his life he consumed only theriac and Falernian wine. The end of his reign, a period of relative peace, stability, and prosperity, is often taken to mark the end of the golden age of Rome. There followed a succession of short-lived emperors, almost none of whom died of natural causes, and who did their best to defend the empire from the onslaught of barbarians from all sides. Lying on his deathbed in 395 CE, the emperor Theodosius I divided the empire into western and eastern halves, each to be ruled by one of his sons, in an attempt to make it easier to defend. But the western empire soon crumbled: The Visigoths, a Germanic tribe, sacked Rome in 410 CE and then established a kingdom covering much of Spain and western Gaul. Rome was plundered again in 455 CE by the Vandals, and before long the western empire had been carved up into a multitude of separate kingdoms.

According to centuries-old Roman and Greek prejudices, the influx of the northern tribes ought to have displaced the civilized wine-drinking culture in favor of beer-drinking barbarism. Yet despite their reputation as vulgar beer lovers, the tribes of northern Europe, where the climate was less suitable for viticulture, had nothing against wine. Of course, many aspects of Roman life were swept away, trade was disrupted, and the availability of wine in some regions diminished; Romanized Britons seem to have switched from wine back to beer as the empire crumbled, for example. But there was also cultural fusion between Roman, Christian, and Germanic traditions as new rulers took over from the Romans. One example of continuity was the widespread survival of Mediterranean wine-drinking culture, which was deep-rooted enough to survive the passing of its Greek and Roman parents. The Visigothic law code, for instance, drawn up between the fifth and seventh centuries, specified detailed punishments for anyone who damaged a vineyard—hardly what you would expect of barbarians.

Another factor in maintaining the wine-drinking culture was its close association with Christianity, the rise of which during the first millennium elevated wine to a position of utmost symbolic significance. According to the Bible, Christ's first miracle, at the beginning of his ministry, was the transformation of six jars of water into wine at a wedding near the Sea of Galilee. Christ told several parables about wine and often likened himself to a vine: "I am the vine, you are the branches," he told his followers. Christ's offering of wine to his disciples at the Last Supper then led to its role in the Eucharist, the central Christian ritual in which bread and wine symbolize Christ's body and blood. This was, in many ways, a continuation of the tradition established by members of the cults of Dionysus and his Roman incarnation, Bacchus. The Greek and Roman wine gods, like Christ, were associated with wine-making miracles and resurrection after death; their worshipers, like Christians, regarded wine drinking as a form of sacred communion. Yet there are also marked differences. The Christian ritual is nothing like its Dionysian counterpart, and while the former involves very small quantities of wine, the latter calls for large quantities drunk in excess.

It has been suggested that the Christian church's need for communion wine played an important role in keeping wine production going during the dark ages after the fall of Rome. That is an exaggeration, however, despite the close links between Christianity and wine. The amount of wine required for the Eucharist was miniscule, and by 1100 it was increasingly the case that only the celebrating priest drank wine from the chalice, while the congregation just received bread. Most wine produced by vineyards on church land, or attached to monasteries, was for everyday consumption by those in religious orders. Benedictine monks, for example, received a daily ration of about half a pint of wine. In some cases, the sale of wine made on church land was a valuable source of income.

Although the wine culture remained reasonably intact in Christian Europe, drinking patterns changed dramatically in other parts of the former Roman world, as a result of the rise of Islam. Its founder, the prophet Muhammad, was born around 570 CE. At the age of forty he felt himself called to become a prophet, and experienced a series of visions during which the Koran was revealed to him by Allah. Muhammad's new teachings made him unpopular in Mecca, a city whose prosperity depended on the traditional Arab religion, so he fled to Medina, where his following grew. By the time of Muhammad's death in 632 CE, Islam had become the dominant faith in most of Arabia. A century later, his adherents had conquered all of Persia, Mesopotamia, Palestine and Syria, Egypt and the rest of the northern African coast, and most of Spain.

Muslims' duties include frequent prayer, almsgiving, and abstention from alcoholic drinks.

Tradition has it that Muhammad's proscription of alcohol followed a fight between two of his disciples during a drinking party. When the prophet sought divine guidance about how to prevent such incidents, Allah's reply was uncompromising: "Wine and games of chance . . . are abominations devised by Satan. Avoid them, so that you may prosper. Satan seeks to stir up enmity and hatred among you by means of wine and gambling, and to keep you from remembrance of Allah and from your prayers. Will you not abstain from them?" The punishment for anyone who broke this rule was duly set at forty lashes. It seems likely, however, that the Muslim ban on alcohol was also the result of wider cultural forces. With the rise of Islam, power shifted away from the peoples of the Mediterranean coast and toward the desert tribes of Arabia. These tribes expressed their superiority over the previous elites by replacing wheeled vehicles with camels, chairs and tables with cushions, and by banning the consumption of wine, that most potent symbol of sophistication. In so doing, Muslims signaled their rejection of the old notions of civilization. Wine's central role in the rival creed of Christianity also predisposed Muslims against it; even its medical use was banned. After much argument the prohibition was extended to other alcoholic drinks too. As Islam spread, so did the prohibition of alcohol.

The ban on alcohol was, however, enforced more rigorously in some places than in others. Wine was celebrated in the work of Abu Nouwas and other Arab poets, and production continued in Spain and Portugal, for example, even though it was technically illegal. And the fact that Muhammad himself was said to have enjoyed lightly fermented date wine led some Spanish Muslims to argue that his objection was not so much to wine itself as to overindulgence. Only wine made from grapes had been explicitly banned, presumably on the basis of its strength; therefore, grape wine ought to be allowed, provided it was diluted so that its strength did not exceed that of date wine. This fancy interpretative footwork was controversial but did provide some leeway. Indeed, wine-drinking parties akin to Greek *symposia* seem to have been popular in some parts of the Muslim world. Mixing wine with water, after all, reduced its potency considerably and seemed to conform with Muhammad's vision of paradise: a garden in which the righteous "shall drink of a pure wine, tempered with the water of Tasnim, a spring at which the favored will refresh themselves."

The advance of Islam into Europe was halted in 732 CE at the Battle of Tours, in central France, where the Arab troops were defeated by Charles Martel, the most charismatic of the princes of the Frankish kingdom that roughly corresponds with modern France. This battle, one of the turning points in world history, marked the high-water mark of Arab influence in Europe. The subsequent crowning of Martel's grandson, Charlemagne, as Holy Roman Emperor in 800 CE heralded the start of a period of consolidation and eventual reinvigoration of European culture.

The King of Drinks

"Woe is me!" wrote Alcuin, a scholar who was one of Charlemagne's advisers, to a friend during a visit to England in the early ninth century CE. "The wine is gone from our wineskins and bitter beer rages in our bellies. And because we have it not, drink in our name and lead a joyful day." Alcuin's lament illustrates that wine was scarce in England, as it was elsewhere in northern Europe. In these parts, where wine could not be produced locally but had to be imported, beer and mead (and a hybrid drink in which cereal grains were fermented with honey) predominated instead. The distinction between beer in northern Europe and wine in the south persists to this day. Modern European drinking patterns crystallized during the middle of the first millennium and were largely determined by the reach of Greek and Roman influences.

Wine drinking, usually in moderation and with meals, still predominates in the south of Europe, within the former boundaries of the Roman Empire. In the north of Europe beyond the reach of Roman rule, beer drinking, typically without the accompaniment of food, is more common. Today, the world's leading producers of wine are France, Italy, and Spain; and the people of Luxembourg, France, and Italy are the leading consumers of wine, drinking an average of around fifty-five liters per person per year. The countries where the most beer is consumed, in contrast, would mostly have been regarded as barbarian territory by the Romans: Germany, Austria, Belgium, Denmark, the Czech Republic, Britain, and Ireland.

Greek and Roman attitudes toward wine, themselves founded on earlier Near Eastern traditions, have survived in other ways, too, and have spread around the world. Wherever alcohol is drunk, wine is regarded as the most civilized and cultured of drinks. In those countries, wine, not beer, is served at state banquets and political summits, an illustration of wine's enduring association with status, power, and wealth.

Wine also provides the greatest scope for connoisseurship and social differentiation. Appreciation of wines from different places began with the Greeks, and the link between the type of wine and the social status of the drinker was strengthened by the Romans. The *symposion* and *convivium* live on in the modern suburban dinner party, where wine fuels an almost ritual discussion of certain topics (politics, business, career advancement, house prices) in a slightly formal atmosphere with particular rules about the order in which food is consumed, the placement of cutlery, and so on. The host is responsible for the choice of wine, and the selection is expected to reflect the importance of the occasion and the social standing of both the host and his guests. It is a scene that a time-traveling Roman would recognize at once.

SPIRITS *in the*
COLONIAL PERIOD

5

High Spirits, High Seas

One can distill wine using a water-bath, and it comes out like rosewater in color.—*Abu Yusuf Yaqub ibn Ishaq al-Sabbah al-Kindi, Arab scientist and philosopher (c. 801–73 CE),* in The Book of the Chemistry of Perfume and Distillations

A Gift from the Arabs

AT THE CLOSE of the first millennium AD, the greatest and most cultured city in western Europe was not Rome, Byzantium, or London. It was Córdoba, the capital of Arab Andalusia, in what is now southern Spain. There were parks, palaces, paved roads, oil lamps to light the streets, seven hundred mosques, three hundred public baths, and extensive drainage and sewage systems. Perhaps most impressive of all was the public library, completed around 970 CE and containing nearly half a million books—more books than any other European library, or indeed most European countries. And it was merely the largest of seventy libraries in the city. No wonder Hroswitha, a tenth-century German chronicler, described Córdoba as "the jewel of the world."

Córdoba was only one of the great centers of learning within the Arab world, a vast dominion that stretched at its height from the Pyrenees in France to the Pamir Mountains in central Asia, and as far south as the Indus Valley in India. At a time when the wisdom of the Greeks had been lost in most of Europe, Arab scholars in Córdoba, Damascus, and Baghdad were building on knowledge from Greek, Indian, and Persian sources to make further advances in such fields as astronomy, mathematics, medicine, and philosophy. They developed the astrolabe, algebra, and the modern numeral system, pioneered the use of herbs as anesthetics, and devised new navigational techniques based on the magnetic compass (an introduction from China), trigonometry, and nautical maps. Among their many achievements, they also refined and popularized a technique that gave rise to a new range of drinks: distillation.

This process, which involves vaporizing and then recondensing a liquid in order to separate and purify its constituent parts, has ancient origins. Simple distillation equipment dating back to the fourth millennium BCE has been found in northern Mesopotamia, where, judging from later cuneiform inscriptions, it was used to make perfumes. The Greeks and Romans were also familiar with the technique; Aristotle, for example, noted that the vapor condensed from boiling salt water was not salty. But it was only later, starting in the Arab world, that distillation was routinely applied to wine, notably by the eighth-century Arab scholar Jabir ibn Hayyan, who is remembered as one of the fathers of chemistry. He devised an improved form of distillation apparatus, or still, with which he and other Arab alchemists distilled wine and other substances for use in their experiments.

Distilling wine makes it much stronger, because the boiling point of alcohol (seventy-eight degrees centigrade) is lower than that of water (one hundred degrees centigrade). As the wine is slowly heated, vapor begins to rise from its surface long before the liquid starts to boil. Due to alcohol's lower boiling point, this vapor contains proportionately more alcohol and less water than the original liquid. Drawing off and condensing this alcohol-rich vapor produces a liquid with a far higher alcohol content than wine, though it is far from being pure alcohol, since some water and other impurities evaporate even at temperatures below one hundred degrees. However, the alcohol content can be increased by repeated redistillation, also known as rectification.

Knowledge of distillation was one of many aspects of the ancient wisdom that was preserved and extended by Arab scholars and, having been translated from Arabic into Latin, helped to rekindle the spirit of learning in western Europe. The word *alembic*, which refers to a type of still, encapsulates this combination of ancient knowledge and Arab innovation. It is derived from the Arabic *al-ambiq*, descended in turn from the Greek word *ambix*, which refers to the specially shaped vase used in distillation. Similarly, the modern word *alcohol* illuminates the origins of distilled alcoholic drinks in the laboratories of Arab alchemists. It is descended from *al-koh'l*, the name given to the black powder of purified antimony, which was used as a cosmetic, to paint or stain the eyelids. The term was used more generally by alchemists to refer to other highly

Distillation equipment in a medieval laboratory. The production of spirits began as an obscure alchemical technique known only to a select few.

purified substances, including liquids, so that distilled wine later came to be known in English as "alcohol of wine."

From their obscure origins in alchemical laboratories, the new drinks made possible by distillation became dominant during the Age of Exploration, as seafaring European explorers established colonies and then empires around the world. Distilled drinks provided a durable and compact form of alcohol for transport on board ship and found a range of other uses. These drinks became economic goods of such significance that their taxation and control became matters of great political importance and helped to determine the course of history. The abstemious Arab scholars who first distilled wine regarded the result as alchemical ingredients or a medicine, rather than an everyday drink. Only when knowledge of distillation spread into Christian Europe did distilled spirits become more widely consumed.

A Miracle Cure?

On a winter night in 1386 the royal doctors were summoned to the bedchamber of Charles II of Navarre, the ruler of a small kingdom in what is now northern Spain. The king was known as "Charles the Bad," a nickname he earned early in his reign when he suppressed a revolt with particular cruelty and ferocity. His favorite pastime was plotting against his father-in-law, the king of France. Now, after a night of debauchery, Charles had been struck down by fever and paralysis. His doctors decided to administer a medicine reputed to have miraculous healing powers, and made using an almost magical process: the distillation of wine.

One of the first Europeans to experiment with this novel process was the twelfth-century Italian alchemist Michael Salernus, who learned of it from Arab texts. "A mixture of pure and very strong wine with three parts salt, distilled in the usual vessel, produces a liquid which will flame up when set on fire," he wrote. Evidently, this process was known only to a select few at the time, since Salernus wrote several of the key words of this sentence (including *wine* and *salt*) in secret code. Since distilled wine could be set on fire, it was called *aqua ardens*, which means "burning water."

Of course, burning also described the unpleasant sensation produced in the throat after swallowing distilled wine. Yet those who tried drinking small quantities of *aqua ardens* found that this initial discomfort, sometimes disguised using herbs, was far outweighed by the sensation of invigoration and well-being that swiftly followed. Wine was widely used as a medicine, so it seemed only logical that concentrated and purified wine should have even greater healing powers. By the late thirteenth century, as universities and medical schools were flowering throughout Europe, distilled wine was being acclaimed in Latin medical treatises as a miraculous new medicine, aqua vitae, or "water of life."

One firm believer in the therapeutic power of distilled wine was Arnald of Villanova, a professor at the French medical school of Montpellier, who produced instructions for distilling wine around 1300. "The true water of life will come over in precious drops, which, being rectified by three or four successive distillations, will afford the wonderful quintessence of wine," he wrote. "We call it aqua vitae, and this name is remarkably suitable, since it is really a water of immortality. It prolongs life, clears away ill-humors, revives the heart, and maintains youth."

Aqua vitae seemed supernatural, and in a sense it was, for distilled wine has a far higher alcohol content than any drink that can be produced by natural fermentation. Even the hardiest yeasts cannot tolerate an alcohol content greater than about 15 percent, which places a natural limit on the strength of fermented alcoholic drinks. Distillation allowed alchemists to circumvent this limit, which had prevailed since the discovery of fermentation thousands of years earlier. Arnald's pupil, Raymond Lully, declared aqua vitae "an element newly revealed to men but hid from antiquity, because the human race was then too young to need this beverage destined to revive the energies of modern decrepitude." Both men lived to be well over seventy, an unusually advanced age for the time, which may have been taken as evidence for aqua vitae's life-prolonging power.

This wonderful new medicine could either be administered as a drink or applied externally to the affected part of the body. Aqua vitae's proponents believed it could preserve youth; improve memory; treat diseases of the brain, nerves, and joints; revive the heart; calm toothache; cure blindness, speech defects, and paralysis; and even protect against the plague. It was, in short, regarded as a panacea, which was why Charles the Bad's doctors decided to administer it to their patient. Working by candlelight, they enveloped the king in sheets soaked with aqua vitae, hoping that contact with the magical fluid would cure his paralysis. But the treatment went disastrously wrong: The sheets were accidentally ignited by a careless servant's candle, and the king instantly went up in flames. His subjects are said to have regarded his fiery and agonizing death as a divine judgment, for one of the king's final acts had been to order a dramatic increase in taxation.

Over the course of the fifteenth century, aqua vitae began to change from a medicinal drink into a recreational one as knowledge of distillation spread. This process was helped by a new invention, the printing press, developed by Johannes Gutenberg during the 1430s. (It was new to Europeans, at least, though the same idea had occurred to the Chinese some centuries earlier.) The first printed book about distillation was written by Michael Puff von Schrick, an Austrian doctor, and published in Augsburg in 1478. It was so popular that fourteen editions of the book had appeared by 1500. Among the claims made by von Schrick were that drinking half a spoon of aqua vitae every morning could ward off illness, and that pouring a little aqua vitae into the mouth of a dying person would give him or her the strength to speak one last time.

But for most people, aqua vitae's appeal came not from its supposed medicinal benefits but from its power to intoxicate people quickly and easily. Distilled drinks proved particularly popular in the cooler climes of northern Europe, where wine was scarce and expensive. By distilling beer, it was possible to make powerful alcholic drinks with local ingredients for the first time. The Gaelic for aqua vitae, *uisge beatha*, is the origin of the modern word *whiskey*. This new drink quickly became part of the Irish lifestyle. One chronicler recorded the death in 1405 of Richard MacRaghnaill, the son of an Irish chieftain, who died "after drinking water of life to excess; and it was water of death to Richard."

Elsewhere in Europe, aqua vitae was called "burnt wine,"

rendered in German as *Branntwein* and in English as *brandywine*, or simply *brandy*. People began distilling wine in their own homes and offering it for sale on feast days, a practice that was widespread and troublesome enough that it was explicitly banned in the German city of Nuremberg in 1496. A local doctor observed: "In view of the fact that everyone at present has got into the habit of drinking aqua vitae it is necessary to remember the quantity that one can permit oneself to drink, and learn to drink it according to one's capacities, if one wishes to behave like a gentleman."

Spirits, Sugar, and Slaves

The emergence of these new distilled drinks occurred just as European explorers were first opening up the world's sea routes, reaching around the southern tip of Africa to the east, and crossing the Atlantic to establish the first links with the New World in the west. The process began with the exploration by Portuguese explorers of the west coast of Africa, and the discovery and colonization of the nearby Atlantic islands, the first stepping stones on the way to the Americas. These expeditions were organized and funded by Prince Henrique of Portugal, also known as Prince Henry the Navigator. Despite his name, Prince Henry himself remained in Portugal for most of his life. He went abroad just three times, and even then only as far as North Africa, on three military excursions that respectively made, destroyed, and restored his reputation as a commander. But from his base in Sagres he masterminded an ambitious program of Portuguese naval exploration. Prince Henry funded expeditions and collated the resulting reports, observations, and maps.

He also encouraged his captains to embrace advances in navigation such as the magnetic compass, along with trigonometry and the astrolabe, an invention which had, like distillation, been introduced by Arabs into western Europe. The chief motive of the Portuguese, Spanish, and other explorers of the time was to find an alternative route to the East Indies, in order to circumvent the Arab monopoly on the spice trade. Ironically, their eventual success was due in part to the use of technology provided by the Arabs.

The Atlantic islands of Madeira, the Azores, and the Canaries proved to be ideal places to produce sugar, another Arab introduction. But growing sugarcane required enormous amounts of water and manpower. The Arabs had amassed a range of irrigation techniques and labor-saving devices during their westward expansion, including the water screw, the Persian innovation of underground aqueducts, and water-powered mills to process sugarcane. Even so, sugar production under the Arabs relied on slaves, mostly brought in from East Africa. The Europeans captured many of the Arab sugar plantations during the religious wars of the Crusades but lacked experience in growing sugar and needed even more manpower to maintain production. During the 1440s the Portuguese began to ship black slaves from their trading posts on the west coast of Africa. At first these slaves were kidnapped, but the Portuguese soon agreed to buy slaves, in return for European goods, from African traders.

Mass slavery had been unseen in Europe since Roman times, in part for religious reasons, for doctrine forbade the enslavement of one Christian by another. Such theological objections to the new slave trade were overlooked or sidestepped using a number of dubious arguments. At first, it was suggested that by buying slaves and converting them to Christianity, Europeans were rescuing them from the false doctrine of Islam. But then another argument emerged: Black Africans, argued some theologians, did not qualify as fully human, could not, therefore, become Christians, and could be enslaved. They were, according to another theory, "children of Ham," so their enslavement was sanctioned by the Bible. This insidious logic was not widely accepted, at least at first. But the remoteness of the Atlantic islands meant the use of slave labor could be kept conveniently out of sight. By 1500 the introduction of slaves had turned Madeira into the largest exporter of sugar in the world, with several mills and two thousand slaves.

The use of slaves in sugar production expanded dramatically after the European discovery of the New World by Christopher Columbus in 1492. He had been looking for a westerly passage to the East Indies but instead found the islands of the Caribbean. There was no gold, spices, or silk to take back to his royal patrons in Spain, but Columbus confidently declared the islands ideal for growing sugar, a business he knew well. On his second voyage to the New World in 1493 he took sugarcane from the Canary Islands. Production was soon under way on the Spanish islands of the Caribbean and on the South American mainland, in what is now Brazil, under the Portuguese. Attempts to enslave the indigenous people failed, as they inexorably succumbed to Old-World diseases, so the colonists began importing slaves directly from Africa instead. Over the course of four centuries, around eleven million slaves were transported from Africa to the New World, though this figure understates the full scale of the suffering, because as many as half the slaves captured in the African interior died on the way to the coast. Distilled drinks played a central role in this evil trade, which intensified as the British, French, and Dutch established sugar plantations in the Caribbean during the seventeenth century.

The African slavers who supplied the Europeans with slaves accepted a range of products in exchange, including textiles, shells, metal bowls, jugs, and sheets of copper. But most sought-after by far were strong alcoholic drinks. The Africans in different regions already drank alcoholic drinks such as palm wine, mead, and various varieties of beer, all of which dated back to antiquity. But alcohol imported from Europe was, in the words of one trader, "everywhere called for," even in Muslim parts of Africa. In the early days of the slave trade, when it was dominated by Portugal, African slavers acquired a taste for strong Portuguese wines. In 1510 the Portuguese traveler Valentim Fernandes wrote that the Wolofs, a people from the Senegal region, "are drunkards who derive great pleasure from our wine."

Wine was a convenient form of currency, but European slave traders quickly realized that brandy was even better. It allowed more alcohol to be packed into a smaller space inside the cramped hold of a ship, and its higher alcohol content acted as a preservative, making it less likely than wine to spoil while in transit. Africans valued distilled spirits because they were far more concentrated, or "hot," than their own grain-based beers and palm wines. Drinking imported alcohol became a mark of distinction among African slavers. Textiles were often the most valuable component of the packages of goods exchanged for slaves, but alcohol, and brandy in particular, was the most prestigious.

It soon became customary for Europeans to present large quantities of alcohol, known as *dashee* or *bizy*, as a gift before beginning negotiations with African traders. The Europeans and Africans conversed in a pidgin language derived from Portuguese, several examples of which were transcribed by a French trader, including *qua qua* (linen) and *singo me miombo* (give me some strong liquor). According to John Atkins, a British naval surgeon who chronicled the slave trade, the African slaver "never cares to treat with dry lips." William Bosman, a Dutch slave trader, recommended that captains of slave ships should make daily gifts of brandy to local leaders and principal traders. The Africans of Whydah, he warned, would not do business at all unless they had first been presented with sufficient *dashee*. "He that intends to trade here, must humour them herein," he wrote.

Brandy oiled the wheels of the slave trade in other ways, too. One account records that the canoemen who ferried goods to and from European ships were paid a bottle of brandy a day as a retainer, plus an extra two to four bottles on days when they worked, and a bonus bottle on Sundays. The guards who marched slaves from holding pens on the coast down to the shore were also paid in brandy. The connections between spirits, slaves, and sugar were further strengthened following the invention of a powerful new drink made from the waste products of the sugar-production process itself. That drink was rum.

The First Global Drink

On a September day in 1647 an Englishman named Richard Ligon caught his first glimpse of the Caribbean island of

Barbados from the deck of the ship *Achilles*. "Being now come in sight of this happy island, the nearer we came, the more beautiful it appeared to our eyes," he wrote in an account of his voyage. Appearances proved deceptive, however, for when Ligon and his fellow travelers disembarked they discovered that Barbados was in the midst of an outbreak of the plague. This disrupted the travelers' plans, so that having only intended to stay for a few days, Ligon remained on the island for three years. During his stay he compiled a detailed account of the island's many plants and animals, the customs of its people, and the workings of its sugar plantations.

The first English settlers had arrived on Barbados in 1627 to find the island uninhabited. They set about trying to grow tobacco, which had become popular in their homeland and had proved to be a profitable crop for farmers in the new North American colony of Virginia. But Barbados tobacco was, Ligon observed, "the worst . . . that growes in the whole world." So the settlers brought in sugarcane, equipment, and expertise from Brazil instead. During Ligon's stay, sugar established itself as the island's most important crop. The industry was heavily dependent on slave labor. Ligon ran into the religious logic used to justify slavery when a black slave, to whom he had explained the workings of a compass, asked if he could convert to Christianity, "for he thought that to be a Christian was to be endued with all those knowledges he wanted." Ligon relayed this request to the slave's master and was told that slaves were not allowed to convert—since "by the Lawes of England . . . we could not make a Christian a slave"—so any slaves who were allowed to convert would have to be freed. And that was unthinkable, since it would have stopped the lucrative sugar business in its tracks. Within a decade Barbados dominated the sugar trade, making its sugar barons among the richest men in the New World.

The planters on Barbados gained more than just sugarcane and equipment from Brazil; they also learned how to ferment the by-products of the sugar-making process and then to distill the result to make a powerful alcoholic drink. The Portuguese called it cane brandy, and they made it from the foam skimmed off the boiling cane juice or from the cane juice itself. This process was further refined on Barbados, however, where the cane brandy was made from molasses, the otherwise worthless leftovers from sugar making. This made it possible to make cane brandy far more cheaply and without any reduction in the output of sugar. The planters of Barbados could literally have their sugar and drink it too.

According to Ligon, the resulting drink, known as "kill-devil," was "infinitely strong, but not very pleasant in taste. . . . The people drink much of it, indeed too much; for it often layes them asleep on the ground." Wine and beer were costly to import, and liable to spoil while in transit from Europe, but kill-devil could be made locally in large quantities. Ligon noted that kill-devil was sold on the island itself "to Planters, as have no sugar-works of their own, yet drink excessively of it, for they buy it at easie rates," and also to passing ships, "and it is transported into foreign parts, and drunk by the way." Only after Ligon's departure was kill-devil given the name by which it is known today. A traveler who visited Barbados in 1651 observed that the islanders' preferred drink or "chief fudling" was "Rumbullion, alias Kill-Devill, and this is made of sugar-canes distilled, a hot, hellish and terrible liquor." Rumbullion, a slang word from southern England that means "a brawl or violent commotion," may have been chosen as the drink's nickname because that was frequently the outcome when people drank too much of it.

Rumbullion, soon shortened to rum, spread throughout the Caribbean and then beyond. It was given to newly arrived slaves as part of the "seasoning" process, which weeded out the weak and subdued the unruly. Slaves were encouraged to become dependent on regular rations of rum, both to withstand the demands placed upon them and to blot out the associated hardship. It was also used as an inducement. Slaves were rewarded with extra rum for catching rats or performing particularly unpleasant tasks. Plantation records suggest slaves were typically issued two or three gallons of rum a year (but in some cases as much as thirteen gallons), which they could either drink themselves or barter for food. As a result, rum became an important tool of social control. Ligon noted that it was also used as a medicine, and that when slaves were unwell, the doctor gave to each one "a dram cup of this Spirit, and that [was] a present cure."

Rum also became popular among sailors, and from 1655 was adopted as a substitute for the traditional ration of beer on Royal Navy ships in the Caribbean. Within a century it became the navy's preferred drink during long cruises. Replacing the usual gallon of perishable, weak beer with a half pint of rum had predictable consequences for discipline and efficiency, however, and prompted Admiral Edward Vernon to issue an order that the rum should be mixed with two pints of water. Diluting the rum had no effect on the total amount of alcohol consumed, though it made the sailors more inclined to drink the otherwise unpalatable water available on board ships. What turned out to be far more important was Vernon's idea to add sugar and lime juice to the mixture to make it more palatable. He had invented a primitive cocktail that was immediately named in his honor. Vernon's nickname was "Old Grogram," because he wore a waterproof cloak made of grogram, a coarse fabric stiffened with gum. His new drink became known as grog.

The problem remained that the strength of rum varied widely, and sailors who saw their rum being watered down to make grog felt shortchanged. Before the invention of an accurate hydrometer in the nineteenth century, there was no easy way to measure the strength of an alcoholic drink. So the navy's pursers, who were responsible for distributing the rum ration, measured the strength of the unmixed rum beforehand using a rule of thumb said to have been devised at the Royal Arsenal. They mixed the rum with a little water and a few grains of black gunpowder, then heated the mixture using a magnifying glass to concentrate the rays of the sun. If the gunpowder failed to ignite, the mixture was too weak, and more rum would be added. Only when the gunpowder just barely ignited was the mixture deemed to be the correct strength, which corresponds to 48 percent alcohol. (If the mixture was too strong, an explosion could ensue, and tradition has it that the sailors were then entitled to help themselves while the purser was incapacitated.)

The use of grog in place of beer played an unseen role during the eighteenth century in establishing British supremacy at sea. One of the main causes of death among sailors at the time was scurvy, a wasting disease that is now known to be caused by a lack of vitamin C. The best way to prevent it, discovered and forgotten many times during the eighteenth century, was to administer regular doses of lemon or lime juice. The inclusion of lemon or lime juice in grog, made compulsory in 1795, therefore reduced the incidence of scurvy dramatically. And since beer contains no vitamin C, switching from beer to grog made British crews far healthier overall. The opposite was true of their French counterparts, for whom the standard drink ration was not beer but three-quarters of a liter of wine (the equivalent of a modern bottle). On long cruises, this ration was replaced by three-sixteenths of a liter of eau-de-vie. Since wine contains small amounts of vitamin C but eau-de-vie does not, the effect was to reduce the French navy's resistance to scurvy, just as the British navy's resistance was increasing. The Royal Navy's unique ability to combat scurvy was said by one naval physician to have doubled its performance and contributed directly to Britain's eventual defeat of the French and Spanish fleets at Trafalgar in 1805. (It also meant that British sailors became known as "limeys.")

All this was far in the future, however, when rum was first invented. Its immediate significance was as a currency, for it closed the triangle linking spirits, slaves, and sugar. Rum could be used to buy slaves, with which to produce sugar, the leftovers of which could be made into rum to buy more slaves, and so on and on. Jean Barbot, a French trader, observed on visiting the west coast of Africa in 1679 that he found "a great alteration: the French brandy, whereof I had always had a good quantity abroad, being much less demanded, by reason that a great quantity of spirits and rum had been bought on that coast." By 1721 one English trader reported that rum had become the "chief barter" on the slave coast of Africa, even for gold. Rum also took over from brandy as the currency in which canoemen and guards were paid. Brandy helped to kick-start the transatlantic trade in sugar and slaves, but rum made it self-fueling and far more profitable.

Unlike beer, which was usually produced and consumed locally, and wine, which was usually made and traded within a specific region, rum was the result of the convergence of materials, people, and technologies from around the world, and the product of several intersecting historical forces. Sugar, which originated in Polynesia, had been introduced to Europe by the Arabs, taken to the Americas by Columbus, and cultivated by slaves from Africa. Rum distilled from its waste products was consumed both by European colonists and by their slaves in the New World. It was a drink that owed its existence to the buccaneering enterprise of the Age of Exploration; but it would not have existed without the cruelty of the slave trade, from which Europeans deliberately averted their gaze for so long. Rum was the liquid embodiment of both the triumph and the oppression of the first era of globalization.

6

The Drinks That Built America

Out of the cheap molasses of the French Islands, New
England made the rum which was the chief source of
her wealth—the rum with which she bought slaves for
Maryland and the Carolinas, and paid her balances to
the English merchants.—*Woodrow Wilson, U.S. President
(1856–1924)*

America's Favorite Drink

ENGLAND'S PLAN TO establish colonies in North
America, starting in the late sixteenth century, was
founded on a fallacy. It was generally assumed that the
region of the North American continent to which England laid
claim—the lands between thirty-four degrees and thirty-eight
degrees north, named Virginia in honor of Queen Elizabeth I,
the virgin queen—would have the same climate as the Mediterranean region of Europe, since it lay at similar latitudes. As a
result, the English hoped that the American colonies, once
established, would be able to supply Mediterranean goods such
as olives and fruit and reduce England's dependence on imports

from continental Europe. One prospectus claimed that the colonies would provide "the Wines, Fruit and Salt of France and Spain . . . the silks of Persia and Italy." Similarly, abundant timber would do away with the need to import wood from Scandinavia. The colonists and their backers in London also hoped to find precious metals, minerals, and jewels. America, in short, was expected to be a land of plenty that would quickly turn a profit.

The reality turned out to be very different. The harsher-than-expected North American climate meant that Mediterranean crops, and other imports such as sugar and bananas, would not grow. Nor were there any precious metals, minerals, or jewels to be found, and attempts to make silk failed. In the decades after the establishment of the first permanent English colony in 1607, the colonists faced many unexpected difficulties as they struggled to make a living from the land. They had to contend with disease, food shortages, infighting, and constant battles with the local Indians, whose lands they had appropriated.

Amid such hardship, securing a reliable supply of alcohol assumed great importance. When two of the three ships that had brought the first permanent settlers to Virginia in 1607 set off back to England, Thomas Studly, one of the inhabitants of the new colony of Jamestown, complained that "there remained neither taverne, beer house, nor place of reliefe." The first supply ship, arriving that winter, brought some beer, though much of it had been drunk by the crew. Further shipments were often substandard or had spoiled during the voyage. In 1613 a Spanish observer reported that the three hundred colonists had nothing but water to drink, "which is contrary to the nature of the English—on account of which they all wish to return and would have done so if they had been at liberty." Little had changed by 1620: The population had grown to three thousand, but, noted one observer, "the greatest want they complain of is good drink"—in other words, something other than water.

That same year, a shortage of beer determined the site of the second English colony, established by the Puritan separatists known as the Pilgrims. The *Mayflower* set out in 1620 aiming for the Hudson River but made landfall farther north at Cape Cod. Bad weather prevented the ship from heading south, so the ship's captain dumped his passengers on the shore. William Bradford, a Pilgrim leader who became governor of the colony, noted in his diary, "We could not now take time for further search or consideration, our victuals being much spent, especially our Beere." The sailors were anxious to ensure sufficient supplies of beer for the return journey since it was wrongly believed at the time that drinking beer on a sea voyage provided protection against scurvy. The Pilgrims, like the colonists in Virginia, had to resort to water. "It is thought that there can be no better water in the world, yet dare I not prefer it before good beer, as some have done," a colonist named William Wood observed, "but any man will choose it before bad beer." When a third English colony was established, in Massachusetts, the settlers made sure they brought plenty of beer. In 1628 the ship *Arbella*, which carried the leader of the Puritan colonists, John Winthrop, had among its provisions "42 Tonnes of Beere," or about ten thousand gallons.

Owing to the harsh climate, European cereal crops, which could be used to make beer, were very difficult to cultivate. Rather than rely on imported beer from England, the settlers tried to make their own from corn, spruce tips, twigs, maple sap, pumpkins, and apple parings. A contemporary song is testimony to the resourcefulness of these brewers: "Oh we can make liquor to sweeten our lips, Of pumpkins, of parsnips, of walnut-tree chips." Nor was wine making an option, as it was for the Spanish and Portuguese colonists farther south. The colonists tried to introduce European vines, but their efforts failed due to the climate, disease, and, since they were from northern Europe, lack of wine-making experience. They tried to make wine from local grapes instead, but the result was revolting. Eventually, the Virginia colonists decided to concentrate on the commercial cultivation of tobacco, and to import malted barley (from which to make beer) from Europe, along with wine and brandy.

Everything changed in the second half of the seventeenth century, however, when rum became available. It was far cheaper than brandy, since it was made from leftover molasses rather than expensive wine, and did not have to be shipped across the Atlantic. As well as being cheaper, rum was stronger too. Rum quickly established itself as the North American colonists' favorite drink. It alleviated hardship, provided a liquid form of central heating in the harsh winters, and conveniently reduced the colonists' dependence on imports from Europe. Rum was generally drunk neat by the poor, and by the better off in the form of punch—a mixture of spirits, sugar, water, lemon juice, and spices served in an elaborately decorated bowl. (This drink, like the cruder naval drink of grog, was a forerunner of the modern cocktail.)

The colonists consumed rum when drawing up a contract, selling a farm, signing a deed, buying goods, or settling a suit.

One custom decreed that anyone who backed out of a contract before signing it had to provide half a barrel of beer, or a gallon of rum, in compensation. Not everyone welcomed the appearance of this cheap, powerful new drink, however. "It is an unhappy thing that in later years a Kind of Drink called Rum has been common among us," lamented the Boston minister Increase Mather in 1686. "They that are poor, and wicked too, can for a penny or two-pence make themselves drunk."

From the late seventeenth century, rum formed the basis of a thriving industry, as New England merchants—primarily in Salem, Newport, Medford, and Boston—began to import raw molasses rather than rum and do the distilling themselves. The resulting rum was not thought to be as good as West Indies rum, but it was even cheaper, which was what mattered to most drinkers. Rum became the most profitable manufactured item produced in New England. In the words of one contemporary observer: "The quantity of spirits which they distil in Boston from the molasses they import is as surprising as the cheapness at which they sell it, which is under two shillings a gallon; but they are more famous for the quantity and cheapness than for the excellency of their rum." Rum became so cheap that in some cases a day's wages could get a laborer drunk for a week.

From Rum to Revolution

In addition to selling rum for local consumption, the New England distillers found a ready market among slave traders, for whom rum had become the preferred form of alcoholic currency with which to purchase slaves on Africa's west coast. Distillers in

Newport even made an extra strong rum specifically for use as a slave currency. Since it packed more alcohol into a given volume, it provided a more concentrated form of wealth. The thriving trade in rum did not sit well with the planters on the British sugar islands or their backers in London, however, for the New England distillers were importing their molasses from the French sugar islands. Since France had banned the manufacture of rum in its colonies in order to protect its domestic brandy industry, French sugar producers were happy to sell their molasses to New England distillers at a low price. At the same time, British sugar producers happened to be losing out to the French in the European sugar market. The New England distillers' use of French molasses added insult to injury. The British producers called for government intervention, and in 1733 a new law, known as the Molasses Act, was passed in London.

The act levied a prohibitive duty of sixpence per gallon on molasses imported into the North American colonies from foreign (in other words, French) colonies or plantations. The idea was to encourage the New England distillers to buy molasses from the British sugar islands, since their exports were not subject to the duty. But the British islands did not produce anywhere near enough molasses to supply the New England rum industry; and the distillers, in any case, regarded the French molasses as superior. If it had been strictly enforced, the act would have forced the distillers both to cut production and to raise their prices, and would have brought a sudden end to New England's prosperity by removing the mainstay of its economy, since rum then accounted for 80 percent of exports. It would also have deprived the North American colonists of their favorite drink; by this time, rum was being consumed at a rate of nearly four American gallons per year for every man, woman, and child in the colonies.

So the distillers ignored the law almost completely, smuggling in molasses from the French islands, and when necessary bribing the officials who were supposed to collect the duty, though most turned a blind eye. Customs officers were appointed in England, and most of them stayed there, drawing their salaries and paying someone else to carry out their duties overseas. Accordingly, these junior functionaries had more sympathy for their fellow colonists than for their masters in London. Within a few years of the law's passage, the vast majority of rum produced—over five-sixths, according to some estimates—was still being made from smuggled molasses. At the same time, the number of distilleries making rum in Boston grew from eight in 1738 to sixty-three in 1750. Rum continued to flow, maintaining its position in all aspects of colonial life. It played an important role in election campaigns: When George Washington ran for election to Virginia's local assembly, the House of Burgesses, in 1758, his campaign team handed out twenty-eight gallons of rum, fifty gallons of rum punch, thirty-four of wine, forty-six of beer, and two of cider—in a county with only 391 voters.

Although the Molasses Act was not enforced, it was resented. Passing the law was a colossal blunder on the part of the British government. By making smuggling socially acceptable, it undermined respect for British law in general and set a vital precedent: Henceforth, the colonists felt entitled to defy other laws that imposed seemingly unreasonable duties on items shipped to and from the colonies. As a result, the widespread defiance of the

Molasses Act was an early step along the road to American independence.

A subsequent step occurred with the passage of the Sugar Act in 1764, at the end of the French and Indian War, during which British troops and American colonists fought together to defeat the French. (This conflict was the American component of a broader war between France and Britain, fought in Europe, North America, and India, that was arguably the first true world war.) Victory ensured British dominance of the North American continent but left Britain with an enormous public debt. Reasoning that the war had been fought largely for the benefit of the colonists in America, the British government concluded that they should help to foot the bill. Furthermore, many of the colonists had continued to trade with the enemy, France, during the war. So the government decided to strengthen and enforce the Molasses Act. The sixpence-per-gallon duty on molasses was halved, but the government took steps to ensure that it would now be collected in full. Customs officers were no longer allowed to remain in Britain while others collected duties on their behalf. Colonial governors were required to enforce the laws strictly and arrest smugglers, and the Royal Navy was given the power to collect duties in American waters.

The new act, with its explicit goal of raising revenues, rather than merely regulating trade, was deeply unpopular in America. New England's rum distillers led the opposition to the new rules by helping to organize a boycott of imports from Britain. Many Americans, not just those whose livelihoods were affected by the act, regarded it as unfair that they should have to pay taxes to a distant parliament where they had no representation. The cry of "no taxation without representation" became a popular slogan. Advocates of independence, known as the "Sons of Liberty," began to mobilize public opinion in favor of a break with Britain. These campaigners often met in distilleries and taverns. One revolutionary leader, John Adams, noted in his diary that he attended a meeting of the Sons of Liberty in 1766 in "a counting-room in Chase and Speakman's distillery," where the participants drank rum punch, smoked pipes, and ate cheese and biscuits.

The Sugar Act was followed by a series of other unpopular laws, including the Stamp Act of 1765, the Townshend Acts of 1767, and the Tea Act of 1773. The result was the Boston Tea Party of 1773, in which three shiploads of tea were dumped into Boston harbor in protest at new tax rules. But although tea is the drink associated with the start of the revolution, rum played just as important a role in the decades leading up to the eventual outbreak of the Revolutionary War in 1775. Fittingly, on the eve of the outbreak of hostilities, when Paul Revere made his famous ride from Boston to Lexington to warn John Hancock and Samuel Adams of the approach of British troops, he stopped off for a rum toddy (rum, sugar, and water, heated by plunging a red-hot poker into the mixture) at a tavern in Medford belonging to Isaac Hall, the captain of the local militia.

Once the fighting started, rum was the preferred drink of American soldiers during the six years of hostilities. General Henry Knox, writing to George Washington in 1780 about the procurement of supplies from the northern states, emphasized the particular importance of rum. "Besides beef and Pork, bread & flour, Rum is too material an article, to be omitted," he wrote. "No exertions ought to be spar'd to provide ample quantities of it." The taxation of rum and molasses, which began the estrangement of Britain from its American colonies, had given rum a distinctly revolutionary flavor. Many years after the British surrender in 1781 and the establishment of the United States of America, John Adams, by then one of the country's founding fathers, wrote to a friend: "I know not why we should blush to confess that molasses was an essential ingredient in American independence. Many great events have proceeded from much smaller causes."

Pioneer Spirit

Rum was the drink of the colonial period and the American Revolution, but many of the citizens of the young nation soon turned their backs on it in favor of another distilled drink. As settlers moved westward, away from the eastern seaboard, they switched to drinking whiskey, distilled from fermented cereal grains. One reason was that many of the settlers were of Scotch-Irish origin and had experience of grain distilling. The supply of molasses, from which rum was made, had also been disrupted during the war. And while grains such as barley, wheat, rye, and corn were difficult to grow near the coast—hence the early colonists' initial difficulties with making beer—they could be cultivated more easily inland. Rum, in contrast, was a maritime product, made in coastal towns from molasses imported by sea. Moving it inland was expensive. Whiskey could be made almost anywhere and did not depend on imported ingredients that could be taxed or blockaded.

By 1791 there were over five thousand pot stills in western Pennsylvania alone, one for every six people. Whiskey took on the duties that had previously been fulfilled by rum. It was a compact form of wealth: A packhorse could carry four bushels of grain but could carry twenty-four bushels once they had been distilled into whiskey. Whiskey was used as a rural currency, traded for other essentials such as salt, sugar, iron, powder, and shot. It was given to farmworkers, used in birth and death rituals, consumed whenever legal documents were signed, given to jurors in courthouses and to voters by campaigning politicians. Even clergymen were paid in whiskey.

So when the secretary of the U.S. Treasury, Alexander Hamilton, began to look for a way to raise money to pay off the vast

The Whiskey Rebellion of 1794 (*The Capture of the Whiskey-Tax Collectors*)

national debt incurred during the Revolutionary War, imposing a federal excise duty on the production of distilled drinks seemed an obvious choice. The excise would raise money and might discourage people from drinking too much. Hamilton believed that such an excise would be "favourable to the agriculture, to the economy, to the morals, and to the health of the society." In March 1791 a law was passed: From July 1, distillers could pay either an annual levy or an excise duty of at least seven cents on each gallon of liquor produced, depending on its strength. An immediate outcry arose, particularly along the western frontier. The excise seemed particularly unfair to the inland settlers because it applied to liquor as it left the still, not at the point of sale. This meant that whiskey produced for private consumption or barter was still subject to excise. Furthermore, many of the settlers had come to America to get away from revenue collectors and government interference. They complained that the new federal government was no better than the British government, whose rule America had just shaken off.

The disagreement over the whiskey excise also reflected a deeper divide over the balance of power between the states and the federal government. By and large, the inhabitants of the eastern territories were happier than those of the southern and western ones with the idea that federal law should take precedence over state law. The new law—which specified, among other things, that offenders would be tried in federal court in Philadelphia, rather than in local courts—seemed to favor eastern, federalist interests. James Jackson of Georgia declared in the House of Representatives that the excise would "deprive the mass of the people of almost the only luxury they enjoy, that of distilled spirits." If it was not opposed, he asked, what might come next? "The time will come," Jackson warned, "when a shirt shall not be washed without an excise."

Once the new law came into force, many farmers refused to pay up. Revenue collectors were attacked, their documents stolen and destroyed, and the saddles taken from their horses and cut into pieces. The opposition was strongest in the fiercely separatist western Pennsylvania frontier counties of Fayette, Allegheny, Westmoreland, and Washington. Groups of farmers opposed to the excise began to coordinate organized resistance. Distillers who paid the excise had holes shot in their stills. Notices advocating disobedience appeared on trees. Congress amended the law in 1792 and 1794 to reduce the tax on rural distillers, and gave the state courts jurisdiction to try offenders. But this failed to quell the opposition. Hamilton, who realized that the authority of the federal government was now at stake, sent federal marshals to western Pennsylvania to serve writs on several farmers who had refused to pay.

Violence flared after one such farmer, William Miller, was served with a writ in July 1794. A shot was fired at the marshal's party by one of Miller's associates, though no one was hurt. Over the next two days the two groups skirmished, the mob of armed "whiskey boys" opposed to the excise swelled to five hundred, and there were deaths on both sides. David Bradford, an ambitious attorney, assumed leadership of the whiskey boys and called on the local people for support. Around six thousand men gathered at Braddock's Field, near Pittsburgh. Bradford was elected major general of this impromptu army. Amid high spirits, military exercises, and target practice, the rebels passed resolutions advocating secession from the United States and the establishment of a new independent state.

Convinced by Hamilton that decisive action was necessary, President George Washington requisitioned thirteen thousand militiamen from eastern Pennsylvania, New Jersey, Virginia, and Maryland. These troops, along with artillery pieces, baggage, and supplies of tax-paid whiskey, were sent over the mountains to Pittsburgh to demonstrate the preeminence of the federal government to the secessionists. The nascent rebellion was, however, already crumbling. As the army approached, Bradford fled and his supporters melted away. Ironically, the arrival of the militia to take on the whiskey boys did much to resolve the problem: At the

George Washington

end of their march, the federal soldiers wanted more whiskey, which they paid for in hard cash. This provided the distillers of western Pennslyvania the funds with which to pay the excise.

A token group of twenty rebels was taken back to Philadelphia and paraded through the streets. But other than being held in jail for a few months, they escaped punishment. Two of their number were sentenced to death but were pardoned by the president. Ultimately, the liquor excise failed and was repealed a few years later. Paying the federal militia to suppress the rebellion cost $1.5 million, nearly one-third of the entire excise duties collected during the ten years the excise law was in force. But while both the rebellion and the excise failed, the suppression of the Whiskey Rebellion, the first tax protest to take place since independence, forcefully illustrated that federal law could not be ignored, and was a defining moment in the early history of the United States.

The failure of the rebellion also led to the development of another drink, as Scotch-Irish rebels moved farther west into the new state of Kentucky. There they began to make whiskey from corn as well as rye. The production of this new kind of whiskey was pioneered in Bourbon County, so that the drink became known as bourbon. The use of corn, an indigenous crop, gave it a unique flavor.

In the last years of his life, George Washington himself established a whiskey distillery. The idea came from his farm manager, a Scot who suggested that the grains produced at Washington's estate, Mount Vernon, could be profitably made into whiskey. Two stills began operating in 1797, and at the peak of production, shortly before Washington's death in December 1799, there were five stills. That year he produced eleven thousand gallons of rye, which he sold locally, making a profit of $7,500. He also gave barrels of it to family and friends. "Two hundred gallons of Whiskey will be ready this day for your call," Washington wrote to his nephew on October 29, 1799, "and the sooner it is taken the better, as the demand (in these parts) is brisk."

Washington's activities as a whiskey maker presented a stark contrast with the attitudes of another of America's founding fathers, Thomas Jefferson. He denounced "the poison of whiskey" and famously remarked that "no nation is drunken where wine is cheap, and none sober where the dearness of wine substitutes ardent spirits as the common beverage." Jefferson did his best to cultivate vines in America and advocated a reduction in the excise duty charged on imported wine as "the only antidote to the bane of whiskey." But his cause was hopeless. Wine was far more expensive, contained less alcohol, and lacked the American connotations of whiskey, an unpretentious drink associated with independence and self-sufficiency.

Colonialism by the Bottle

Throughout the colonial period, spirits provided an escape from hardship—both the self-imposed kind experienced by the European colonists and the far greater hardships they imposed on African slaves and indigenous peoples. For as well as using spirits to purchase, subdue, and control slaves, European colonists in the Americas deliberately exploited the local Indians' enthusiasm for distilled drinks as a means of subjugation.

The origin of this enthusiasm is the subject of much debate, but it seems to have arisen from the Indian assumption that spirits, like indigenous hallucinogenic plants, had supernatural powers that the drinker could only access by allowing himself to become completely intoxicated. A late-seventeenth-century observer in New York remarked that the Indian tribesmen were "great lovers of strong drink, yet they do not care for drinking unless they have enough to make themselves drunk." If there was not enough for everyone in a group to get drunk, the alcohol would be shared among a smaller number, while the others became spectators. The insistence on complete intoxication also explains why some Indians found it puzzling that Europeans sometimes preferred wine over rum. "They wonder much of the English for purchasing wine at so dear a rate when Rum is much cheaper & will make them sooner drunk," noted one colonist in 1697.

Whatever its origins, this custom was widely exploited by Europeans, who took care to supply large quantities of alcohol when trading with Indians for goods or land. In practice, this meant rum in British-controlled areas and brandy in French areas. The use of brandy by French fur traders in Canada was criticized by a French missionary, who denounced "the infinity of disorder, brutality, violence . . . and insult, which the deplorable and infamous traffic in brandy has spread universally among the Indians of these parts. . . . In the despair in which we are plunged, nothing remains for us but to abandon them to the brandy sellers as a domain of drunkenness and debauchery." Rather than suppressing the brandy trade, local French troops regarded the maintenance of supply, both for themselves and for sale to the Indians, as their main duty.

In Mexico, the introduction of distillation by the Spanish led to the development of mescal, a distilled version of pulque, the mildly alcoholic indigenous drink made by the Aztecs from the fermented juice of the agave plant. (Pulque was the everyday, staple drink; Aztec warriors, priests, and nobles drank chocolate, the drink of the elite.) The Aztecs and other local Indians were then encouraged to drink mescal rather than pulque, and indeed to overindulge in this far stronger drink. In 1786 the viceroy of Mexico suggested that the Indian fondness for drink and its effectiveness in fostering dependency on the colonial power meant that the same approach should perhaps be tried with the Apaches to the north. This would, he suggested, create "a new need which forces them to recognize very clearly their obligatory dependence with regard to ourselves."

Distilled drinks, alongside firearms and infectious diseases, helped to shape the modern world by helping the inhabitants of the Old World to establish themselves as rulers of the New World. Spirits played a role in the enslavement and displacement of millions of people, the establishment of new nations, and the subjugation of indigenous cultures. Today, spirits are no longer associated with slavery and exploitation. But other echoes of their uses in colonial times persist. Air passengers who throw a bottle of duty-free spirits into their hand luggage do so because it is a compact form of alcohol that is hardy enough to survive a long journey unspoiled. And in their desire to avoid excise duties, purchasers of duty-free spirits are maintaining the antiestablishment tradition of rum runners and whiskey boys.

COFFEE *in* *the* AGE *of* REASON

7

The Great Soberer

Coffee, the sober drink, the mighty nourishment of
the brain, which unlike other spirits, heightens purity
and lucidity; coffee, which clears the clouds of the
imagination and their gloomy weight; which illuminates
the reality of things suddenly with the flash of truth.
—*Jules Michelet, French historian (1798–1874)*

Enlightenment by the Cup

THE GREEKS WERE fallible. Heavy objects do not fall
faster than lighter ones. The Earth is not the center of
the universe, and the heart is not a furnace that heats
the blood but a pump that circulates it around the body. But only
in the early seventeenth century, as astronomers and anatomists
uncovered previously unseen worlds, did European thinkers seri-
ously begin to challenge the old certainties of Greek philosophy.
Pioneers such as Galileo Galilei in Italy and Francis Bacon in England rejected blind faith in ancient texts in favor of direct observation and experiment. "There is no hope of any major increase
in scientific knowledge by grafting or adding the new on top of

the old," Bacon declared in his book *The New Logic,* published in 1620. "The restoration of the sciences must start from the bottom-most foundations—unless we prefer to go round in perpetual circles at a contemptibly slow rate." Bacon led the denunciation of the influence of the Greek philosophers. He and his followers wanted to demolish the edifice of human knowledge and rebuild it, one brick at a time, on solid new foundations. Everything could be challenged, nothing assumed. The way had been cleared by the religious wars of the Restoration, which reduced the authority of the church, particularly in northern Europe. The new rationalism flourished in England and the Netherlands, driven in part by the challenges of exploiting and maintaining far-flung overseas colonies, and giving rise to the flurry of intellectual activity known as the Scientific Revolution.

This spirit of rational inquiry spread into the mainstream of Western thought over the next two centuries, culminating in the movement called the Enlightenment, as the empirical, skeptical approach adopted by scientists was applied to philosophy, politics, religion, and commerce. During this Age of Reason, Western thinkers moved beyond the wisdom of the ancients and opened themselves to new ideas, pushing out the frontiers of knowledge beyond Old-World limits in an intellectual counterpoint to the geographic expansion of the Age of Exploration. Out went dogmatic reverence for authority, whether philosophical, political, or religious; in came criticism, tolerance, and freedom of thought.

The diffusion of this new rationalism throughout Europe was mirrored by the spread of a new drink, coffee, that promoted sharpness and clarity of thought. It became the preferred drink of scientists, intellectuals, merchants, and clerks—today we would call them "information workers"—all of whom performed mental work sitting at desks rather than physical labor in the open. It helped them to regulate the working day, waking them up in the morning and ensuring that they stayed alert until the close of the business day, or longer if necessary. And it was served in calm, sober, and respectable establishments that promoted polite conversation and discussion and provided a forum for education, debate, and self-improvement.

The impact of the introduction of coffee into Europe during the seventeenth century was particularly noticeable since the most common beverages of the time, even at breakfast, were weak "small beer" and wine. Both were far safer to drink than water, which was liable to be contaminated, particularly in squalid and crowded cities. (Spirits were not everyday staples like wine and beer; they were for getting drunk.) Coffee, like beer, was made using boiled water and, therefore, provided a new and safe alternative to alcoholic drinks. Those who drank coffee instead of alcohol began the day alert and stimulated, rather than relaxed and mildy inebriated, and the quality and quantity of their work improved. Coffee came to be regarded as the very antithesis of alcohol, sobering rather than intoxicating, heightening perception rather than dulling the senses and blotting out reality. An anonymous poem published in London in 1674 denounced wine as the "sweet Poison of the Treacherous Grape" that drowns "our very Reason and our Souls." Beer was condemned as "Foggy Ale" that "beseig'd our Brains." Coffee, however, was heralded as

> . . . that Grave and Wholesome Liquor,
> That heals the Stomach, makes the Genius quicker,

Relieves the Memory, revives the Sad,
and cheers the Spirits, without making Mad.

Western Europe began to emerge from an alcoholic haze that had lasted for centuries. "This coffee drink," wrote one English observer in 1660, "hath caused a greater sobriety among the Nations. Whereas formerly Apprentices and clerks with others used to take a morning draught of Ale, Beer, or Wine, which, by the dizziness they cause in the Brain, made many unfit for business, they use now to play the Good-fellows in this wakeful and civil drink." Coffee was also regarded as an antidote to alcohol in a more literal sense. "Coffee sobers you up instantaneously," declared Sylvestre Dufour, a French writer, in 1671. The notion that coffee counteracts drunkenness remains prevalent to this day, though there is little truth to it; coffee makes someone who has drunk alcohol feel more alert, but actually reduces the rate at which alcohol is removed from the bloodstream.

Coffee's novelty further contributed to its appeal. Here was a drink that had been unknown to the Greeks and Romans; drinking it was yet another way seventeenth-century thinkers could emphasize that they had moved beyond the limits of the ancient world. Coffee was the great soberer, the drink of clear-headedness, the epitome of modernity and progress—the ideal beverage, in short, for the Age of Reason.

The Wine of Islam

Coffee's stimulating effect had been known about for some time in the Arab world, where coffee originated. There are several romantic stories of its discovery. One tells of an Ethiopian goatherd who noticed that his flock became particularly frisky after consuming the brownish purple cherries from a particular tree. He then tried eating them himself, noted their stimulating powers, and passed his discovery on to a local imam. The imam, in turn, devised a new way to prepare the berries, drying them and then boiling them in water to produce a hot drink, which he used to keep himself awake during overnight religious ceremonies. Another story tells of a man named Omar who was condemned to die of starvation in the desert outside Mocha, a city in Yemen, on the southwestern corner of the Arabian peninsula. A vision guided him to a coffee tree, whereupon he ate some of its berries. This gave him sufficient strength to return to Mocha, where his survival was taken as a sign that God had spared him in order to pass along to humankind knowledge of coffee, which then became a popular drink in Mocha.

As with the legends associated with the discovery of beer, these tales may contain a grain of truth, for the custom of drinking coffee seems to have first become popular in Yemen in the mid–fifteenth century. While coffee berries may have been chewed for their invigorating effects before this date, the practice of making them into a drink seems to be a Yemeni innovation, often attributed to Muhammad al-Dhabhani, a scholar and a member of the mystical Sufi order of Islam, who died around 1470. By this time, coffee (known in Arabic as *qahwah*) had undoubtedly been adopted by Sufis, who used it to ward off sleep during nocturnal religious ceremonies in which the participants reached out to God through repetitive chanting and swaying.

As coffee percolated throughout the Arab world—it had

reached Mecca and Cairo by 1510—the exact nature of its physical effects became the subject of much controversy. Coffee shook off its original religious associations and became a social drink, sold by the cup on the street, in the market square, and then in dedicated coffeehouses. It was embraced as a legal alternative to alcohol by many Muslims. Coffeehouses, unlike the illicit taverns that sold alcohol, were places where respectable people could afford to be seen. But coffee's legal status was ambiguous. Some Muslim scholars objected that it was intoxicating and therefore subject to the same religious prohibition as wine and other alcoholic drinks, which the prophet Muhammad had prohibited.

Religious leaders invoked this rule in Mecca in June 1511, the earliest known of several attempts to ban the consumption of coffee. The local governor, a man named Kha'ir Beg, who was responsible for maintaining public morality, literally put coffee on trial. He convened a council of legal experts and placed the accused—a large vessel of coffee—before them. After a discussion of its intoxicating effects, the council agreed with Kha'ir Beg that the sale and consumption of coffee should be prohibited. The ruling was proclaimed throughout Mecca, coffee was seized and burned in the streets, and coffee vendors and some of their customers were beaten as a punishment. Within a few months, however, higher authorities in Cairo overturned Kha'ir Beg's ruling, and coffee was soon being openly consumed again. His authority undermined, Kha'ir Beg was replaced as governor the following year.

But was coffee really an intoxicant? Muslim scholars had already spent much effort debating whether the prophet had meant to ban intoxicating drinks altogether or merely the act of drinking to intoxication. Everyone agreed on the need for a legal definition of intoxication, and several such definitions were duly devised. An intoxicated person was variously defined as someone who "becomes absent-minded and confused," "departs from whatever he has in the way of mild virtue and tranquility into foolishness and ignorance," or "comprehends absolutely nothing at all, and who does not know a man from a woman, or the earth from the heavens." These definitions, devised as part of the scholarly argument about alcoholic drinks, were then applied to coffee.

Yet coffee clearly failed to produce any such effects in the drinker, even when consumed in large quantities. In fact, it did quite the opposite. "One drinks coffee with the name of the Lord on his lips and stays awake," noted one coffee advocate, "while the person who seeks wanton delight in intoxicants disregards the Lord, and gets drunk." Coffee's opponents tried to argue that any change in the drinker's physical or mental state was grounds on which to ban coffee. The drink's defenders successfully parried this argument too, noting that spicy foods, garlic, and onions also produced physical effects, such as watering eyes, but that their consumption was perfectly legal.

Although Kha'ir Beg's superiors in Cairo did not uphold his ban on the sale and consumption of coffee, they did echo his disapproval of gatherings and places where it was drunk. Indeed, it was not so much coffee's effects on the drinker but the circumstances in which it was consumed that worried the authorities, for coffeehouses were hotbeds of gossip, rumor, political debate, and satirical discussion. They were also popular venues for chess and backgammon, which were regarded as morally dubious.

Technically, board games were only banned under Islamic law if bets were placed on their outcome. But the fact that they were played at all added to the perception, among opponents of coffeehouses, that such establishments were at best places of lax morality and at worst dens of plotting and sedition.

There were many further attempts to close down coffeehouses, for example in Mecca in 1524 and Cairo in 1539, though such closures were usually short-lived. For despite these efforts, and the denunciation of coffee drinkers as layabouts or gossips, no law was actually being broken, so attempts to ban coffee ultimately failed. By the early seventeenth century, visiting Europeans were commenting on the widespread popularity of coffeehouses in the Arab world, and their role as meeting places and sources of news. William Biddulph, an English traveler, noted in 1609 that "their Coffa houses are more common than Ale-houses in England. . . . If there be any news it is talked of there." George Sandys, another English traveler who visited Egypt and Palestine in 1610, observed that "although they be destitute of Taverns, yet have they their Coffa-houses, which something resemble them. There they sit chatting most of the day; and sippe of a drinke called Coffa (of the berry that it is made of) in little China dishes, as hot as they can suffer it; blacke as soote, and tasting not much unlike it."

One possible objection to the adoption of coffee in Europe— its association with Islam—was dispelled around this time. Shortly before his death in 1605, Pope Clement VIII was asked to state the Catholic church's position on coffee. At the time, the drink was a novelty little known in Europe except among botanists and medical men, including those at the University of

Padua, a leading center for medical research. Coffee's religious opponents argued that coffee was evil: They contended that since Muslims were unable to drink wine, the holy drink of Christians, the devil had punished them with coffee instead. But the pope had the final say. A Venetian merchant provided a small sample for inspection, and Clement decided to taste the new drink before making his decision. The story goes that he was so enchanted by its taste and aroma that he approved its consumption by Christians.

Within half a century, this exotic novelty was fast becoming commonplace in parts of western Europe. Coffeehouses opened in Britain in the 1650s and in Amsterdam and The Hague during the 1660s. As coffee moved west, it took the Arab notion of the coffeehouse as a more respectable, intellectual, and above all nonalcoholic alternative to the tavern along with it—and more than a whiff of controversy.

The Triumph of Coffee

Coffee could have been tailor-made for the London of the 1650s and 1660s. The first coffeehouses appeared during the rule of the puritanical Oliver Cromwell, who came to power at the end of the English civil war after the dethronement and execution of King Charles I. England's coffeehouses got their start, in Puritan times, as more respectable and temperate alternatives to taverns. They were well lit, and adorned with bookshelves, mirrors, pictures in gilt frames, and good furniture, in stark contrast to the gloom and squalor of the taverns where alcohol was served. Following Cromwell's death in 1658, public opinion turned in favor of restoring the monarchy, and during this time, coffeehouses became centers of political debate and intrigue as the way was cleared for the accession of Charles II in 1660. William Coventry, one of the king's advisers, noted that Charles's supporters had often met in coffeehouses during Cromwell's rule, and that "the King's friends had then used more liberty of speech in these places than they durst to do in any other." He suggested that the king might not have gained his throne but for the gatherings that took place in coffeehouses.

At the same time, London was emerging as the hub of a thriving commercial empire. The embrace of coffeehouses by businessmen, for whom they provided convenient and respectable public places in which to meet and do business, ensured their continued popularity after the Restoration. By appealing to Puritans, plotters, and capitalists alike, London's coffeehouses matched the city's mood perfectly.

The city's first coffeehouse was opened in 1652 by Pasqua Rosee, the Armenian servant of an English merchant named Daniel Edwards who had acquired a taste for coffee while traveling in the Middle East. Edwards introduced his friends in London to coffee, which Rosee would prepare for him several times a day. So enthusiastic were they for the new drink that Edwards decided to set Rosee up in business as a coffee seller. The handbill announcing the launch of Rosee's business, titled *The Vertue of the Coffee Drink*, shows just how much of a novelty coffee was. It assumes total ignorance of coffee on the part of the reader, explaining the drink's origins in Arabia, the method of its preparation, and the customs associated with its consumption. Much of the handbill was concerned with coffee's supposed medicinal qualities. It was said to be effective against sore eyes, headache, coughs, dropsy, gout, and scurvy, and to prevent "Mis-carryings in Child-bearing Women." But it was perhaps the explanation of the commercial benefits of coffee that drew Rosee's customers in: "It will prevent Drowsiness, and make one fit for business, if one have occasion to Watch; and therefore you are not to Drink of it after Supper, unless you intend to be watchful, for it will hinder sleep for 3 or 4 hours."

Such was Rosee's success that the local tavern keepers protested to the lord mayor that Rosee had no right to set up a business in competition with them, since he was not a freeman of the City. Rosee was ultimately forced out of the country, but the idea of the coffeehouse had taken hold, and further examples sprung up during the 1650s. By 1663 the number of coffeehouses in London had reached eighty-three. Many of them were destroyed in the Great Fire of London in 1666, but even more arose in their place, and by the end of the century there were hundreds of them. One authority puts the total at three thousand, though that seems unlikely in a city with a population of just six hundred thousand at the time. (Coffeehouses sometimes served other drinks too, such as hot chocolate and tea, but their orderly and convivial atmosphere was inspired by Arabian coffeehouses, and coffee was the predominant drink.)

Not everyone approved, however. Alongside the tavern keepers and vintners, who had commercial reasons for objecting to coffee, the drink's opponents included medical men who believed the new drink was poisonous and commentators who, echoing Arab critics of coffee, worried that coffeehouses encouraged time-wasting and trivial discussion at the expense of more important activities. Others simply objected to the taste of coffee, which was disparaged as "syrup of soot" or "essence of old shoes." (Coffee, like beer, was taxed by the gallon, which meant it had to be made up in advance. Cold coffee from a barrel was then reboiled before serving, which cannot have done much for the taste.)

The result was a stream of pamphlets and broadsides on both sides of the debate, with such titles as *A Coffee Scuffle* (1662), *A Broadside Against Coffee* (1672), *In Defence of Coffee* (1674), and *Coffee Houses Vindicated* (1675). One notable attack on London's coffeehouses came from a group of women, who published *The Women's Petition Against Coffee, representing to public consideration the grand inconveniences accruing to their sex from the excessive use of the drying and enfeebling Liquor.* The women complained that their husbands were drinking so much coffee that they were becoming "as unfruitful as the deserts, from where that unhappy berry is said to be brought." Furthermore, since the men were spending all their time in coffeehouses, from which women were prohibited, "the whole race was in danger of extinction."

The simmering debate over the merits of coffee prompted the British authorities to act. King Charles II had, in fact, been looking for a pretext to move against the coffeehouses for some time. Like his counterparts in the Arab world, he was suspicious of the freedom of speech allowed in coffeehouses and their suitability for hatching plots. Charles was particularly aware of this, since coffeehouse machinations had played a small part in his own accession to the throne. On December 29, 1675, the king issued a "Proclamation for the suppression of

Coffee-houses," declaring that since such establishments "have produced very evil and dangerous effects . . . for that in such Houses . . . divers False, Malitious and Scandalous Reports are devised and spread abroad, to the Defamation of His Majestie's Government, and to the Disturbance of the Peace and Quiet of the Realm; His Majesty hath thought it fit and necessary, That the said Coffee-Houses be (for the future) Put down and Suppressed."

The result was a public outcry, for coffeehouses had by this time become central to social, commercial, and political life in London. When it became clear that the proclamation would be widely ignored, which would undermine the government's authority, a further proclamation was issued, announcing that coffee sellers would be allowed to stay in business for six months if they paid five hundred pounds and agreed to swear an oath of allegiance. But the fee and time limit were soon dropped in favor of vague demands that coffeehouses should refuse entry to spies and mischief makers. Not even the king could halt the march of the coffee.

Similarly, doctors in Marseilles, where France's first coffeehouse had opened in 1671, attacked coffee on health grounds at the behest of wine merchants who feared for their livelihood. Coffee, they declared, was a "vile and worthless foreign novelty . . . the fruit of a tree discovered by goats and camels [which] burned up the blood, induced palsies, impotence and leanness" and would be "hurtful to the greater part of the inhabitants of Marseilles." But this attack did little to slow the spread of coffee; it had already caught on as a fashionable drink among the aristocracy, and coffeehouses were flourishing in Paris by the end of the century. When coffee became popular in Germany, the composer Johann Sebastian Bach wrote a "Coffee Cantata" satirizing those who unsuccessfully opposed coffee on medical grounds. Coffee was also embraced in Holland, where one writer observed in the early eighteenth century that "its use has become so common in our country that unless the maids and seamstresses have their coffee every morning, the thread will not go through the eye of the needle." The Arab drink had conquered Europe.

Empires of Coffee

Until the end of the seventeenth century, Arabia was unchallenged as supplier of coffee to the world. As one Parisian writer explained in 1696, "Coffee is harvested in the neighbourhood of Mecca. Thence it is conveyed to the port of Jiddah. Hence it is shipped to Suez, and transported by camels to Alexandria. Here, in the Egyptian warehouses, French and Venetian merchants buy the stock of coffee-beans they require for their respective homelands." Coffee was also shipped, on occasion, directly from Mocha by the Dutch. But as coffee's popularity grew, European countries began to worry about their dependency on this foreign product and set about establishing their own supplies. The Arabs understandably did everything they could to protect their monopoly. Coffee beans were treated before being shipped to ensure they were sterile and could not be used to seed new coffee plants; foreigners were excluded from coffee-producing areas.

First to break the Arab monopoly were the Dutch, who displaced the Portuguese as the dominant European nation in the

East Indies during the seventeenth century, gaining control of the spice trade in the process and briefly becoming the world's leading commercial power. Dutch sailors purloined cuttings from Arab coffee trees, which were taken to Amsterdam and successfully cultivated in greenhouses. In the 1690s coffee plantations were established by the Dutch East India Company at Batavia in Java, an island colony in what is now Indonesia. Within a few years, Java coffee shipped directly to Rotterdam had granted the Dutch control of the coffee market. Arabian coffee was unable to compete on price, though connoisseurs thought its flavor was superior.

Next came the French. The Dutch had helpfully demonstrated that coffee flourished in a similar climate to that required by sugar, which suggested that it would grow as well in the West Indies as it did in the East Indies. A Frenchman, Gabriel Mathieu de Clieu, who was a naval officer stationed on the French island of Martinique, took it upon himself to introduce coffee to the French West Indies. During a visit to Paris in 1723, he embarked on an entirely unofficial scheme to get hold of a cutting of a coffee tree to take back to Martinique. The only coffee tree in Paris was a well-guarded specimen in a greenhouse in the Jardin des Plantes, presented by the Dutch as a gift to Louis XIV in 1714; Louis, however, seems to have taken little interest in coffee. De Clieu could not simply help himself to a cutting from this royal tree, so he used his connections instead. He prevailed upon an aristocratic young lady to obtain a cutting from the royal doctor, who was entitled to use whatever plants he wanted in the preparation of medical remedies. This cutting was then passed back to de Clieu, who tended it carefully and took it, installed in a glass box, onto a ship bound for the West Indies.

If de Clieu's self-aggrandizing account is to be believed, the plant faced numerous dangers on its journey across the Atlantic. "It is useless to recount in detail the infinite care that I was obliged to bestow upon this delicate plant during a long voyage, and the difficulties I had in saving it," de Clieu wrote many years later, at the start of a detailed account of his perilous journey. First the plant had to brave the attentions of a mysterious passenger who spoke French with a Dutch accent. Every day de Clieu would carry his plant on deck to expose it to the sun, and after dozing next to his plant one day he awoke to find the Dutchman had snapped off one of its shoots. The Dutchman, however, disembarked at Madeira. The ship then had a brush with a pirate corsair and only narrowly escaped. The coffee plant's glass box was damaged in the fight, so de Clieu had to ask the ship's carpenter to repair it for him. Then followed a storm, which again damaged the box and soaked the plant with seawater. Finally, the ship was becalmed for several days, and drinking water had to be rationed. "Water was lacking to such an extent that for more than a month I was obliged to share the scanty ration of it assigned to me with my coffee plant, upon which my happiest hopes were founded," de Clieu wrote.

Eventually, de Clieu and his precious cargo arrived at Martinique. "Arriving at home my first care was to set out my plant with great attention in the part of my garden most favorable to its growth," he wrote. "Although keeping it in view, I feared many times that it would be taken from me; and I was at last obliged to surround it with thorn bushes and to establish a guard about it

Gabriel Mathieu de Clieu shares his water ration with his coffee plant, while becalmed en route to Martinique.

until it arrived at maturity . . . this precious plant which had become still more dear to me for the dangers it had run and the cares it had cost me." Two years later, de Clieu gathered his first harvest from the plant. He then began to give cuttings of the plant to his friends, so that they could begin cultivation too. De Clieu also sent coffee plants to the islands of Santo Domingo and Guadeloupe, where they flourished. Coffee exports to France began in 1730, and production so exceeded domestic demand that the French began shipping the excess coffee from Marseilles to the Levant. Once again, Arabian coffee found it difficult to compete. In recognition of his achievement, de Clieu was presented in 1746 to Louis XV, who was keener on coffee than his father had been. At around the same time, the Dutch introduced coffee to Suriname, a colony in South America.

Descendants of de Clieu's original plant were also proliferating in the region, in Haiti, Cuba, Costa Rica, and Venezuela. Ultimately, Brazil became the world's dominant coffee supplier, leaving Arabia far behind.

Coffee had come a long way from its obscure origins as a religious drink in Yemen. After permeating the Arab world, it had been embraced throughout Europe and was then spread around the world by European powers. Coffee had come to worldwide prominence as an alternative to alcohol, chiefly favored by intellectuals and businessmen. But of even greater significance than this new drink was the novel way in which it was consumed: in coffeehouses, which dispensed conversation as much as coffee. In doing so, coffeehouses provided an entirely new environment for social, intellectual, commercial, and political exchange.

8

The Coffeehouse Internet

You that delight in Wit and Mirth, and long to hear
   such News,
As comes from all parts of the Earth, Dutch, Danes, and
   Turks and Jews,
I'le send you a Rendezvous, where it is smoking new:
Go hear it at a Coffee-house—it cannot but be true . . .
There's nothing done in all the World, From Monarch
   to the Mouse,
But every Day or Night 'tis hurl'd into the Coffee-house.
—from "News from the Coffee-House"
   by Thomas Jordan (1667)

A Coffee-Powered Network

WHEN A SEVENTEENTH-CENTURY European businessman wanted to hear the latest business news, follow commodity prices, keep up with political gossip, find out what other people thought of a new book, or stay abreast of the latest scientific developments, all he had to do was walk into a coffeehouse. There, for the price of a cup (or "dish") of coffee, he could read the latest pamphlets and newsletters, chat with other patrons, strike business deals, or take part in literary or political discussions. Europe's coffee-houses functioned as information exchanges for scientists, businessmen, writers, and politicians. Like modern Web sites, they were vibrant and often unreliable sources of information, typically specializing in a particular topic or political viewpoint. They became the natural outlets for a stream of newsletters, pamphlets, advertising free-sheets, and broadsides. One contemporary observer noted: "The Coffee-houses particularly are very commodious for a free Conversation, and for reading at an easie Rate all manner of printed News, the Votes of Parliament when sitting, and other Prints that come out Weekly or casually. Amongst which the London Gazette comes out on Mundays and Thursdays, the Daily Courant every day but Sunday, the Postman, Flying-Post, and Post-Boy, Tuesdays, Thursdays, and Saturdays, and the English Post, Mundays, Wednesdays, and Fridays; besides their frequent Postscripts." These publications also carried coffeehouse wit out into the provinces and country towns.

Depending on the interests of their customers, some coffee-houses displayed commodity prices, share prices, or shipping lists on their walls; others subscribed to foreign newsletters filled with news from other countries. Coffeehouses became associated with specific trades, acting as meeting places where actors, musicians, or sailors could go if they were looking for work. Coffeehouses catering to a particular clientele, or dedicated to a given subject, were often clustered together in the same neighborhood.

This was especially true in London, where hundreds of coffeehouses, each with its own distinctive name and sign over the door, had been established by 1700. Those around St. James's and Westminster were frequented by politicians; those near St. Paul's Cathedral by clergymen and theologians. The literary set, meanwhile, congregated at Will's coffeehouse in Covent Garden, where for three decades the poet John Dryden and his circle reviewed and discussed the latest poems and plays. The coffeehouses around the Royal Exchange were thronged with businessmen, who would keep regular hours at particular coffeehouses so that their associates would know where to find them, and who used coffeehouses as offices, meeting rooms, and venues for trade. Books were sold at Man's coffeehouse in Chancery Lane, and goods of all kinds were bought and sold in several coffeehouses that doubled as auction rooms. So closely were some coffeehouses associated with certain topics that the *Tatler*, a London magazine founded in 1709, used the names of coffeehouses as subject headings for its articles. Its first issue declared: "All accounts of Gallantry, Pleasure, and Entertainment shall be under the Article of White's Chocolate-house; Poetry, under that of Will's Coffee-house; Learning, under the title of Grecian; Foreign and Domestick News, you will have from St. James's Coffee-house."

Richard Steele, the *Tatler*'s editor, gave its postal address as the Grecian coffeehouse, the preferred haunt of the scientific community. This was another coffeehouse innovation: After the establishment of the London penny post in 1680, it became a common practice to use a coffeehouse as a mailing address. Regulars at a particular coffeehouse could pop in once or twice a day, drink a dish of coffee, hear the latest news, and check to see if there was any new mail waiting for them. "Foreigners remarked that the coffee-house was that which especially distinguished London from all other cities," wrote the nineteenth-century historian Thomas Macauley in his *History of England*. "The coffee-house was the Londoner's home, and that those who wished to find a gentleman commonly asked, not whether he lived in Fleet Street or Chancery Lane, but whether he frequented the Grecian or the Rainbow." Some people frequented multiple coffeehouses, the choice of which depended on their interests. A merchant, for example, might oscillate between a financial coffeehouse and one specializing in Baltic, West Indian, or East Indian shipping. The wide-ranging interests of the English scientist Robert Hooke were reflected in his visits to around sixty London coffeehouses during the 1670s, as recorded in his diary.

Rumors, news, and gossip were carried between coffeehouses by their patrons, and on occasion runners would flit from one coffeehouse to another to report major events such as the outbreak of war or the death of a head of state. ("The Grand Vizier strangled," noted Hooke after learning the news at Jonathan's coffeehouse on May 8, 1693.) News traveled fast across this coffee-powered network; according to one account published in the *Spectator* in 1712: "There was a fellow in town some years ago, who used to divert himself by telling a lye at Charing Cross in the morning at eight of the clock, and then following it through all parts of town until eight at night; at which time he came to a club of his friends, and diverted them with an account [of] what censure it had drawn at Will's in Covent Garden, how dangerous it was believed at Child's and what inference they drew from it with relation to stocks at Jonathan's."

A coffeehouse in late-seventeenth-century London

Coffeehouse discussions both molded and reflected public opinion, forming a unique bridge between the public and private worlds. In theory, coffeehouses were public places, open to any man (since women were excluded, at least in London); but their homely decor and comfortable furniture, and the presence of regular customers, also gave them a cosy, domestic air. Patrons were expected to respect certain rules that did not apply in the outside world. According to custom, social differences were to be left at the coffeehouse door; in the words of one contemporary rhyme, "Gentry, tradesmen, all are welcome hither, and may without affront sit down together." The alcohol-related practice of toasting to other people's health was banned, and anyone who started a quarrel had to atone for it by buying a dish of coffee for everyone present.

The significance of coffeehouses was most readily apparent in London, a city that, between 1680 and 1730, consumed more coffee than anywhere else on Earth. The diaries of intellectuals of the time are littered with coffeehouse references: "Thence to the coffee-house" appears frequently in the celebrated diary of Samuel Pepys, an English public official. His entry for January 11, 1664, gives a flavor of the cosmopolitan, serendipitous atmosphere that prevailed within the coffeehouses of the period, where matters both profound and trivial were discussed, and you never knew who you might meet, or what you might hear: "Thence to the Coffee-house, whither comes Sir W. Petty and Captain Grant, and we fell in talke (besides a young gentleman, I suppose a merchant, his name Mr. Hill, that has travelled and I perceive is a master in most sorts of musique and other things) of musique; the universal character; art of memory . . . and other most excellent discourses to my great content, having not been in so good company a great while, and had I time I should covet the acquaintance of that Mr. Hill. . . . The general talke of the towne still is of Collonell Turner, about the robbery; who, it is thought, will be hanged."

Similarly, Hooke's diary shows that he used coffeehouses as places for academic discussions with friends, negotiations with builders and instrument makers, and even as venues for scientific experiments. One entry from February 1674 notes the subjects of discussion at Garraway's, his preferred coffeehouse at the time: the supposed custom, among tradesmen in the Indies, to hold things with their feet as well as their hands; the prodigious height of palm trees; and "the extreme deliciousness of the queen pine apple," then a new and exotic fruit from the West Indies.

Coffeehouses were centers of self-education, literary and philosophical speculation, commercial innovation, and, in some cases, political fermentation. But above all they were clearinghouses for news and gossip, linked by the circulation of customers, publications, and information from one establishment to the next. Collectively, Europe's coffeehouses functioned as the Internet of the Age of Reason.

Innovation and Speculation

The first coffeehouse in western Europe opened not in a center of trade or commerce but in the university city of Oxford, where a Lebanese man named Jacob set up shop in 1650, two years before Pasqua Rosee's London establishment. Although the connection between coffee and academia is now taken for granted—coffee is the drink customarily served in between sessions at academic conferences and symposia—it was initially controversial. When coffee became popular in Oxford and the coffeehouses selling it began to multiply, the university authorities tried to clamp down, worrying that coffeehouses promoted idleness and distracted members of the university from their studies. Anthony Wood, a chronicler of the time, was among those who denounced the enthusiasm for the new drink. "Why doth solid and serious learning decline, and few or none follow it now in the university?" he asked. "Answer: Because of coffee-houses, where they spend all their time."

But coffee's opponents could not have been more wrong, for coffeehouses became popular venues for academic discussion, particularly among those who took an interest in the progress of science, or "natural philosophy" as it was known at the time. Far from discouraging intellectual activity, coffee actively promoted it. Indeed, coffeehouses were sometimes called "penny universities," since anyone could enter and join the discussion for a penny or two, the price of a dish of coffee. As one ditty of the time put it: "So great a Universitie, I think there ne'er was any; In which you may a Scholar be, for spending of a Penny."

One of the young men who acquired a taste for coffeehouse discussions while studying at Oxford was the English architect and scientist Christopher Wren. Chiefly remembered today as the architect of St. Paul's Cathedral in London, Wren was also one of the leading scientists of his day. He was a founding member of the Royal Society, Britain's pioneering scientific institution, which was formed in London in 1660. Its members, including Hooke, Pepys, and Edmond Halley (the astronomer after whom the comet is named), would often decamp to a coffeehouse after the society's meetings to continue their discussions. To give a typical example, on May 7, 1674, Hooke recorded in his diary that he demonstrated an improved form of astronomical quadrant at the Royal Society, and repeated his demonstration afterward at Garraway's coffeehouse, where he discussed it with John Flamsteed, an astronomer appointed by Charles II as the first astronomer royal the following year. In contrast with the formal atmosphere of the society's meetings, coffeehouses provided a more relaxed atmosphere which encouraged discussion, speculation, and exchange of ideas.

Hooke's diary gives examples of how information could be exchanged in coffeehouse discussions. At one meeting, at Man's coffeehouse, Hooke and Wren traded information about the behavior of springs. "Discoursed much about Demonstration of spring motion. He told a pretty thought of his about a poysd weather glass. . . . I told him an other. . . . I told him my philosophicall spring scales. . . . He told me his mechanick rope scale." On another occasion Hooke exchanged recipes for medical remedies with a friend at St. Dunstan's coffeehouse. Such discussions also allowed scientists to try out half-formed theories and ideas. Hooke, however, had a reputation for being boastful, argumentative, and overstating his case. After an argument with Hooke in Garraway's, Flamsteed complained that he had "long observed it is in his nature to make contradictions at randome, and with little judgmt, & to defend ym with unproved assertions." Hooke, claimed Flamsteed, "bore mee downe with wordes enough &

psuaded the company that I was ignorant in these thinges which that hee onely understood not I."

But Hooke's coffeehouse boastfulness was the unwitting trigger for the publication of the greatest book of the Scientific Revolution. On a January evening in 1684, a coffeehouse discussion between Hooke, Halley, and Wren turned to the theory of gravity, the topic of much speculation at the time. Between sips of coffee, Halley wondered aloud whether the elliptical shapes of planetary orbits were consistent with a gravitational force that diminished with the inverse square of distance. Hooke declared that this was the case, and that the inverse-square law alone could account for the movement of the planets, something for which he claimed to have devised a mathematical proof. But Wren, who had tried and failed to produce such a proof himself, was unconvinced. Halley later recalled that Wren offered to "give Mr Hook or me 2 months time to bring him a convincing demonstration thereof, and besides the honour, he of us that did it, should have from him a present of a book of 40 shillings." Neither Halley nor Hooke took up Wren's challenge, however, and this prize went unclaimed.

A few months later Halley went to Cambridge, where he visited another scientific colleague, Isaac Newton. Recalling his heated coffeehouse discussion with Wren and Hooke, Halley asked Newton the same question: Would an inverse-square law of gravity give rise to elliptical orbits? Like Hooke, Newton claimed to have proved this already, though he could not find the proof when Halley asked to see it. After Halley's departure, however, Newton devoted himself to the problem. In November he sent Halley a paper which showed that an inverse-square law of gravity did indeed imply elliptical planetary orbits. But this paper, it turned out, was just a foretaste of what was to come. For Halley's question had given Newton the impetus he needed to formalize the results of many years of work, and to produce one of the greatest books in the history of science: *Philosophiae naturalis principia mathematica* (Mathematical principles of natural philosophy), generally known as the *Principia*. In this monumental work, published in 1687, Newton demonstrated how his principle of universal gravitation could explain the motions of both earthly and celestial bodies, from the (probably apocryphal) falling apple to the orbits of the planets. With the *Principia*, Newton at last provided a new foundation for the physical sciences to replace the discredited theories of the Greeks; he had made the universe submit to reason. Such was the impact of his work that Newton is widely regarded as the greatest scientist in history.

Hooke insisted that he had given Newton the idea of the inverse-square law in letters exchanged a few years earlier. But when he made his case in another coffeehouse discussion following the presentation of the first volume of the *Principia* to the Royal Society in June 1686, Hooke failed to convince his scientific colleagues. There was a world of difference between advancing an idea in a coffeehouse and proving its correctness; Hooke had not published his ideas or formally presented them to the society; and he had a reputation for claiming to have thought of everything before anyone else (though, in many cases, he actually had). "Being adjourned to the coffee-house," Halley wrote to Newton, "Mr Hooke did there endeavour to gain belief, that he had such thing by him, and that he gave you the first hint of this invention. But I found that they were all of the opinion, that . . .

you ought to be considered as the inventor." Despite Hooke's protestations, the coffeehouse had given its verdict, which still stands today.

Toward the end of the seventeenth century, the dissemination of scientific knowledge through London's coffeehouses took on a new, more structured form. A series of lectures on mathematics was given at the Marine Coffee House, near St. Paul's, starting in 1698, after which coffeehouses became popular venues for lectures of increasing complexity. Equipped with the latest microscopes, telescopes, prisms, and pumps, James Hodgson, a former assistant of Flamsteed's, established himself as one of London's foremost popularizers of science. His course of lectures in natural philosophy promised to provide "the best and surest Foundation for all useful knowledge" and included demonstrations of the properties of gases, the nature of light, and the latest findings in astronomy and microscopy. Hodgson also gave private lessons and published a book about navigation. Similarly, the Swan Coffee-House in Threadneedle Street was the venue for lectures on mathematics and astronomy, while another coffeehouse, in Southwark, was owned by a family who taught mathematics, published books on navigation, and sold scientific instruments. Special lectures on astronomy were organized at both Button's coffeehouse and the Marine to coincide with an eclipse of the sun.

These lectures served both commercial and scientific interests. Seamen and merchants realized that science could contribute to improvements in navigation, and hence to commercial success, while the scientists were keen to demonstrate that their apparently esoteric findings had practical value. As one English mathematician observed in 1703, mathematics had become "the business of Traders, Merchants, Seamen, Carpenters, Surveyors of lands, or the like." Entrepreneurs and scientists teamed up to form companies to exploit new inventions and discoveries in navigation, mining, and manufacturing, paving the way for the Industrial Revolution. It was in coffeehouses that science and commerce became intertwined.

The coffeehouse spirit of innovation and experiment extended into the financial sphere too, giving rise to new business models in the form of innumerable novel variations on insurance, lottery, or joint-stock schemes. Of course, many of the ventures hatched in coffeehouses never got off the ground or were spectacular failures; the drama of the South Sea Bubble, a fraudulent investment scheme that collapsed in September 1720, ruining thousands of investors, was played out in coffeehouses such as Garraway's. But among the successful examples, the best known began in the coffeehouse opened in London in the late 1680s by Edward Lloyd. It became a meeting place for ship captains, shipowners, and merchants, who went to hear the latest maritime news and to attend auctions of ships and their cargoes. Lloyd began to collect and summarize this information, supplemented with reports from a network of foreign correspondents, in the form of a regular newsletter, initially handwritten and later printed and sent to subscribers. Lloyd's became the natural meeting place for shipowners and the underwriters who insured their ships. Some underwriters began to rent regular booths at Lloyd's, and in 1771 a group of seventy-nine of them collectively established the Society of Lloyds, which survives to this day as Lloyd's of London, the world's leading insurance market.

Coffeehouses also functioned as stockmarkets. Initially, stocks were traded alongside other goods at the Royal Exchange, but as the number of listed companies grew (rising from 15 to 150 during the 1690s) and trading activity increased, the government passed an act "to Restrain the Number and Practice of Brokers and Stockjobbers," imposing strict rules on stock trading within the exchange. In protest, the stockbrokers abandoned the exchange and moved into the coffeehouses in the surrounding streets, and one in particular: Jonathan's, in Exchange Alley. One broker's advertisement from 1695 reads: "John Castaing at Jonathan's Coffee House on Exchange, buys and sells all Blank and Benefit Tickets; and all other Stocks and Shares."

As the volume of trade grew, the drawbacks of the informal nature of coffeehouse trading became apparent. Brokers who defaulted on payment were prevented from entering Jonathan's; although there was no way to stop them trading elsewhere, banishment from Jonathan's meant a significant loss of business. Defaulters' names were written on a blackboard to prevent readmission a few months later. Nevertheless, problems remained, so in 1762 a group of 150 brokers struck an agreement with the proprietor of Jonathan's: In return for an annual subscription of eight pounds each, they would be granted use of the premises, with the right to exclude or expel untrustworthy brokers. But this scheme was successfully challenged by a banished broker, who argued that coffeehouses were public places that anyone should be able to enter. In 1773 a group of traders from Jonathan's broke away and decamped to a new building, initially known as New Jonathan's. But this name did not last long, as the *Gentlemen's Magazine* reported: "New Jonathan's came to the resolution that instead of its being called New Jonathan's, it should be called The Stock Exchange, which is to be wrote over the door." This establishment was the forerunner of the London Stock Exchange.

This period of rapid innovation in public and private finance, with the floating of joint-stock companies, the buying and selling of shares, the development of insurance schemes, and the public financing of government debt, all of which culminated in London's eventual displacement of Amsterdam as the world's financial center, is known today as the Financial Revolution. The need to fund expensive colonial wars made it necessary, and the fertile intellectual environment and speculative spirit of the coffeehouses made it possible. The financial equivalent of the *Principia* was *The Wealth of Nations*, written by the Scottish economist Adam Smith. It described and championed the emerging doctrine of laissez-faire capitalism, according to which the best way for governments to encourage trade and prosperity was to leave people to their own devices. Smith wrote much of his book in the British Coffee House, his base and postal address in London, and a popular meeting place for Scottish intellectuals, among whom he circulated chapters of his book for criticism and comment. So it was that London's coffeehouses were the crucibles of the scientific and financial revolutions that shaped the modern world.

Revolution by the Cup

As the Financial Revolution was under way in England, revolution of a different kind was brewing in France. During the eighteenth century, Enlightenment thought in France had flowered under thinkers, such as the philosopher and satirist François-Marie Arouet de Voltaire, who extended the new scientific rationalism into the social and political spheres. After offending a nobleman with a witticism in 1726, Voltaire had been imprisoned in the Bastille prison in Paris and was only released on condition that he went to England. While there he immersed himself in the scientific rationalism of Isaac Newton and the empiricism espoused by the philosopher John Locke. Just as Newton had rebuilt physics from first principles, Locke set out to do the same for political philosophy. Men were born equal, he believed, were intrinsically good and were entitled to the pursuit of happiness. No man should interfere with another's life, health, liberty, or possessions. Inspired by these radical ideas, Voltaire returned to France and detailed his views in a book, *Lettres philosophiques*, which compared the French system of government unfavorably with a somewhat idealized description of the English system. As a result, the book was immediately banned.

A similar fate befell the *Encyclopédie* compiled by Denis Diderot and Jean Le Rond d'Alembert, the first volume of which appeared in 1751. Its contributors included Voltaire, along with other leading French thinkers such as Jean-Jacques Rousseau and Charles-Louis de Secondat Montesquieu who, like Voltaire, had been greatly influenced by Locke. With such a lineup of contributors, it is hardly surprising that the *Encyclopédie* came to be seen as the definitive summary of Enlightenment thinking. It promoted a rational, secular view of the world founded on scientific determinism, denounced ecclesiastical and legal abuses of power, and infuriated the religious authorities, who successfully lobbied for it, too, to be banned. Diderot quietly continued his work even so, and the *Encyclopédie* was eventually completed in 1772, with each of its twenty-eight volumes delivered to subscribers in secret.

As in London, the coffeehouses of Paris were meeting places for intellectuals and became centers of Enlightenment thought. Diderot actually compiled the *Encyclopédie* in a Paris coffeehouse, the Café de la Régence, which he used as his office. He recalled in his memoirs that his wife used to give him nine *sous* each morning to pay for a day's worth of coffee. Yet it was in the coffeehouses that the contrast between France and England was especially apparent. In London, coffeehouses were places of unrestrained political discussion and were even used as the headquarters of political parties. The English writer Jonathan Swift remarked that he was "not yet convinced that any Access to men in Power gives a man more Truth or Light than the Politicks of a Coffee House." Miles's coffeehouse was the meeting place of a regular discussion group, founded in 1659 and known as the "Amateur Parliament." Pepys observed that its debates were "the most ingeniose, and smart, that I ever heard, or expect to heare, and bandied with great eagernesse; the arguments in the Parliament howse were but flatte to it." After debates, he noted, the group would hold a vote using a "wooden oracle," or ballot box—a novelty at the time. No wonder one French visitor to London, the Abbé Prévost, declared that London's coffeehouses, "where you have the right to read all the papers for and against the government," were the "seats of English liberty."

The situation in Paris was very different. Coffeehouses abounded—six hundred had been established by 1750—and, as in London, they were associated with particular topics or lines of business. Poets and philosophers gathered at the Café Parnasse and the Café Procope, whose regular patrons included Rousseau, Diderot, d'Alembert, and the American scientist and statesman Benjamin Franklin. Voltaire had a favorite table and chair at the Procope, and a reputation for drinking dozens of cups of coffee a day. Actors gathered at the Café Anglais, musicians at Café Alexandre, army officers at the Café des Armes, while the Café des Aveugles doubled as a brothel. Unlike the salons frequented by the aristocracy, the French coffeehouses were open to all, even to women. According to one eighteenth-century account, "The coffee-houses are visited by respectable persons of both sexes: we see among them many various types: men-about-town, coquettish women, abbés, country bumpkins, journalists, the parties to a law-suit, drinkers, gamesters, parasites, adventurers in the field of love or industry, young men of letters—in a word, an unending series of persons." Within a coffeehouse, the egalitarian society to which Enlightenment thinkers aspired might, on the surface, appear to have been brought to life.

But the circulation of information in French coffeehouses, in both spoken and written form, was subject to strict government oversight. With tight curbs on freedom of the press and a bureaucratic system of state censorship, there were far fewer sources of news than in England or Holland. This led to the emergence of handwritten newsletters of Paris gossip, transcribed by dozens of copyists and sent by post to subscribers in Paris and beyond. (Since they were not printed, they did not need government approval.) The lack of a free press also meant that poems and songs passed around on scraps of paper, along with coffeehouse gossip, were important sources of news for many Parisians. Even so, patrons had to watch what they said, for the coffeehouses were filled with government spies. Anyone who spoke out against the state risked being imprisoned in the Bastille. The archives of the Bastille contain reports of hundreds of trivial coffeehouse conversations, noted down by police informers. "At the Café de Foy someone said that the king had taken a mistress, that she was named Gontaut, and that she was a beautiful woman, the niece of the duc de Noailles," reads one report from the 1720s. "Jean-Louis Le Clerc made the following remarks in the Café de Procope: that there never has been a worse king; that the court and the ministers make the king do shameful things, which utterly disgust his people," reads another, from 1749.

French coffeehouses highlighted the paradox that despite the intellectual advances of the Enlightenment, progress in the social and political spheres had been hindered by the dead hand of the *ancien régime*. The wealthy aristocracy and clergy, a mere 2 percent of the population, were exempt from taxes, so the burden of taxation fell on everyone else: the rural poor and the wealthier members of the bourgeoisie, who resented the aristocracy's firm grip on power and privilege. In coffeehouses the contrast between radical new ideas about how the world might be and how it actually was became most apparent. As France struggled to deal with a mounting financial crisis largely caused by its support for America in the Revolutionary War, coffeehouses became centers of revolutionary ferment. According to one eyewitness in Paris in July 1789, coffeehouses "are not only crowded within, but other expectant crowds are at the doors and windows, listening *à gorge déployée* [open-mouthed] to certain orators who from chairs or tables harangue each his little audience; the eagerness with which they are heard, and the thunder of applause they receive for every sentiment of more than common hardiness or violence against the government, cannot easily be imagined."

As the public mood darkened, a meeting of the Assembly of Notables (the clergy, aristocrats, and magistrates) failed to sort out the financial crisis, prompting King Louis XVI to convene the States-General, an elected national assembly, for the first time in over 150 years. The meeting at Versailles degenerated into confusion, however, prompting the king to sack his finance minister, Jacques Necker, and call out the army. Ultimately, it was at the Café de Foy, on the afternoon of July 12, 1789, that a young lawyer named Camille Desmoulins set the French Revolution in motion. Crowds had gathered in the nearby gardens of the Palais Royal, and tensions rose as the news of Necker's dismissal spread, since he was the only member of the government trusted by the people. Revolutionaries stoked fears that the army would soon descend to massacre the crowd. Desmoulins leaped onto a table outside the café, brandishing a pistol and shouting, "To arms, citizens! To arms!" His cry was taken up, and Paris swiftly descended into chaos; the Bastille was stormed by an angry mob two days later. The French historian Jules Michelet subsequently observed that those "who assembled day after day in the Café de Procope saw, with penetrating glance, in the depths of their black drink, the illumination of the year of the revolution." It literally began at a café.

Camille Desmoulins gives a speech outside the Café de Foy on July 12, 1789, setting the French Revolution in motion.

The Drink of Reason

Today, the consumption of coffee and other caffeinated drinks is so widespread, both in and out of the home, that the impact of coffee's introduction and the appeal of the first coffeehouses is difficult to imagine. Modern cafés pale by comparison with their illustrious historical forebears. Yet some things have not changed. Coffee remains the drink over which people meet to discuss, develop, and exchange ideas and information. From neighborhood coffee klatches to academic conferences to business meetings, it is still the drink that facilitates exchange and cooperation without the risk of the loss of self-control associated with alcohol.

The original coffeehouse culture is echoed perhaps best in

A coffeehouse in late-eighteenth-century Paris

Internet cafés and wireless-Internet hot spots that facilitate the caffeine-fueled exchange of information, and in coffee-shop chains that are used as ad hoc offices and meeting rooms by mobile workers. Is it any surprise that the current center of coffee culture, the city of Seattle, home to the Starbucks coffeehouse chain, is also where some of the world's largest software and Internet firms are based? Coffee's association with innovation, reason, and networking—plus a dash of revolutionary fervor— has a long pedigree.

TEA *and the* BRITISH EMPIRE

9

Empires of Tea

Better to be deprived of food for three days than of tea for one.—*Chinese proverb*

Thank God for tea! What would the world do without tea? How did it exist?—*Sydney Smith, British writer (1771–1845)*

The Drink That Conquered the World

WITH FAR-FLUNG TERRITORIES stretched around the world, the British Empire was famously described in 1773 by Sir George Macartney, an imperial administrator, as "this vast empire on which the sun never sets." At its height, it encompassed a fifth of the world's surface and a quarter of its population. Despite the loss of its North American colonies following American independence, Britain expanded its sphere of influence dramatically from the mid–eighteenth century, establishing control of India and Canada, setting up new colonies in Australia and New Zealand, and displacing the Dutch to dominate European sea trade with the East. Intertwined with Britain's emergence as the first global superpower was its pioneering adoption of a new system of manufacturing. Workers were brought together in large factories where tireless labor-saving machines driven by steam engines amplified human skill and effort—a cluster of innovations collectively known today as the Industrial Revolution.

Linking these imperial and industrial expansions was a new drink—new to Europeans, at least—that became associated with the English and remains so to this day. Tea provided the basis for the widening of European trade with the East. Profits from its trade helped to fund the advance into India of the British East India Company, the commercial organization that became Britain's de facto colonial government in the East. Having started as a luxury drink, tea trickled down to become the beverage of the working man, the fuel for the workers who operated the new machine-powered factories. If the sun never set on the British Empire, it was perpetually teatime, somewhere at least.

With its associated drinking rituals of genteel afternoon tea and the worker's tea break, tea perfectly matched Britain's self-image as a civilizing, industrious power. How odd, then, that this quintessentially English drink initially had to be imported at great cost and effort from China, that vast and mysterious dominion on the other side of the world, and that the cultivation and processing of tea were utter mysteries to its European drinkers. As far as they were concerned, the chests of tea leaves simply materialized on the dock in Canton; tea might as well have come from Mars. Even so, tea somehow became a central part of British culture. The drink that already lubricated China's immense empire could then conquer vast new territories: Having won over the

British, tea spread throughout the world and became the most widely consumed beverage on Earth after water. The story of tea is the story of imperialism, industrialization, and world domination, one cup at a time.

The Rise of Tea Culture

According to Chinese tradition, the first cup of tea was brewed by the emperor Shen Nung, whose reign is traditionally dated to 2737–2697 BCE. He was the second of China's legendary emperors and was credited with the inventions of agriculture and the plow, along with the discovery of medicinal herbs. (Similarly, his predecessor, the first emperor, is said to have discovered fire, cooking, and music.) Legend has it that Shen Nung was boiling some water to drink, using some branches from a wild tea bush to fuel his fire, when a gust of wind carried some of the plant's leaves into his pot. He found the resulting infusion a delicate and refreshing drink. He later wrote a medical treatise, the *Pen ts'ao*, on the medicinal uses of various herbs, in which he supposedly noted that an infusion of tea leaves "quenches the thirst, lessens the desire for sleep, and gladdens and cheers the heart." Yet tea is not, in fact, such an ancient Chinese beverage; the story of Shen Nung is a far later invention. The earliest edition of the *Pen ts'ao*, dated to the Neo-Han dynasty (25–221 CE), makes no mention of tea. The reference to tea was added in the seventh century.

Tea is an infusion of the dried leaves, buds, and flowers of an evergreen bush, *Camellia sinensis*, which seems to have evolved in the jungles of the eastern Himalayas on what is now the India-

China border. In prehistoric times, people noticed the invigorating effect of chewing its leaves, and the healing effect of rubbing them on wounds, practices that survived for thousands of years. Tea was also consumed in a medicinal gruel in southwest China, the chopped leaves being mixed with shallot, ginger, and other ingredients; tribal peoples in what is now northern Thailand steamed or boiled the leaves and formed them into balls, then ate them with salt, oil, garlic, fat, and dried fish. So tea was a medicine and a foodstuff before it was a drink.

Exactly how and when it spread into China is unclear, but it seems to have been helped along by Buddhist monks, adherents of the religion founded in India in the sixth century BCE by Siddhartha Gautama, known as the Buddha. Both Buddhist and Taoist monks found that drinking tea was an invaluable aid to meditation, since it enhanced concentration and banished fatigue—qualities that are now known to be due to the presence of caffeine. Lao-tzu, the founder of Taoism who lived in the sixth century BCE, believed that tea was an essential ingredient in the elixir of life.

The earliest unambiguous Chinese reference to tea is from the first century BCE, some twenty-six centuries after Shen Nung's supposed discovery. Having started out as an obscure medicinal and religious beverage, tea first seems to have become a domestic drink in China around this time; a contemporary book, *Working Rules of Servants,* describes the proper ways to buy and serve it. Tea had become so popular by the fourth century CE that it became necessary to begin the deliberate cultivation of tea, rather than simply harvesting the leaves from wild bushes. Tea spread throughout China and became the national beverage during the

Tang dynasty (618–907 CE), a period that is regarded as a golden age in Chinese history.

During this time, China was the largest, wealthiest, and most populous empire in the world. Its overall population tripled between 630 and 755 to exceed fifty million, and its capital, Changan (modern Xi'an), was the greatest metropolis on Earth, home to around two million people. The city was a cultural magnet at a time when China was particularly open to outside influences. Trade thrived along the trade routes of the Silk Road and by sea with India, Japan, and Korea. Clothing, hairstyles, and the sport of polo were imported from Turkey and Persia, new foodstuffs from India, and musical instruments and dances from central Asia, along with wine in goatskin bags. China exported silk, tea, paper, and ceramics in return. Amid this diverse, dynamic, and cosmopolitan atmosphere, Chinese sculpture, painting, and poetry flourished.

The prosperity of the period and the surge in population were helped along by the widespread adoption of the custom of drinking tea. Its powerful antiseptic properties meant it was safer to drink than previous beverages such as rice or millet beer, even if the water was not properly boiled during preparation. Modern research has found that the phenolics (tannic acid) in tea can kill the bacteria that cause cholera, typhoid, and dysentery. Tea could be prepared quickly and easily from dried leaves and did not spoil like beer. It was, in effect, an efficient and convenient water-purification technology that dramatically reduced the prevalence of waterborne diseases, reducing infant mortality and increasing longevity.

Tea also had a more visible economic impact. As the size and value of the Chinese trade in tea grew during the seventh century, the tea merchants of Fujian, who were required to handle large sums of money, pioneered the use of a new invention: paper money. Tea itself, in the form of bricks, also came into use as a currency. It was ideally suited to the purpose, providing a light and compact store of value that could also be consumed if necessary. Paper money had the drawback that its value diminished the farther it was taken from the imperial center, whereas tea actually increased in value in remote areas. Brick tea remained in use as a currency in some parts of central Asia into modern times.

Tea's popularity during the Tang dynasty was reflected by the imposition of the first tax on tea in 780, and by the success of a book published the same year: *The Classic of Tea*, written by Lu Yu, a celebrated Taoist poet. Written at the behest of the merchants who sold tea, it describes the cultivation, preparation,

Tea production in China. Processing leaves into tea was a complicated process, all of which was done by hand.

and serving of tea in great detail. Lu Yu wrote many more books about tea, no aspect of which escaped his gaze. He described the merits of the various kinds of leaves, the best sort of water to use in its preparation (ideally, from slow-flowing mountain streams; well water only if no other is available), and even enumerated the stages in the process of boiling water: "When the water is boiling, it must look like fishes' eyes and give off but the hint of a sound. When at the edges it clatters like a bubbling spring and looks like pearls innumerable strung together, it has reached the second stage. When it leaps like breakers majestic and resounds like a swelling wave, it is at its peak. Any more and the water will be boiled out and should not be used." Lu Yu's palette was so sensitive that he was said to be able to identify the source of water from its taste alone, and even to determine the part of the river from which it had been drawn. More than anyone else, Lu Yu transformed tea from a mere thirst-quenching drink to a symbol of culture and sophistication. Tea tasting and appreciation, particularly the ability to recognize different types, became highly regarded. Making tea became an honor reserved for the head of the household; an inability to make tea well, in an elegant manner, was considered a disgrace. Drinking parties and banquets centered on tea became popular at the court, where the emperor drank special teas made with water transported from particular springs. This led to the tradition of presenting special "tribute teas" to the emperor every year.

Tea's popularity continued in the prosperous Sung dynasty (960–1279), but it fell from official favor as China came under the rule of the Mongols during the thirteenth century. The Mongols were originally a nomadic, pastoral people who tended herds of horses, camels, and sheep on the open steppes. Under Genghis Khan and his sons, they established the largest connected land empire in history, encompassing much of the Eurasian landmass, from Hungary in the west to Korea in the east, and as far south as Vietnam. Fittingly for a nation of skilled horsemen, the traditional Mongol drink was koumiss, made by churning and then fermenting mare's milk in a leather bag, to transform the lactose sugars in the milk into alcohol. This explains why the Venetian traveler Marco Polo, who spent many years at the Chinese court during this period, made no mention of tea other than to note the tradition of the tea tribute to the emperor (though he did remark that koumiss was "like white wine and very good to drink"). China's new rulers showed no interest in the local drink and maintained their own cultural traditions. Kublai Khan, ruler of the eastern portion of the Mongol Empire, had grass from the steppes grown in the courtyards of his Chinese palace and drank koumiss specially prepared from the milk of white mares.

To emphasize the extent and diversity of the Mongol Empire, Kublai's brother Mangu Khan installed a silver drinking fountain at the Mongol capital of Karakorum. Its four spouts dispensed rice beer from China, grape wine from Persia, mead from northern Eurasia, and koumiss from Mongolia. Tea was nowhere to be seen. But the sprawling empire symbolized by this fountain proved unsustainable and collapsed during the fourteenth century. A renewed enthusiasm for drinking tea was then one way in which Chinese culture reasserted itself following the expulsion of the Mongols and the establishment of the Ming dynasty (1368–1644). The preparation and consumption of tea began to become increasingly elaborate; the meticulous attention to detail advocated by Lu Yu was revived and extended. Harking back to its religious roots, tea came to be seen as a form of spiritual as well as bodily refreshment.

The idea of the tea ceremony was, however, taken to its greatest heights in Japan. Tea had been drunk in Japan as early as the sixth century, but in 1191 the latest Chinese knowledge about the growing, picking, preparation, and drinking of tea was brought into the country by a Buddhist monk named Eisai, who wrote a book extolling tea's health benefits. When Japan's military ruler, or shogun, Minamoto Sanetomo, fell ill, Eisai cured him with the help of some homegrown tea. The shogun became a strong advocate of the new drink, and its popularity spread from his court to the country as a whole. By the fourteenth century, tea had become widespread at every level in Japanese society. The climate was well suited for the cultivation of tea; even the smallest households could maintain a couple of bushes, picking a leaf or two when needed.

The full Japanese tea ceremony is an immensely intricate, almost mystical ritual that can take more than an hour. Merely to describe the steps of grinding the tea, boiling the water, mixing and stirring the tea is to overlook the significance of the particular form of the utensils, and the order and the nature of their use. The water must be transferred from a specific kind of jar to the kettle using a delicate bamboo dipper; a special spoon is used to measure out the tea; there must be a special stirrer, a square silk cloth to wipe the jar and spoon, a rest for the kettle lid, and so on. All of these items are to be brought in by the host in the correct sequence and placed on the correct mats. Ideally, the host is even to gather the firewood himself, and the whole ceremony should take place in a teahouse situated in an appropriately laid-out garden.

In the words of Japan's greatest tea-master, Rikyu, who lived in the seventeenth century, "If the tea and eating utensils are of bad taste, and if the natural layout and planning of the trees and rocks in the tea-garden are unpleasing, then it is as well to go straight back home." Although incredibly formal, some of Rikyu's rules, such as the decree that the conversation was not to turn to worldly matters, are not so different from the unwritten rules that govern a ceremonious European dinner party. The Japanese tea ceremony was the very pinnacle of tea culture, the result of taking a drink from southern Asia, imbuing it with a diverse range of cultural and religious influences, and filtering it through hundreds of years of accumulated customs and rituals.

Tea Reaches Europe

In the early sixteenth century, when the first Europeans reached China by sea, the Chinese justifiably regarded their country as the greatest on Earth. It was the world's largest and most populous nation, with a civilization far older and more enduring than any in Europe. The Celestial Empire, as it was known, was assumed by its inhabitants to be located at the center of the universe. Nobody could compete with its cultural and intellectual achievements; outsiders were dismissed as barbarians or "foreign devils" who might understandably wish to imitate China but whose corrupting influence was best kept at arm's length. Nor was any European technology of the time unknown to the Chinese, who were ahead of Europe in almost every field; the magnetic compass, gunpowder, and printed books on board European ships were all Chinese innovations. The Portuguese explorers who had sailed from their trading post at Malacca on the Malay Peninsula in search of the legendary riches of the East were met with condescension. China was self-sufficient and lacked nothing.

The Portuguese agreed to pay tribute to the emperor in return for the right to trade, and they maintained sporadic commercial contact with China for several years. European manufactured goods were of no interest to the Chinese, though they were happy to sell silk and porcelain in return for gold and silver. Eventually, in 1557, the Chinese authorities allowed the Portuguese to establish a trading post on the tiny peninsula of Macao in the Canton estuary, through which all goods were to be shipped. This allowed the Chinese to levy duties and minimized contact with the foreigners; other Europeans were excluded from direct Chinese trade altogether. When the Dutch arrived in the East Indies toward the end of the sixteenth century, they had to buy Chinese goods through intermediaries in other countries in the region.

Tea is first mentioned in European reports from the region in the 1550s. But shipping it to Europe did not occur to the earliest traders. Small quantities may have been brought to Lisbon privately by Portuguese sailors, but it was not until 1610 that a Dutch ship brought the first small commercial consignment of tea to Europe, where it was regarded as a novelty. From the Netherlands, tea reached France in the 1630s and England in the 1650s. This first tea was green tea, the kind that had always been consumed by the Chinese. Black tea, which is made by allowing the newly picked green leaves to oxidize by leaving them overnight, only appeared during the Ming dynasty; its origins are a mystery. It came to be regarded by the Chinese as suitable only for consumption by foreigners and eventually dominated exports to Europe. Clueless as they were to the origins of tea, Europeans wrongly assumed green and black tea were two entirely different botanical species.

Although it was available in Europe a few years earlier than coffee, tea had far less impact during the seventeenth century, largely because it was so much more expensive. It began as a luxury and medicinal drink in the Netherlands, where arguments raged over its health benefits from the 1630s. An early opponent of tea (and of coffee and chocolate, the other two newfangled hot drinks) was Simon Pauli, a German doctor and physician to the king of Denmark. He published a tract in 1635 in which he conceded that tea had some medical benefits, but that they were far outweighed by its drawbacks. Transporting the tea from China, he claimed, made it poisonous, so that "it hastens the death of those that drink it, especially if they have passed the age of forty years." Pauli boasted that he had used "the utmost of my Endeavours to destroy the raging epidemical Madness of importing Tea into Europe from China."

Taking the opposite view was Nikolas Dirx, a Dutch doctor who championed tea and regarded it as a panacea. "Nothing is comparable to this plant," he declared in 1641. "Those that use it are for that reason, alone, exempt from all maladies and reach an extreme old age." An even more enthusiastic advocate of tea was another Dutch doctor, Cornelius Bontekoe, who wrote a book recommending the consumption of several cups of tea each day. "We recommend tea to the entire nation, and to all peoples!" he declared. "We urge every man, every woman, to drink it every day; if possible, every hour; beginning with ten cups a day and subsequently increasing the dosage—as much as the stomach can take." People who were ill, he suggested, should consume as many as fifty cups a day; he proposed two hundred as an upper limit. Bontekoe was honored by the Dutch East India Company for his help in boosting tea sales; indeed, the company may have put him up to writing his book in the first place. It is notable that he disapproved of the practice of adding sugar to tea, which had by this time started to become popular. (Some medical authorities of the time regarded sugar as harmful.)

Another European addition to tea was milk. As early as 1660 an English advertisement for tea declared that among its many supposed medical benefits, "it (being prepared and drank with Milk and Water) strengtheneth the inward parts, and prevents consumption, and powerfully assuageth the pains of the Bowels or griping of the Guts or Looseness." In France, where tea enjoyed a brief spell of popularity among the aristocracy between 1650 and 1700, people also began to drank tea with milk, both for the flavor and to reduce its temperature. Cooling tea using milk protected both the drinker and the fine porcelain cup in which the tea was served. But tea was soon eclipsed in France by coffee and chocolate. Ultimately it was Britain, rather than France or the Netherlands, that emerged as the most tea-loving European nation, with momentous historical consequences.

Britain's Peculiar Enthusiasm for Tea

It is not too much of an exaggeration to say that almost nobody in Britain drank tea at the beginning of the eighteenth century, and nearly everybody did by the end of it. Official imports grew from around six tons in 1699 to eleven thousand tons a century later, and the price of a pound of tea at the end of the century was one-twentieth of the price at the beginning. Furthermore, those figures do not include smuggled tea, which probably doubled the volume of imports for much of the century until the duty levied on tea was sharply reduced in 1784. Another confounding factor was the widespread practice of adulteration, the stretching of tea by mixing it with ash and willow leaves, sawdust, flowers, and more dubious substances—even sheep's dung, according to one account—often colored and disguised using chemical dyes. Tea was adulterated in one way or another at almost every stage along the chain from leaf to cup, so that the amount consumed was far greater than the amount imported. Black tea began to become more popular, partly because it was more durable than green tea on long voyages, but also as a side effect of this adulteration. Many of the chemicals used to make fake green tea were poisonous, whereas black tea was safer, even when adulterated. As black tea started to displace the smoother, less bitter green tea, the addition of sugar and milk helped to make it more palatable.

Whatever the true extent of smuggling and adulteration, it is clear that by the end of the eighteenth century there was easily enough tea coming into Britain for everyone in the country to drink one or two cups a day, no matter what their station in life. As early as 1757 one observer noted that "there is a certain lane near Richmond, where beggars are often seen, in the summer season, drinking their tea. You may see labourers who are mending the roads drinking their tea; it is even drank in cinder-carts;

and what is not less absurd, sold out in cups to haymakers." What explains the speed and enthusiasm with which the British took to tea? The answer consists of several interlocking parts.

Tea got its start when it became fashionable at the English court following the marriage in 1662 of Charles II to Catherine of Braganza, daughter of King John IV of Portugal. Her enormous dowry included the Portuguese trading posts of Tangier and Bombay, the right to trade with Portuguese possessions overseas, a fortune in gold, and a chest of tea. Catherine was a devoted tea drinker and brought the custom with her. Sipping tea in small cups—"not bigger than thimbles," according to one contemporary account—caught on almost immediately among the aristocracy. The year after Catherine's marriage to the king,

Catherine of Braganza, the wife of Charles II, introduced tea to the English court.

the poet Edmund Waller wrote her a birthday poem, "On Tea," in which he highlighted her two gifts to the nation: tea and easier access to the East Indies.

> *The best of Queens, and best of herbs, we owe*
> *To that bold nation, which the way did show*
> *To the fair region where the sun doth rise,*
> *Whose rich productions we so justly prize.*
> *The Muse's friend, tea does our fancy aid,*
> *Repress those vapors which the head invade,*
> *And keep the palace of the soul serene,*
> *Fit on her birthday to salute the Queen.*

After the initial impetus provided by the tea-drinking queen, the second factor in the rise of tea was the role of the British East India Company, which had been granted a monopoly on imports to England from the East Indies. Though it initially lacked direct access to China, the company's records show that it began to bring in small quantities of "good thea" from the Netherlands during the 1660s as gifts for the king, to ensure that he would "not find himself totally neglected by the Company." This and other gifts won Charles's favor, and he gradually granted sweeping powers to the company, including the rights to acquire territory, issue currency, maintain an army, form alliances, declare war and make peace, and dispense justice. Over the course of the next century, what had started out as a simple trading company ended up as the manifestation of British power in the East, wielding more power than any other commercial organization in history. As the Scottish economist and writer William Playfair observed in 1799, "From a limited body of merchants, the India Company have become the Arbiters of the East." This was due in large part to the way the company fostered, expanded, and profited from the trade in tea.

Tea was served at meetings of the company's directors in London from the mid-1660s, and it was imported on a private basis by the captains and other officers of the company's ships, who were granted an allowance of space on each ship for "private trade." Tea was an ideal commodity for such purposes, given its scarcity and high value; the profit on a ton of tea could be worth several years' wages, and an allowance of ten tons was not unusual for a ship's captain. The private trade in tea probably helped to stimulate early demand, but it was banned in 1686 for fear it would undermine the company's small but growing official trade.

The company's first tea imports from the East Indies (from Bantam, in what is now Indonesia) arrived in 1669, and tea slowly became more widely available. It was initially a minor commodity as the company concentrated first on importing pepper, and then cheap textiles, from Asia. But opposition from Britain's domestic textile producers encouraged the company to place more emphasis on tea; there was no problem with offending domestic producers, since there were none. Tea's retail cost varied dramatically due to the sporadic nature of the supply, but the price per pound of the most expensive teas, which started at around six to ten pounds in 1660, had fallen to around four pounds by 1700. The price per pound of lesser teas was one pound. But a poor family at the time might have had an annual income of twenty pounds, so tea was still far too expensive to become universal. It remained a luxury item until the end of the seventeenth century, overshadowed by coffee, which cost much less; a cup of tea cost about five times as much as a cup of coffee.

Only when the company established trading posts in China in the early eighteenth century, and began direct imports of tea, did volumes increase and prices fall, making tea available to a far wider public. By 1718 tea was displacing silk as the mainstay of imports from China; by 1721 imports had reached five thousand tons a year. In 1744 one writer observed that "opening a Trade with the East-Indies . . . brought the Price of Tea . . . so low that the meanest labouring Man could compass the Purchase of it." At its height, tea represented more than 60 percent of the company's total trade, and the duty on tea accounted for around 10 percent of British government revenue. As a result, control of the tea trade granted the company an enormous degree of political influence and enabled it to have laws passed in its favor. Imports of tea from other European countries were banned; the duty on tea was reduced to increase sales and expand the market; adulteration of tea was punishable by huge fines. Smuggling and adulteration remained rife, but that just showed how much pent-up demand there was for tea. Finally, all that stood between Britain and total dominance of the East Indies trade were the Dutch. A series of wars ended in 1784 with a Dutch defeat, and the rival Dutch East India Company was dissolved in 1795, granting its British counterpart almost total control of the global tea trade.

Catherine of Braganza made it fashionable, and the East India Company made it available; but tea also became sociable, with the invention of new ways to consume it, both in private and in public. In 1717 Thomas Twining, the proprietor of a London coffeehouse, opened a shop next door specifically to sell tea, and to women in particular. Women were unable to buy tea over the counter in coffeehouses, which were men-only establishments. Nor did they wish to send their servants out to buy expensive tea with other household items, since that would mean entrusting them with large sums of money. (Tea's expense was reflected in the use of tea caddies—special boxes with lockable lids in which tea was stored, and to which only the lady of the house had access.) At Twining's shop, however, women could buy this fashionable new drink by the cup for immediate consumption, and as dried leaves for preparation at home. "Great ladies flocked to Twining's house in Devereaux Court in order to sip the enlivening beverage in small cups for which they paid their shillings," noted a contemporary observer. They could also have special blends of tea made up for them by Twining to match their tastes.

Knowledge of tea and its ceremonial consumption in genteel surroundings at home became a means of demonstrating one's sophistication. Elaborate tea parties emerged as the British equivalent of the Chinese and Japanese tea ceremonies; tea was served in porcelain cups, imported in vast quantities as ballast in the same ships that brought the tea from China. Authors offered advice on how to prepare tea, the order in which guests of different rank should be served, what food to serve, and how guests ought to express thanks to the host. Tea was not just a drink; it eventually became an entirely new afternoon meal.

An English tea party around 1750. The ceremonial consumption of tea in genteel surroundings became an emblem of sophistication.

Another innovation in the serving of tea was the emergence of the tea gardens of London. The first to open, in 1732, was Vauxhall Gardens, a park with lit walkways, bandstands, performers of all kinds, and stalls selling food and drink, primarily bread and butter to be washed down with tea. Other tea gardens soon followed. Their appeal was that they provided an elegant, respectable public venue, and a good place to meet members of the opposite sex. Young men at one tea garden, the White Conduit House, would "accidentally" tread on the trains of young women's gowns and offer a dish of tea in recompense; at another tea garden, the Parthenon, women would make the first move, asking their chosen young man to treat them to a dish of tea, according to a contemporary account in the *Gentleman's Magazine*. Tea gardens were particularly popular with women, who had always been excluded from coffeehouses, which were in decline by this time. The more respectable coffeehouses had begun to transform themselves into private gentleman's clubs and commercial institutions; that left only the less respectable ones, which relied on sales of alcohol and were increasingly difficult to distinguish from taverns. As the writer Daniel Defoe remarked, such establishments "are but ale houses, only they think that the name coffee-house gives a better air."

For the poor, tea gradually became an affordable luxury and then a necessity; tricks such as stretching a small quantity of tea with the addition of more water, or reusing tea leaves, finally brought the drink within everyone's reach, in some form at least. Special tea allowances were added to household servants' wages from the mid–eighteenth century; an Italian visitor to England in 1755 remarked that "even the common maid servants must have their tea twice a day." Despite having come from the other side of the world, tea eventually became cheaper than any drink except water. "We are so situated in our commercial and financial system, that tea brought from the eastern extremity of the world, and sugar brought from the West Indies . . . compose a drink cheaper than beer," noted one early nineteenth-century Scottish observer. And when consumed along with cold food, tea provided the illusion of a hot meal. Some people decried the adoption of tea by the poor and argued that rather than aping the habits of the rich, they should spend their money on more nutritious food instead. One lawmaker even suggested that tea should be made illegal for anyone with an annual income less than fifty pounds. But the truth, as one eighteenth-century writer pointed out, was that "were they now to be deprived of this, they would immediately be reduced to bread and water. Tea-drinking is not the cause, but the consequences of the distresses of the poor." The drink of queens had also become the drink of last resort.

From the top of British society to the bottom, everyone was drinking tea. Fashion, commerce, and social changes all played their part in the embrace of tea by the English, a phenomenon that was noted by foreigners even before the end of the eighteenth century. In 1784 a French visitor remarked that "throughout the whole of England the drinking of tea is general. . . . The humblest peasant has his tea twice a day just like the rich man; the total consumption is immense." A Swedish visitor noted that "next to water, tea is the Englishman's proper element. All classes consume it, and if one is out on the London streets early in the morning, one may see in many places small tables set up under the open sky, round which coal-carters and workmen empty their cups of delicious beverage." Tea had reached around the world from the world's oldest empire and planted itself at the heart of the newest. As they drank their cups of tea at home, the British were reminded of the extent and might of their empire overseas. The rise of tea was entangled with the growth of Britain as a world power and set the stage for further expansion of its commercial and imperial might.

10

Tea Power

The progress of this famous plant has been something
very like the progress of truth; suspected at first, though
very palatable to those who had the courage to taste it;
resisted as it encroached; abused as its popularity
spread; and establishing its triumph at last, in cheering
the whole land from the palace to the cottage, only by
slow and resistless efforts of time and its own virtues.
—*Isaac D'Israeli, English critic and historian (1766–1848)*

Tea and Industry

IN 1771 RICHARD ARKWRIGHT, a British inventor,
began the construction of a large building at Cromford in
Derbyshire. Arkwright, the youngest of thirteen children,
had first displayed his entrepreneurial talent when he began collecting human hair, dyeing it using his own secret formula, and
then fashioning it into wigs. The success of this business provided him with the means to embark on a more ambitious venture, and in 1767 he began developing a "spinning frame."
This was a machine for spinning thread in preparation for
weaving; but unlike the spinning jenny, a hand-operated device

that required a skilled operator, the spinning frame was to be a powered machine that anyone could operate. With the help of a clockmaker, John Kay, from whom he gleaned details of an earlier design, Arkwright built a working prototype and established his first spinning mill, powered by horses, in 1768. This mill so impressed two wealthy businessmen that they gave Arkwright the funds to build a far larger one on a river at Cromford, where the spinning frames would be powered by a waterwheel. Here, at the first modern factory, Arkwright pioneered a new approach to manufacturing. Its success made him a pivotal figure in the revolution that turned Britain into the world's first industrialized nation.

The Industrial Revolution, which started with textile manufacturing and then spread into other fields, depended on both technological and organizational innovations. The starting point was the replacement of skilled human laborers by tireless, accurate machines. These machines required new sources of power, such as water and steam. And that, in turn, made it advantageous to put lots of machines in a large factory around a source of power such as a waterwheel or steam engine. Craftsmen who could perform a range of tasks then gave way to laborers who specialized in a single stage of a manufacturing process. Having machines and workers together under one roof meant that the whole process could be closely supervised, and the use of shifts ensured maximum utilization of the expensive machinery. Arkwright built cottages for his employees next to his mill, so that they arrived at work on time. All of this had an astonishing effect on productivity. Each laborer in Arkwright's mill could do the work of fifty hand spinners, and as other aspects of textile production were automated, including scribbling, carding, and ultimately weaving, production soared. So cheap and abundant were British-made textiles by the end of the eighteenth century that Britain began to export textiles to India, devastating that country's traditional weaving trade in the process.

Just as deskbound clerks, businessmen, and intellectuals had taken to coffee in the seventeenth century, the workers in the new factories of the eighteenth century embraced tea. It was the beverage best suited to these new working arrangements and helped industrialization along in a number of ways. Mill owners began to offer their employees free "tea breaks" as a perk. Unlike beer, the drink traditionally given to agricultural workers, tea did not gently dull the mind but sharpened it, thanks to the presence of caffeine. Tea kept workers alert on long and tedious shifts and improved their concentration when operating fast-moving machines. A hand weaver or spinner could take rests when needed; a worker in a factory could not. Factory workers had to function like parts in a well-oiled machine, and tea was the lubricant that kept the factories running smoothly.

The natural antibacterial properties of tea were also an advantage, since they reduced the prevalence of waterborne disease, even when the water used to make tea had not been properly boiled. The number of cases of dysentery in Britain went into decline starting in the 1730s, and in 1796 one observer noted that dysentery and other waterborne diseases "have so decreased, that their very name is almost unknown in London." By the early nineteenth century doctors and statisticians agreed that the most likely cause of the improvement in the nation's health was the popularity of tea. This allowed the workforce to be more densely packed in their living quarters around factories in the industrial cities of the British Midlands without risk of disease. Infants benefited too, since the antibacterial phenolics in tea pass easily into the breast milk of nursing mothers. This lowered infant mortality and provided a large labor pool just as the Industrial Revolution took hold.

The popularity of tea also stimulated commerce by boosting the demand for crockery and bringing into being a flourishing new industry. Ownership of a fine "tea service" was of great social importance, for rich and poor alike. In 1828 one observer noted that "the operative weavers on machine yarns" lived in "dwellings and small gardens clean and neat, all the family well clad, the men with each a watch in his pocket, and the women dressed to their own fancy . . . every house well furnished with a clock in elegant mahogany or fancy case, handsome tea services in Staffordshire ware, with silver or plated sugar-tongs and spoons." The most famous of the Staffordshire potters was Josiah Wedgwood, whose company produced tea services so efficiently that it could compete with Chinese porcelain, imports of which declined and eventually stopped in 1791.

Wedgwood was a pioneer of mass production and an early adopter of steam engines to grind materials and drive stamping machinery. No longer did individual craftsmen in his factories make each item from beginning to end; instead, they specialized in one aspect of production and became particularly skilled at it. Items moved in a continuous flow from one worker to the next. This division of labor enabled Wedgwood to use the most talented designers for his tea services, without requiring them to be potters too. Wedgwood also pioneered the use of celebrity endorsements to promote his products: When Queen Charlotte, the wife of George III, ordered "a complete sett of tea things," he secured her permission to sell similar items to the public under the name "Queen's ware." He took out newspaper advertisements and staged special invitation-only exhibitions of his tea services, such as the one he produced for Empress Catherine II of Russia. At the same time, the marketing of tea was also becoming more sophisticated; the names of Richard Twining (son of Thomas) and other tea merchants became well known. Twining put up a specially designed sign over the door of his shop in 1787 and labeled his tea with the same design, which is now thought to be the oldest commercial logo in continuous use in the world. The marketing of tea and tea paraphernalia laid the first foundations of consumerism.

Other Western nations took up to a century to catch up with Britain's industrialization. There are many reasons why Britain was well placed to be the cradle of industry: its scientific tradition, the Protestant work ethic, an unusually high degree of religious tolerance, ample supplies of coal, efficient transportation networks of roads and canals, and the fruits of empire, which provided the funds to bankroll British entrepreneurs. But the uniquely British love of tea also played its part, keeping disease at bay in the new industrial cities and fending off hunger during long shifts. Tea was the drink that fueled the workers in the first factories, places where both men and machines were, in their own ways, steam powered.

Policy from the Teapot

The political power of the British East India Company, the organization that supplied Britain's tea, was vast. At its height the company generated more revenue than the British government and ruled over far more people, while the duty on the tea it imported accounted for as much as 10 percent of government revenue. All this gave the company both direct and indirect influence over the policies of the most powerful nation on Earth. The company had many friends in high places, and many of its officials simply bought their way into Parliament. Supporters of the East India Company also cooperated on occasion with politicians with interests in the West Indies; the demand for West Indian sugar was driven by the consumption of tea. All this ensured that in many cases company policy became government policy.

The best-known example involves the role of tea policy in the establishment of American independence. In the early 1770s the smuggling of tea into Britain and its American colonies was at its peak. In Britain smuggled tea appealed because it was cheaper than legal tea, since smugglers did not pay customs duties. In America the colonists had taken to smuggling tea from the Netherlands to avoid paying the duty imposed on tea imports by the government in London, since they were opposed to paying any such taxes in principle. (The tea duty was the last remaining of the various commodity taxes imposed by London with the aim of raising money to pay off the debt arising from the successful prosecution of the French and Indian War.) Rampant smuggling reduced the sales of legal tea, and the company found itself with huge stockpiles: Nearly ten thousand tons of tea were sitting in its London warehouses. And since the company had to pay import duty on this tea whether it sold it or not, it owed the government over one million pounds. The company's solution, as usual, was to get the government to intervene in its favor.

The result was the Tea Act of 1773. Its terms, dictated by the company, included a government loan of 1.4 million pounds to enable it to pay off its debts, and the right to ship tea directly from China to America. This meant the company would not have to pay the British import duty, just the much lower American duty of three pence per pound. Furthermore, the duty would be paid by the company's agents in America, who would be granted exclusive rights to sell the tea, thereby giving the company a monopoly. As well as establishing the government's right to tax the colonists, the lower rate of duty would undercut the price of smuggled tea and undermine the smugglers. But the colonists would be grateful, company officials argued, since the overall effect would be to reduce the price of tea.

This was a huge miscalculation. The American colonists, particularly those in New England, depended for their prosperity on being able to carry out unfettered trade without interference from London, whether buying molasses from the French West Indies with which to make rum, or dealing in smuggled tea from the Netherlands. They boycotted British goods and refused to pay tax to the government in London as a matter of principle. They also resented the way the government was handing the East India Company a monopoly on the retailing of tea. What would be next? "The East India Company, if once they get Footing in this (once) happy Country, will leave no

The Boston Tea Party of 1773, in which protesters
emptied three shiploads of tea into Boston Harbor

Stone unturned to become your Masters," declared a broadside published in Philadelphia in December 1773. "They have
a designing, depraved and despotic Ministry to assist and support them. They themselves are well versed in Tyranny, Plun-
der, Oppression and Bloodshed. . . . Thus they have enriched
themselves, thus they are become the most powerful Trading
company in the Universe." Many British merchants felt the same

way; once again the government was allowing the company to dictate policy for its own benefit.

When the act came into force and the company's ships arrived in America with their cargoes of tea, the colonists prevented them from unloading. And on December 16, 1773, a group of protesters dressed up as Mohawk Indians—many of them merchants involved in the tea-smuggling trade who feared for their livelihoods—boarded three company ships in Boston Harbor. Over the course of three hours they tipped all 342 chests of tea on board into the water. Other similar "tea parties" followed in other ports. The British government responded in March 1774 by declaring the port of Boston closed until the East India Company had been compensated for its losses. This was the first of the so-called Coercive Acts—a series of laws passed in 1774 in which the British attempted to assert their authority over the colonies but instead succeeded only in enraging the colonists further and ultimately prompted the outbreak of the Revolutionary War in 1775. It is tempting to wonder whether a government less influenced by the interests of the company might have simply shrugged off the tea parties or come to some compromise with the colonists. (On the American side, Benjamin Franklin, for example, advocated paying compensation for the tea destroyed.) But instead the dispute over tea proved a decisive step toward Britain's loss of its American colonies.

Opium and Tea

The East India Company's fortunes revived in 1784, when the duty on tea imports to Britain was slashed, which lowered the price of legal tea, doubling the company's sales and wiping out smuggling. But the company's power was gradually curtailed amid growing concern over its enormous influence and the corrupt and self-enriching behavior of its officials. It was placed under the supervision of a board of control, answerable to Parliament. And in 1813, as enthusiasm for Adam Smith's advocacy of free trade gained ground, the company's monopoly on Asian trade was removed, except for China. The company concentrated less on trade and more on the administration of its vast territories in India; after 1800 the bulk of its revenue came from the collection of Indian land taxes. In 1834 the company's monopoly on trade with China was removed too.

But even as its political influence diminished and rival traders were allowed in the market, the company still exerted a vital grasp on the tea trade through its involvement in the trading of opium. This powerful narcotic, made from the juice extracted from unripe poppy seeds, had been in use as a medicine since ancient times. But it is highly addictive, and opium addiction had become enough of a problem in China that the authorities outlawed the use of the drug in 1729. An illicit opium trade continued even so, and in the early nineteenth century the company, with the collusion of the British government, organized and massively expanded it. An enormous semiofficial drug-smuggling operation was established in order to improve Britain's unfavorable balance of payments with China—the direct result of the British love of tea.

The problem, from the British point of view, was that the Chinese were not interested in trading tea in return for European goods. One notable exception, during the eighteenth century, had been clocks and clockwork toys, or automata, the production of which was one of the rare areas where European technological expertise visibly outstripped that of the Chinese. In fact, European technology was pulling ahead of the Chinese in many areas by this time, as China's desire to isolate itself from outside influences inspired a general distrust of change and innovation. But the appeal of automata soon wore off, and the problem remained: The company had to pay for its tea in hard cash, in the form of silver. Not only was it difficult to get hold of the vast quantities of silver required—the equivalent of about a billion dollars' worth a year, in today's money—but to make matters worse, the company found that the price of silver was rising more quickly than the price of tea, which ate into its profits.

Hence the appeal of opium. Like silver, it was regarded as a valuable commodity, at least by those Chinese merchants who were prepared to deal in it. The cultivation and preparation of opium in India was, conveniently, a monopoly controlled by the company, which had been quietly allowing small quantities of opium to be sold to smugglers or corrupt Chinese merchants since the 1770s. So the company set about increasing the production of opium in order to use it in place of silver to buy tea. It would then, in effect, be able to grow as much currency as it needed.

Of course, it would never do to be seen to be directly trading an illegal drug in return for tea, so the company devised an elaborate scheme to keep the opium trade at arm's length. The opium was produced in Bengal and sold at an annual auction in Calcutta, after which the company professed ignorance as to its subsequent destination. The opium was bought by Indian-based "country firms," which were independent trading organizations that had been granted permission by the company to trade with China. These firms, in turn, shipped the opium to the Canton estuary, where it was traded for silver and unloaded at the island of Lintin. From here, the opium was transferred into oared galleys by Chinese merchants and smuggled ashore. The country firms could then claim that they were not doing anything illegal, since they were not actually shipping the opium into China; and the company could deny that it was in any way involved in the trade. Indeed, company ships were strictly forbidden to carry opium.

The Chinese customs officials were well aware of what was going on, but they were involved in the scheme too, having been bribed by the Chinese opium merchants, as W. C. Hunter, an American merchant, explained in a contemporary account: "So perfect a system of bribery existed (with which foreigners had nothing whatever to do) that the business was carried on with ease and regularity. Temporary obstructions occurred, as for instance on the arrival of newly installed magistrates. Then the question of fees arose. . . . In good time, however, it would be arranged satisfactorily, the brokers re-appeared with beaming faces, and peace and immunity reigned in the land." Occasionally, local officials would issue threatening edicts demanding that foreign vessels loitering at Lintin should either come into port on the mainland or sail away; and both sides would sometimes go through the motions of a chase, with Chinese customs vessels chasing foreign ships, at least until they were over the horizon. The officials could then issue a report claiming to have driven off a foreign smuggler.

This villainous scheme was, from the point of view of the company and its friends in government, extremely effective: Exports of opium to China increased 250-fold to reach 1,500 tons a year in 1830. Its sale produced enough silver to pay for Britain's tea; more than enough, indeed, since the value of China's opium imports exceeded those of its tea exports from 1828. The silver traveled by a circuitous route: The country firms sent it back to India, where the company purchased it using bankers' drafts drawn on London. Since the company was also the government of India, these drafts were as good as cash. The silver was then shipped to London and passed to company agents, who took it all the way back to Canton to buy tea. Although China illegally produced as much opium, at the time, as was imported, that is no justification for state-sanctioned drug running on a massive scale, which created thousands of addicts and blighted countless lives merely to maintain Britain's supply of tea.

The Chinese government's best efforts to stop the trade with new laws had little effect, since the Canton bureaucracy had been utterly corrupted. Eventually, in December 1838, the emperor sent Commissioner Lin Tze-su to Canton to put an end to the opium trade once and for all. The atmosphere was already highly charged when Lin arrived: Ever since the end of the company's monopoly in 1834, local officials had been bickering with the British government's representative about trade rules. Lin immediately ordered the Chinese merchants and their British associates to destroy their stocks of opium. They ignored him, since they had been given such orders before and had ignored them with impunity. So Lin's men set fire to the stocks of opium, burning an entire year's supply. When the smugglers treated this as a temporary setback and resumed their business as usual, Lin arrested them, British and Chinese alike. Then, after two British sailors murdered a Chinese man in a brawl and the British authorities refused to hand them over, Lin expelled the British from Canton.

This caused outrage in London, where representatives of the company and other British merchants had been putting pressure on the British government to force China to open itself up to wider trade, rather than forcing everything to pass through Canton. The volatile situation in Canton had to be addressed, the merchants argued, in the interests of free trade in general, and to protect the tea trade (and its associated opium trade) in particular. The government did not want to endorse the opium trade openly but instead took the position that China's internal ban on opium did not give Chinese officials the right to seize and destroy goods (that is, opium) belonging to British merchants. On the pretext of defending the right to free trade, war was declared.

The Opium War of 1839–42 was short and one-sided, due to the superiority of European weapons, which came as a complete surprise to the Chinese. In the first skirmish alone, in July 1839, two British warships defeated twenty-nine Chinese ships. On land, the Chinese and their medieval weapons were no match for British troops armed with state-of-the-art muskets. By the middle of 1842 British troops had seized Hong Kong, taken control of the key river deltas, and occupied Shanghai and several other cities. The Chinese were forced to sign a peace treaty that granted Hong Kong to the British, opened five ports for the free trade of all goods, and required the payment of reparations to the British in silver, including compensation for the opium that had been destroyed by Commissioner Lin.

All of this was a victory for the British merchants and utterly humiliating for China. The myth of Chinese invincibility and superiority had been laid bare. The authority of the ruling Manchu dynasty was already being eroded by its inability to quell repeated religious rebellions; now it had been defeated by a small, distant island and forced to open its ports to barbarian merchants and missionaries. This set the pattern for the rest of the nineteenth century, as further wars were waged by Western powers, ostensibly to compel China to open up to foreign trade. In each case Chinese defeat entailed additional concessions to the commercial aims of foreign powers. The trade in opium, which still dominated imports, was legalized; Britain took control of the Chinese customs service; imported textiles and other industrial goods undermined Chinese craftsmen. China became an arena in which Britain, France, Germany, Russia, the United States, and Japan played out their imperialist rivalries, carving up the country and competing for political dominance. Meanwhile, Chinese ill-feeling toward foreigners grew, and rampant corruption, a withering economy, and soaring opium consumption caused a once-mighty civilization to crumble. The independence of America and the ruin of China; such was the legacy of tea's influence on British imperial policy and, through it, on the course of world history.

From Canton to Assam

Even before the outbreak of the Opium War, concern had been growing in Britain about its dangerous reliance on China for the supply of tea. Many years earlier, in 1788, the East India Company had asked Sir Joseph Banks, the leading botanist of his day, for advice on what crops might be profitably grown in the mountainous region of Bengal. Though tea was at the top of his list, the company ignored this advice. In 1822 the Royal Society of Arts offered a prize of fifty guineas "to whoever could grow and prepare the greatest quantity of China tea in the British West Indies, Cape of Good Hope, New South Wales or the East Indies." But the prize was never awarded. The East India Company was reluctant to investigate other sources of supply, since it did not wish to undermine the value of its trade monopoly with China.

The company characteristically changed its mind in 1834, when its monopoly with China came to an end. Lord William Cavendish Bentinck, who as the head of the company was also governor general of India, enthusiastically embraced the idea of growing tea after a subordinate suggested in a report that "some better guarantee should be provided for the supply of tea than that already furnished by the toleration of the Chinese Government." Bentinck established a committee to investigate the possibility. A delegation set out to solicit advice from the Dutch, who had been trying to cultivate tea in Java since 1728, and to visit China, in the hope of procuring seeds and skilled workers. Meanwhile, the search began for the most suitable part of India in which to grow tea.

Proponents of the idea argued that cultivating tea in India, if it could be done, would benefit both British and Indians alike. British consumers would be assured of a more reliable supply. And since the new Indian tea industry would need a lot of manpower, it would provide plenty of jobs for Indian workers, a great many of whom had lost their livelihoods when the company's imports of cheap cloth from British factories wiped out

India's traditional weaving industry. Furthermore, as well as producing tea, the people of India might be encouraged to consume it, which would create an enormous new market. The Indian farmer, suggested one tea advocate, "would then have a healthy beverage to drink, besides a commodity that would be of great value in the market."

Tea cultivation also promised to be hugely profitable. The traditional Chinese manner of producing tea was anything but industrial and had remained unchanged for hundreds of years. Small producers in the countryside sold their tea to local middlemen. The tea then traveled to the coast, carried by boat along rivers where possible, and by human porters over mountain passes where necessary. Finally, the tea was purchased by merchants who blended it, packed it, and sold it to European traders at Canton. All the middlemen along the route took their cut; together with the cost of transport, tolls, and taxes, that brought the price paid for each pound of tea to nearly twice the original producer's selling price. An enterprise that produced its own tea in India, however, could pocket the difference. Furthermore, applying the new industrial methods, running plantations as though they were "tea factories," and automating as much of the processing as possible could be expected to boost productivity, and hence profits, still further. With the cultivation of tea in India, imperialism and industrialism were to go hand in hand.

The enormous irony of the situation was that there were already tea bushes in India, right under the noses of Bentinck's committee members. In the 1820s Nathaniel Wallich, a government botanist in Calcutta, had been sent a sample of a tealike

A tea plantation in India in 1880. By this time, tea could be produced more cheaply in India than in China.

plant that had been found growing in Assam. He identified it as an unremarkable species of camellia but did not realize that it was in fact from a tea plant. After being appointed to Bentinck's committee in 1834, Wallich sent out a questionnaire to establish which parts of India had the appropriate climate for growing tea. The reply from Assam came in the form of further samples of the cuttings, seeds, and finished product of the tea plant. This time even Wallich was convinced, and the committee gleefully reported to Bentinck "that the Tea Shrub is, beyond all doubt, indigenous in Upper Assam. . . . We have no hesitation in declaring this discovery . . . to be by far the most important and valuable that has ever been made on matters connected with the agricultural or commercial resources of the empire."

An expedition confirmed that tea was indeed growing in Assam, an obscure border region the company had conveniently invaded a few years earlier to provide a buffer against Burmese incursions into India. At the time, the company had decided to install a puppet king in the poorer region of upper Assam, while it concentrated on collecting taxes—on land, crops, and anything else it could think of—in lower Assam. Inevitably, the king did not remain on his throne for long once tea had been found growing within his territory. But turning Assam's wild tea plants into a thriving tea industry proved rather more difficult than expected. The officials and scientists in charge of establishing production bickered over the best way to proceed: Did tea grow best on the plains or the hills, in the hot or the cold? None of them really knew what they were talking about. Plants and seeds were brought in from China, but even the best efforts of a couple of Chinese tea workers, who accompanied the plants, could not induce them to flourish in India.

The problem was finally solved by Charles Bruce, an adventurer and explorer familiar with the people, language, and customs of Assam. By combining the knowledge of the local people with the expertise of some Chinese tea workers, he gradually worked out how to bring the wild tea trees into cultivation, where best to grow them, how to transplant trees from the jungle into ordered tea gardens, and how to wither, roll, and dry the leaves. In 1838 the first small shipment of Assam tea arrived in London, where tea merchants declared themselves very impressed by its quality. Now that the feasibility of producing tea in India had been established, the East India Company resolved to let others do the hard work. It decided to allow entrepreneurs in to establish tea plantations; the company would make money by renting out the land and taxing the resulting tea.

A group of London merchants duly established a new company, the Assam Company, to exploit this opportunity. Deploring the "humiliating circumstances" in which the British were forced to trade with Chinese merchants—this was just as the Opium War was about to break out—they jumped at the chance to establish a new source of production in India, since tea was "a great source of profit and an object of great national importance." A report drawn up by Bruce speculated, "When we have a sufficient number of manufacturers . . . as they have in China, then we may hope to compare with that nation in cheapness of produce; nay we might, and ought, to undersell them." The main problem, Bruce noted, would be finding enough laborers to work in the tea plantations. He blamed widespread opium addiction for the unwillingness of the local people to do such work, but confidently predicted that unemployed workers from neighboring Bengal would pour into Assam once they heard that jobs were available.

The Assam Company had no trouble raising funds; its share offering was hugely oversubscribed, with many would-be investors turned away. In 1840 it took control of most of the East India Company's experimental tea gardens. But the new venture was disastrously mismanaged. It hired all the Chinese workers it could find, falsely assuming that their nationality alone qualified them to grow tea. Company officials, meanwhile, spent the firm's money with wild abandon. The little tea that resulted was of low quality, and the Assam Company's shares lost 99.5 percent of their value. Only in 1847 did the tide start to turn after Bruce, by then the director of the company's operations, was fired. By 1851 the company had started to become profitable, and that year its teas were displayed to great acclaim at the Great Exhibition in London, a showcase for the might and riches of the British Empire. This proved, in the most public way possible, that one did not have to be Chinese in order to make tea.

A tea boom ensued as dozens of new tea companies were set up in India, though many of them failed as clueless speculators bankrolled new ventures without discrimination. Eventually, in the late 1860s, the industry recovered from this tea mania, and production really took off when industrial methods and machinery were applied. The tea plants were arranged in regimented lines; the workers were housed in rows of huts and required to work, eat, and sleep according to a rigid timetable. Picking the tea could not (and still cannot) be automated, but starting in the 1870s its processing could be. A succession of increasingly elaborate machines automated the rolling, drying, sorting, and packing of tea. Industrialization reduced costs dramatically: In 1872 the production cost of a pound of tea was roughly the same in India and China. By 1913 the cost of production in India had fallen by three-quarters. Meanwhile, railways and steamships reduced the cost of transporting the tea to Britain. The Chinese export producers were doomed.

In the space of a few years China had been dethroned as Britain's main supplier of tea. The figures tell the story: Britain imported thirty-one thousand tons of tea from China in 1859, but by 1899 the total had fallen to seven thousand tons, while imports from India had risen to nearly one hundred thousand tons. The rise of India's tea industry had a devastating impact on China's tea farmers and further contributed to the instability of the country, which descended into a chaotic period of rebellions, revolutions, and wars during the first half of the twentieth century. The East India Company did not survive to witness the success of its plan to wean Britain off Chinese tea, however. The Indian Mutiny, a widespread uprising against company rule that was triggered by the revolt of the Bengal army in 1857, prompted the British government to take direct control of India, and the company was abolished in 1858.

India remains the world's leading producer of tea today, and the leading consumer in volume terms, consuming 23 percent of world production, followed by China (16 percent) and Britain (6 percent). In the global ranking of tea consumption per capita, Britain's imperial influence is still clearly visible in the consumption patterns of its former colonies. Britain, Ireland, Australia, and New Zealand are four of the top twelve tea-consuming countries, and the only Western nations in the top twelve: apart from Japan, the rest are Middle Eastern nations, where tea, like coffee, has benefited from the prohibition of alcoholic drinks. The United States, France, and Germany are much farther down the list, each consuming around a tenth of the amount of tea per head that is drunk in Britain or Ireland, and favoring coffee instead.

America's enthusiasm for coffee over tea is often mistakenly attributed to the Tea Act and the symbolic rejection of tea at the Boston Tea Party. But while British tea was shunned during the

Revolutionary War, the American colonists' enthusiasm for the drink was undimmed, prompting them to go to great trouble to find local alternatives. Some brewed "Liberty Tea" from four-leaved loosestrife; others drank "Balm Tea," made from rib-wort, currant leaves, and sage. Putting up with such tea, despite its unpleasant taste, was a way for American drinkers to display their patriotism. A small quantity of real tea was also covertly traded, often labeled as tobacco. But as soon as the war ended, the supply of legal tea began to flow again. Ten years after the Boston Tea Party, tea was still far more popular than coffee, which only became the more popular drink in the mid-nineteenth century. Coffee's popularity grew after the duty on imports was abolished in 1832, making it more affordable. The duty was briefly reintroduced during the Civil War but was abolished again in 1872. "America now admits coffee free of duty, and the increase in consumption has been enormous," noted the *Illustrated London News* that year. Meanwhile, tea's popularity declined as patterns of immigration shifted and the proportion of immigrants coming from tea-drinking Britain diminished.

The story of tea reflects the reach and power, both innovative and destructive, of the British Empire. Tea was the preferred beverage of a nation that was, for a century or so, an unrestrained global superpower. British administrators drank tea wherever they went, as did British soldiers on the battlefields of Europe and the Crimea, and British workers in the factories of the Midlands. Britain has remained a nation of tea drinkers ever since. And around the world, the historical impact of its empire and the drink that fueled it can still be seen today.

COCA-COLA *and*

the RISE

of AMERICA

11

From Soda to Cola

> Stronger! stronger! grow they all,
> Who for Coca-Cola call.
> Brighter! brighter! thinkers think,
> When they Coca-Cola drink.
> —*Coca-Cola advertising slogan, 1896*

Industrial Strength

INDUSTRIALISM AND CONSUMERISM first took root in Britain, but the United States is where they truly flourished, thanks to a new approach to industrial production. The preindustrial way to make something was for a craftsman to work on it from start to finish. The British industrial approach was to divide up the manufacturing process into several stages, passing each item from one stage to the next, and using labor-saving machines where possible. The American approach went even farther by separating manufacturing from assembly. Specialized machines were used to crank out large numbers of inter-changeable parts, which were then assembled into finished products. This approach became known as the American system of manufactures, starting with guns, and then applied to sewing machines, bicycles, cars, and other products. It was the foundation of America's industrial might, since it made possible the mass production and mass marketing of consumer goods, which quickly became an integral part of the American way of life.

The circumstances of nineteenth-century America provided the ideal environment for this new mass consumerism. It was a country where raw materials were abundant and skilled workers were always at a premium; but the new specialized machines allowed even unskilled workers to produce parts as good as those made by skilled machinists. The United States also mostly lacked the regional and class preferences of European countries; that meant a product could be mass-produced and sold everywhere, without the need to tailor it to local tastes. And the nation's railway and telegraph networks, which spread across the country after the end of the Civil War in 1865, made the whole country into a single market. Soon even the British were importing American industrial machinery, a sure sign that industrial leadership had passed from one country to the other. By 1900 the American economy had overtaken Britain's to become the largest on Earth.

During the nineteenth century America focused its economic power inward; during the twentieth century the nation directed it outward to intervene decisively in two world wars. The United States then settled into a third, a cold war with the Soviet Union; the two sides were evenly matched in military terms, so the contest became one of economic power, and ultimately the Soviets could no longer afford to compete. By the end of the century, justly called the American century, the United States stood unchallenged as the world's only superpower, the dominant military and economic force in a world where different nations are interconnected more tightly than ever by trade and communications on a global scale.

The rise of America, and the globalization of war, politics, trade, and communications during the twentieth century, are mirrored by the rise of Coca-Cola, the world's most valuable and widely recognized brand, which is universally regarded as the embodiment of America and its values. For those who approve of the United States, that means economic and political freedom of choice, consumerism and democracy, and the American dream; for those who disapprove, it stands for ruthless global capitalism, the hegemony of global corporations and brands, and the dilution of local cultures and values into homogenized and Americanized mediocrity. Just as the story of Britain's empire can be seen in a cup of tea, so the story of America's rise to global preeminence is paralleled in the story of Coca-Cola, that brown, sweet, and fizzy beverage.

Soda Water Bubbles Up

The direct ancestor of Coca-Cola and all other artificially carbonated soft drinks was produced, oddly enough, in a brewery in Leeds around 1767 by Joseph Priestley, an English clergyman and scientist. Priestley was first and foremost a clergyman, despite his unconventional religious views and a pronounced stutter, but he still found time to pursue scientific research. He lived next door to a brewery and became fascinated by the gas that bubbled from the fermentation vats, known simply at the time as "fixed air." Using the brewery as his laboratory, Priestley set about investigating the properties of this mysterious gas. He started by holding a candle just above the surface of the fermenting beer and noted that the layer of gas extinguished the flame. The smoke from the candle was then carried along by the gas, rendering it briefly visible, and revealing that it ran over the sides of the vat and fell to the floor. This meant the gas was heavier than air. And by pouring water quickly and roughly between two glasses held over a vat, Priestley could cause the gas to dissolve in the water, producing "exceedingly pleasant sparkling water." Today we know the gas as carbon dioxide, and the water as soda water.

One of the theories circulating about fixed air at the time was that it was an antiseptic, which suggested that a drink containing fixed air might be useful as a medicine. This would also explain the health-giving properties of natural mineral waters, which were often effervescent. Priestley presented his findings to the Royal Society in London in 1772 and published a book, titled *Impregnating Water with Fixed Air*, the same year. By this time he had devised a more efficient way to make his sparkling water, by generating the gas in one bottle from a chemical reaction and passing it into a second bottle, inverted and filled with water. Once enough gas had built up in the second bottle, he shook it to combine the gas with the water. For the medical potential of his work Priestley was awarded the Copley Medal, the Royal Society's highest honor. (Carbonated water was wrongly expected to be particularly useful at sea, for use against scurvy; this was before the effectiveness of lemon juice had become widely understood.)

Priestley himself made no attempt to commercialize his

From Soda to Cola

Joseph Priestley, who in 1772 published a book explaining how to make soda water

findings, and it seems that Thomas Henry, a chemist and apothecary who lived in Manchester, was the first to offer artificially carbonated water for sale as a medicine, sometime in the early 1770s. He followed the efforts to make artificial mineral waters very closely and was convinced of their health benefits, particularly in "putrid fevers, dysentery, bilious vomitings, etc." Using a machine of his own invention, Henry was able to produce up to twelve gallons of his sparkling water at a time. In a pamphlet published in 1781, he explained that it had to be "kept in bottles very closely corked and sealed." He also recommended taking it in conjunction with lemonade—a mixture of sugar, water, and lemon juice—so that he may have been the first to sell a sweet, artificially fizzy drink.

During the 1790s scientists and entrepreneurs across Europe went into business making artificial mineral waters for sale to the public with varying degrees of success. Torbern Bergman, a Swedish scientist, encouraged one of his pupils to set up a small factory, but it was so inefficient that the woman employed to do the bottling had only three bottles an hour to seal. More successful was the venture established by a mechanic named Nicholas Paul in Geneva, in conjunction with Jacob Schweppe, a financier. Paul's method for carbonating the water was declared by physicians of Geneva in 1797 to surpass all others, and the firm was soon doing a thriving trade, even exporting its bottled water to other countries by 1800. Paul and Schweppe parted company and set up rival firms in Britain. Schweppe's firm produced more mildy carbonated water, which seems to have better suited British tastes; it was generally believed that water with fewer bubbles more closely imitated natural mineral water, and a cartoon from the period depicts drinkers of Paul's beverage as overinflated balloons.

Some of the new artificial mineral waters were prepared using sodium bicarbonate, or soda, so that *soda water* became the generic term for such drinks. They were strictly medical beverages until 1800; doctors prescribed them for various ailments, and they were considered a form of patent medicine by the British government, which imposed a duty of three pence on each bottle. One medical writer referred in 1798 to the "soda water" made and sold by Schweppe, and a London advertisement of 1802 states that "the gaseous alkaline water commonly called soda water has long been used in this country to a considerable effect."

However, soda water proved to be most popular in America. As in Europe, there was much scientific interest in the properties of natural mineral waters, and the possibilities of imitating them.

The eminent Philadelphia physician Benjamin Rush investigated the mineral waters of Pennsylvania and reported his findings to the American Philosophical Society in 1773. Two other states-man-scientists, James Madison and Thomas Jefferson, also took an interest in the medicinal properties of mineral waters. The natural springs of Saratoga in upper New York State were particularly renowned at the time. George Washington visited them in 1783 and expressed sufficient interest that the following year a friend wrote to him to describe attempts to bottle the waters: "What distinguishes these waters . . . from all others . . . is the great quantity of fixed air they contain. . . . The water . . . cannot be confined so that the air will not, somehow or another, escape. Several persons told us that they had corked it tight in bottles, and that the bottles broke. We tried it with the only bottle we had, which did not break, but the air found its way through a wooden stopper and the wax with which it was sealed."

In the United States, soda water moved from scientific curiosity to commercial product with the help of Benjamin Silliman, the first professor of chemistry at Yale University. He went to Europe in 1805 to collect books and apparatus for his new department and was struck by the popularity of the bottled soda water being sold in London by Schweppe and Paul. On his return he began to make and bottle soda water for his friends and was immediately overwhelmed by demand. "Finding it quite impossible with my present means to oblige as many as call upon me for soda water, I have determined to undertake the manufacture of it on the large scale as it is done in London," he wrote to a business associate. He began selling bottled water in 1807 in New Haven, Connecticut.

Others soon followed in other cities, notably Joseph Hawkins in Philadelphia, who devised a new way to dispense soda water: through a fountain. Hawkins's aim was to imitate the spas and pump rooms built over natural springs in Europe, where the mineral water could be dispensed directly into glasses. According to a description of his spa-room from 1808, "The mineral water . . . is raised from the fountain or reservoir in which it is prepared under ground, through perpendicular wooden columns, which enclose metallick tubes, and by turning a cock at the top of the columns, the water may be drawn without the necessity of bottling." Hawkins was granted a patent for this invention in 1809. But the idea of selling soda water in spalike settings proved unpopular. Instead, apothecaries came to dominate the trade. By the late 1820s the soda fountain had become a standard feature of the apothecary's shop; the soda water was prepared and dispensed on the spot, rather than being sold in bottles (though bottled waters were imported from Europe, and Saratoga water was successfully bottled for sale starting in 1826).

Like so many other drinks before it, soda water started out as a specialist medicine and ended up in widespread use as a refreshment, with its medical origins granting it a comforting underlying respectability. As early as 1809 an American chemistry book noted that "soda water is also very refreshing, and to most persons a very grateful drink, especially after heat and fatigue." As well as being consumed on its own, it could be used to make sparkling lemonade, almost certainly the first modern fizzy drink. It was also being mixed with wine on both sides of the Atlantic by the early nineteenth century; one English observer noted that "when mixed with wine it is found that a much smaller quantity of wine satisfies the stomach and the palate, than wine does alone." Today we call this mixture a wine spritzer. But from the 1830s, and particularly in the United States, soda water was principally flavored using specially made syrups.

The *American Journal of Health* noted in 1830 that such syrups "are employed to flavor drinks and are much used as grateful additions to carbonic acid water." Syrups were originally handmade from mulberries, strawberries, raspberries, pineapples, or sarsaparilla. Special dispensers were added to soda fountains, which started to become increasingly elaborate. Blocks of ice were added to chill both the soda water and the syrups. By the 1870s the largest soda fountains were enormous contraptions. At the Centennial Exposition in Philadelphia in 1876, James Tufts, a soda-fountain magnate from Boston, displayed his Arctic Soda Water Apparatus. It was thirty feet high, towering over the spectators, and was adorned with marble, silver fittings, and potted plants. It was manned by immaculately dressed waiters and had to be housed in its own specially designed building. A testament to inventiveness and marketing prowess, this display generated plenty of orders for Tuft's American Soda Fountain Company.

The soda-water business was also becoming industrialized behind the scenes, thanks to businessmen such as John Matthews, a veteran of the British soda-water trade who moved to New York. Initially, he focused on making and selling his own soda water, and then on selling soda fountains, but when his son (also called John) joined the business, he expanded in a new direction. A prolific inventor, the younger Matthews devised specialized machinery to automate every aspect of the soda-water business, from carbonation to bottle washing, and he began selling this machinery to other firms. By 1877 the company had amassed over one hundred patents and had sold over twenty thousand machines. Its catalog offered "a complete establishment for making and bottling soda water, ginger ale, etc using corks" for the sum of $1,146.45. This included the apparatus and raw materials to generate the gas, two fountains to carbonate the water, a bottling machine, fifty gross of bottles, flavoring extracts, and colorings. Matthews's inventions were displayed at exhibitions and won awards around the world. They epitomized the American approach to mass production: Specialized machines handled each step of the process, the bottles and stoppers were standardized, interchangeable parts, and the resulting drink, produced cheaply in large quantities, had mass appeal.

Indeed, soda water, produced on an industrial scale and consumed by rich and poor alike, seemed to capture something of the spirit of America itself. Writing in *Harper's Weekly* in 1891, the author and social commentator Mary Gay Humphreys observed that "the crowning merit of soda-water, and that which fits it to be the national drink, is its democracy. The millionaire may drink champagne while the poor man drinks beer, but they both drink soda water." Her suggestion that soda water could claim to be America's national drink was, however, only half right. A new national drink was indeed emerging at the time— but soda water was only the half of it.

Coca-Cola's Creation Myth

In May 1886 John Pemberton, a pharmacist who lived in Atlanta, Georgia, invented a drink. According to the Coca-Cola

Company's official version of the story, he was a tinkerer who stumbled on the right combination of ingredients by accident, while trying to devise a cure for headaches. One afternoon he mixed various ingredients in a three-legged pot to create a caramel-colored liquid, which he then took to a nearby pharmacy, combining the liquid with soda water to create the sweet, fizzy, and invigorating drink—Coca-Cola—that would eventually reach nearly every corner of the world. The real story is rather more complicated, however.

Pemberton was, in fact, an experienced maker of patent medicines, the quack remedies that were hugely popular in America in the late nineteenth century. These pills, balsams, syrups, creams, and oils were generally triumphs of advertising over pharmacology. Some were harmless, but many contained large amounts of alcohol, caffeine, opium, or morphine. They were sold through newspaper advertisements, and their production became a huge industry after the Civil War, as veterans took to dosing themselves. The popularity of patent medicines reflected a general distrust of conventional medicines, which were often expensive and ineffective. Patent medicines offered an alluring alternative, marketed as they were on the basis of exotic ingredients or the medical knowledge of Native Americans, and under names with religious, patriotic, or mythological overtones: Munson's Paw-Paw Pills to Coax Your Liver into Action, Dr. Morse's Indian Root Pills, and so on.

There was nothing to stop manufacturers of such medicines from making outrageous claims about their effectiveness. The Elixir of Life sold by a Dr. Kidd, for example, claimed to cure "every known ailment. . . . The lame have thrown away crutches and walked after two or three trials of the remedy. . . . Rheumatism, neuralgia, stomach, heart, liver, kidney, blood and skin diseases disappear as by magic." The newspapers that printed such advertisements did not ask any questions. They welcomed the advertising revenues, which enabled the newspaper industry to expand enormously; by the end of the nineteenth century patent medicines accounted for more newspaper advertising than any other product. The makers of St. Jacob's Oil, which was said to remedy "sore muscles," spent five hundred thousand dollars on advertising in 1881, and some advertisers were spending more than one million dollars a year by 1895.

The patent-medicine business was among the first to recognize the importance of trademarks and advertising, of slogans, logos, and hoardings. Since the remedies themselves usually cost very little to make, it made sense to spend money on marketing. With so many competing products on the market, however, only 2 percent of them made a profit, according to one estimate. But those that did succeed made fortunes for their inventors. One of the most famous was Lydia E. Pinkham's Vegetable Compound. It was said to be "a positive cure for all those painful Complaints and Weaknesses so common to our best female population. . . . It removes faintness, flatulency, destroys all craving for stimulants, and relieves weakness of the stomach." Customers were encouraged to write to Pinkham for medical advice, even after her death in 1883, which was kept quiet. They received form letters in return, invariably recommending the use of more of her compound. When analyzed in the early twentieth century, it was found to contain 15 to 20 percent alcohol. Ironically, women temperance campaigners were among its most fervent users.

Pemberton's own attempts to make patent medicines had met with mixed success. At times his remedies produced a solid income, but during the 1870s he had a run of bad luck. He was declared bankrupt in 1872, and his attempts to get back on his feet were hampered by two fires that destroyed his stock. But he continued to develop new patent medicines in the hope that one of them would make him rich. Finally, in 1884, he started to get somewhere, thanks to the popularity of a new patent-medicine ingredient: coca.

The leaves of the coca plant had long been known among South American peoples for their stimulating effect; coca was known as "the divine plant of the Incas." Chewing a small ball of the leaves releases tiny quantities of an alkaloid drug, cocaine. In small doses this sharpens the mind, much like caffeine, and suppresses the appetite, making possible long treks across the Andes with very little food or sleep. Cocaine was isolated from coca leaves in 1855, and it then became the subject of much interest among Western scientists and doctors, who thought it might help to cure opium addicts by providing an alternative. (They were unaware that cocaine was just as addictive.) Pemberton followed the discussion of coca in the medical journals closely, and by the 1880s he and other patent-medicine makers were incorporating it into their tablets, elixirs, and ointments. Pemberton's contribution to this burgeoning field was a drink called French Wine Coca.

As its name suggests, this was a coca-infused wine. In fact, it was just one of many attempts to imitate a particularly successful patent medicine called Vin Mariani, which consisted of French wine in which coca leaves had been steeped for six months. Vin Mariani was popular in Europe and the United States, thanks to its high cocaine content and the marketing prowess of its creator, a Corsican named Angelo Mariani. The letters of endorsement for his drink from celebrities and heads of state, including three popes, two American presidents, Queen Victoria, and the inventor Thomas Edison, were published as a book in thirteen volumes. Pemberton copied the coca-infused wine formula and added kola extract too. The nuts of the kola plant from West Africa were another supposed wonder-cure that had become known in the West at around the same time as coca, and also had an invigorating effect when chewed, since they contain about 2 percent caffeine. As with coca leaves in South America, kola nuts were valued as a stimulant by indigenous peoples in West Africa, from Senegal in the north to Angola in the south. They were used in religious ceremonies by the Yoruba people in Nigeria; the people of Sierra Leone wrongly believed that kola nuts cured malaria. In nineteenth-century America, coca and kola often ended up being lumped together in patent medicines due to the similarity of their effects.

Just as he copied and slightly modified Mariani's formula for the drink, Pemberton also borrowed from Mariani's advertisements, claiming several celebrity endorsements as testimonials for his own drink. Sales of his French Wine Coca began to grow. But just when it seemed that Pemberton was on the right track, Atlanta and Fulton County voted to prohibit the sale of alcohol from July 1, 1886, for a two-year trial period. With the temperance movement gaining

A Coca-Cola logo on an early bottlecap

ground, Pemberton needed to produce a successful nonalcoholic remedy, and fast. He went back to his elaborate home laboratory and started work on a "temperance drink" containing coca and kola, with the bitterness of the two principal ingredients masked using sugar. This would be no ordinary patent medicine, though; he intended it to be dispensed as a medicinal soda-water flavoring. As he refined his formula, Pemberton sent batches of it to the neighborhood pharmacy, where it was offered to customers alongside the other flavorings. On occasion he would ask his nephew to loiter in the pharmacy to hear what other people had to say about the new drink's taste.

By May 1886 Pemberton was happy with the formula; now it needed a name. One of his business associates, a man named Frank Robinson, made the obvious suggestion: Coca-Cola. The name was derived directly from the two main ingredients;

Robinson later recalled that he thought "the two Cs would look well in advertising." This original version of Coca-Cola contained a small amount of coca extract and therefore a trace of cocaine. (It was eliminated early in the twentieth century, though other extracts derived from coca leaves remain part of the drink to this day.) Its creation was not the accidental concoction of an amateur experimenting in his garden, but the deliberate and painstaking culmination of months of work by an experienced maker of quack remedies.

Having invented Coca-Cola, Pemberton stood back to let Robinson, his associate, handle the manufacturing and marketing. The first advertisement for the new drink, which appeared in the *Atlanta Journal* on May 29, 1886, was short and to the point: "Coca-Cola. Delicious! Refreshing! Exhilarating! Invigorating! The new and popular soda fountain drink containing the properties of the wonderful Coca plant and the famous Cola nut." The new drink had been launched just in time for Atlanta's experiment with Prohibition. It was nonalcoholic, and it appealed as both a soda-water flavoring and a patent medicine. This was reflected in the wording of Pemberton's label, attached to the flasks of syrup supplied to pharmacists, which declared: "This Intellectual Beverage and Temperance Drink contains the valuable Tonic and Nerve Stimulant properties of the Coca plant and Cola (or Kola) nuts, and makes not only a delicious, exhilarating, refreshing and invigorating Beverage (dispensed from the soda water fountain or in other carbonated beverages), but a valuable Brain Tonic, and a cure for all nervous affections—Sick Head-Ache, Neuralgia, Hysteria,

Melancholy, etc. The peculiar flavor of Coca-Cola delights every palate."

Robinson promoted the drink in a number of ways. He sent out tickets that entitled their holders to free samples of Coca-Cola, in the hope that they would acquire a taste for it and come back for more as paying customers. He put up posters in streetcars and banners at soda fountains that read "Drink Coca-Cola, 5c." Robinson also developed the distinctive Coca-Cola logo, in cursive script, which first appeared in a newspaper advertisement on June 16, 1887. Sales of the Coca-Cola syrup to pharmacists were running at around two hundred gallons a month at the height of the summer soda-fountain season, equivalent to about twenty-five thousand drinks. By the time Atlanta voted to discontinue its experiment with Prohibition in November 1887, Coca-Cola had established itself.

Despite the new drink's promising start, Pemberton's business associates were unhappy. For several months there was much bickering over who owned the rights to the Coca-Cola name and formula. Shares in the Pemberton Chemical Company, the entity that formally owned the rights to his patent medicines, were sold and resold, so that it was unclear who owned what. To further complicate matters, Pemberton had sold two-thirds of his Coca-Cola rights to two businessmen in July 1887, apparently because he was unwell and wanted to raise some money quickly. (He was, by this time, dying of stomach cancer.) This transaction took place behind Robinson's back; when he found out about it, he insisted that he was still entitled to use the Coca-Cola formula too. Pemberton then set up a new company that also claimed ownership over the rights. The businessmen to whom he had previously sold out became disillusioned and sold their rights to another party.

The whole mess was finally sorted out by Asa Candler, another Atlanta-based maker of patent medicines and the brother of Robinson's lawyer. He heard about the fuss surrounding the new drink, teamed up with Robinson, and then began buying out the various other parties. Nevertheless, during the summer of 1888 the ownership of Coca-Cola was still so confused that Atlanta druggists were being offered three rival versions of it: one by Candler and Robinson's new company, another by Pemberton's new company, and a third by Pemberton's rebellious son Charley.

Ultimately, it was John Pemberton's death from cancer, on August 16, 1888, that enabled Candler to consolidate his control over Coca-Cola. Candler called the city's druggists together and delivered a moving and entirely insincere speech. Pemberton was not just one of Atlanta's foremost druggists, he declared, but a good man and close friend; he suggested that the druggists ought to close their shops on the day of Pemberton's funeral as a mark of respect. With this speech, and by acting as a pallbearer at the funeral, Candler succeeded in convincing everyone that he had Pemberton's best interests at heart, and that his version of Coca-Cola was, as it were, the real thing. Pretending that Pemberton had been a close friend was an outright lie. Yet in a way it became true retrospectively. For it is only thanks to Candler that Pemberton is remembered today at all. Without Asa Candler's efforts, Coca-Cola would never have become the success that it did.

Caffeine for All

When he first secured the rights to Coca-Cola, for a mere $2,300, Asa Candler regarded it as merely one of his many patent medicines. But as sales continued to grow—they quadrupled in 1890, to reach 8,855 gallons—Candler decided to abandon his other remedies, none of which was anything like as popular. Coca-Cola was even selling during the winter, outside the usual soda-fountain season. So Candler hired traveling salesmen to sell Coca-Cola to pharmacists in neighboring states, gave away more free tickets to lure new customers, and pumped money into advertising. By the end of 1895 annual sales exceeded 76,000 gallons, and Coca-Cola was being sold in every state in America. The company's newsletter boasted that "Coca-Cola has become a National drink."

This rapid growth was possible because the Coca-Cola Company only sold syrup; it did not sell the finished product of syrup mixed with soda water. Candler was strongly opposed to the idea of selling Coca-Cola in bottles, since he was worried that the drink's taste might suffer during storage. Expanding into a new city or state, then, simply meant striking deals with local pharmacists and then shipping the syrup and its associated advertising materials: banners, calendars, and other items that featured the company's red-and-white logo. Since Atlanta was a major hub on the nation's railway network, distribution was not a problem. And pharmacists liked the drink because it was profitable: Each five-cent Coca-Cola they sold only required one cent's worth of syrup, and most of the rest was pure profit.

The Coca-Cola Company, in turn, could make the syrup for around three-quarters of a cent per drink, so it made a profit on every drink sold too.

Downplaying Coca-Cola's supposed medical attributes, a sudden shift in strategy, also helped to boost sales. Until 1895 it was still being sold as a primarily medicinal product—described as a "Sovereign Remedy for Headache" and so on. But selling Coca-Cola as a remedy risked limiting the market to those who identified with the symptoms it was supposed to cure. Selling it simply as a refreshing drink, in contrast, gave it universal appeal; not everyone is ill, but everyone is thirsty at one time or another. So out went the gloomy advertisements listing ailments and maladies, and in came a cheerier, more direct approach: "Drink Coca-Cola. Delicious and Refreshing." Where previous advertisements had aimed Coca-Cola at harried, overworked businessmen looking for a headache cure or tonic, the new advertisements recommended the drink to women and children. This change of emphasis was, it turned out, fortuitously timed. In 1898 a tax was imposed on patent medicines, a category which was initially deemed to include Coca-Cola. The company fought the decision and ultimately won exemption from the tax, but it could only do so because it had repositioned Coca-Cola as a drink rather than a drug.

Sales were also driven, ironically, by the introduction of bottled Coca-Cola. Candler had always been opposed to the idea, but in July 1899 he granted two businessmen, Benjamin Thomas and Joseph Whitehead, the right to bottle and sell Coca-Cola. At the time Candler thought this was an unimportant deal, and did not even make the two men pay for the bottling rights; instead,

Coca-Cola's distinctive
glass bottle, introduced
in 1916

he simply agreed to sell them the syrup, just as he sold it to
soda-fountain owners. If bottling took off, he would sell more
syrup; if it failed, as he expected, he would not lose anything. In
fact, bottling proved enormously successful. Bottled Coca-Cola
opened up entirely new markets, because it could now be sold
anywhere—at grocery stores and at sporting events, for example—not just at soda fountains. Thomas and Whitehead soon
realized that rather than doing the bottling themselves, it made
much more sense to sell subsidiary bottling rights to others, in
return for a large cut of the profits. In so doing, they created a
lucrative franchise business and made Coca-Cola available in
every town and village in the United States. The characteristic

Coca-Cola bottle, with its distinctive shape, was introduced by the company in 1916.

Bottled Coca-Cola took off just as public concern was growing over the dangers of patent medicines, and harmful additives and adulterants in food. Leading the charge was Harvey Washington Wiley, a government scientist, who was particularly concerned about the danger posed by quack remedies to children. His years of campaigning were rewarded in 1906 with the passage of the Pure Food and Drug Act, generally known as "Dr. Wiley's Law." At first it seemed that the new rules would benefit Coca-Cola, which proudly advertised that it was "Guaranteed under the Pure Food and Drugs Act," by doing away with some of its more dubious rivals. But the following year Wiley announced his intention to investigate Coca-Cola on the grounds that it contained caffeine. His complaint was that, unlike tea and coffee, Coca-Cola, which was now available across America, was drunk by children. Parents were, he argued, generally unaware of the presence of caffeine and did not realize that their children were taking a drug.

Just as Kha'ir Beg had put coffee on trial in Mecca in 1511, Wiley put Coca-Cola on trial in 1911, in a federal case titled *The United States v. Forty Barrels and Twenty Kegs of Coca-Cola*. In court, religious fundamentalists railed against the evils of Coca-Cola, blaming its caffeine content for promoting sexual transgressions; government scientists expounded on the effects of Coca-Cola on rabbits and frogs; and expert witnesses put forward by the Coca-Cola Company spoke up in the drink's favor. The month-long trial made for great theater, with accusations of jury rigging and sensationalist coverage: "Eight

Coca-Colas Contain Enough Caffeine to Kill," screamed one headline, entirely incorrectly. The problem with Wiley's case was that it was founded on moral rather than scientific objections. Nobody disputed that there was caffeine in Coca-Cola; the question was whether it was harmful, and to children in particular. The scientific evidence suggested that it was not. Besides, Wiley was not trying to ban tea or coffee.

So in the end the case came down to the narrow question of whether the Coca-Cola Company misrepresented its product, and whether it could claim that the drink was indeed "pure." Ultimately, the court found in Coca-Cola's favor: Its name accurately reflected the presence of kola, which contains caffeine. And since caffeine had always been part of the formula for Coca-Cola, it did not count as an additive—so the drink was indeed "pure." That said, this second part of the ruling was subsequently overturned on appeal, and an out-of-court settlement was agreed in which the amount of caffeine in Coca-Cola was reduced by half. The company also promised not to depict children in its advertisements, a policy it maintained until 1986. But the important thing was that the sale to children of Coca-Cola, a caffeinated drink, was now legally sanctioned. Together with the popularity of the bottled drink, this meant that Coca-Cola had successfully extended the use of caffeine, the world's most popular drug, into realms where coffee and tea had been unable to reach.

The Coca-Cola Company found other ways of selling its product to children without depicting them directly in advertisements. By far the most famous examples are the jolly posters depicting Santa Claus drinking Coca-Cola that first appeared in 1931. It is widely but wrongly believed that through these posters, the Coca-Cola Company was responsible for creating the modern image of Santa Claus as a bearded man in a white-trimmed red suit, choosing the colors to match its own red-and-white logo. In fact, the idea of a red-suited Santa was already firmly established. The *New York Times* reported on November 27, 1927 that "a standardized Santa Claus appears to New York children. . . . Height, weight, stature are almost exactly standardized, as are the red garments, the hood and the white whiskers. . . . The pack full of toys, ruddy cheeks and nose, bushy eyebrows and a jolly, paunchy effect are also inevitable parts of the requisite make-up." Putting Santa in its advertisements, however, enabled the company to appeal directly to children, and to associate its drink with fun and merriment.

The Sublimated Essence of America

The 1930s brought three challenges to the might of Coca-Cola: the end of Prohibition; the Great Depression that followed the Wall Street stockmarket crash of 1929; and the rise of a vigorous competitor, PepsiCo, with its rival drink, Pepsi-Cola. The resumption of legal sales of alcoholic drinks, which had been banned since 1920, was expected to have a particularly devastating effect on the sales of Coca-Cola. "Who would drink 'soft stuff' when real beer and 'he-man's whiskey' could be obtained legally?" asked one press report. "Why, the case was an open and shut one: The Coca-Cola Co. was on the skids." In fact, the repeal of Prohibition had very little effect on sales; Coca-Cola, it seemed, met a different need from alcoholic drinks. Indeed, the range of circumstances in which it was consumed continued to expand.

For some people, Coca-Cola took the place of coffee as a social drink. Unlike alcoholic drinks, it was deemed suitable for consumption at all times of day—even at breakfast—and, of course, by people of all ages. During Prohibition, the company's brilliant publicist, Archie Lee, carefully pushed the consumption of Coca-Cola at soda fountains as a cheery and family-friendly replacement for drinking beer or other forms of alcohol in a bar, and a way to escape the gloomy reality of the economic climate. Lee also pioneered the new technology of radio to sell Coca-Cola, and the prominent placement of the drink in numerous movies— another way of associating it with glamour and escapism. Coca-Cola's advertisements depicted an appealingly happy, carefree world. As a result, Coca-Cola prospered during the Depression.

"Regardless of depression, weather, and intense competition, Coca-Cola continues in ever-increasing demand," noted an investment analyst at the time. Here was a hot-weather drink that still sold in the winter, a nonalcoholic drink that could hold its own against alcoholic beverages, a drink that made caffeine consumption universal, and an affordable treat that maintained its appeal even in an economic downturn. As Harrison Jones, a company executive, put it in a rousing speech that marked the finale of the company's fiftieth anniversary celebrations in 1936, "the Four Horsemen of the Apocalypse may charge over the earth and back again—and Coca-Cola will remain!"

Some of these factors also helped Coca-Cola's rival, Pepsi-Cola. Its origins went back to 1894, but after going through two bankruptcies it only became a serious competitor to Coca-

Cola in the 1930s, in the hands of a New York businessman named Charles Guth, who owned a chain of confectionery stores and soda fountains. Rather than buy Coca-Cola for his stores, he took over the ailing Pepsi-Cola company and offered its drink instead. Sales took off when he started to offer twelve-ounce bottles at the same price (five cents) that Coca-Cola charged for a six-ounce bottle. The larger drink cost very little more to make, since most of the cost was in bottling and distribution, and it had great appeal to cash-strapped consumers. A huge legal battle ensued as the Coca-Cola Company accused its rival of trademark infringement. The case dragged on for years, doing neither company any good, and prompting an out-of-court settlement in 1942. Coca-Cola agreed to stop contesting Pepsi-Cola's trademark, and Pepsi adopted a red, white, and blue logo that clearly distinguished it from Coca-Cola. Another outcome was that the word *cola* became a generic term for brown, carbonated, caffeinated soft drinks. Ultimately, the two firms benefited from each other's existence: The existence of a rival kept Coca-Cola on its toes, and Pepsi-Cola's selling proposition, that it offered twice as much for the same price, was only possible because Coca-Cola had established the market in the first place. The rivalry was a classic example of how vigorous competition can benefit consumers and increase demand.

By the end of the 1930s Coca-Cola was stronger than ever. Unquestionably a national institution, accounting for nearly half of all sparkling soft-drink sales in the United States, Coca-Cola was a mass-produced, mass-marketed product, consumed by rich and poor alike. In 1938 the veteran journalist William Allen White, a famous and respected social commentator, declared it to be "a sublimated essence of all that America stands for, a decent thing honestly made, universally distributed, conscientiously improved with the years." Coca-Cola had taken over the United States; now it was ready to take over the world, going wherever American influence extended.

12

Globalization in a Bottle

A billion hours ago, human life appeared on earth.
A billion minutes ago, Christianity emerged.
A billion seconds ago, the Beatles changed music.
A billion Coca-Colas ago was yesterday morning.
—*Robert Goizueta, chief executive of the Coca-Cola Company,*
April 1997

The American Century

THE TWENTIETH CENTURY was a period defined by the struggle for individual political, economic, and personal liberty against various forms of oppression, and marked by war, genocide, and the threat of nuclear annihilation. But it ended with a remarkable degree of consensus that people are happiest when granted freedom of choice in the political, economic, and personal spheres, in the form of democracy, consumerism, and the rejection of many long-standing forms of discrimination. The idea that a mere drink could come to embody these values seems absurd. And yet that is what happened during the second half of the twentieth century.

The nation that most strongly identified itself with the struggle for individual freedom was the United States, and its values have come to be inextricably associated with its national drink, Coca-Cola.

Although it was being sold in several countries outside the United States by the time of the outbreak of World War II, Coca-Cola only became a truly global brand in the wake of America's emergence as a global superpower, with the abandonment of its longtime policy of isolationism. Throughout the nineteenth century, the country had followed the line advocated by George Washington, who declared in his farewell address in 1796, "It is our true policy to steer clear of permanent alliances with any portion of the foreign world." America's intervention in World War I, which helped to tip the balance of the European conflict against the Germans and Austrians, was an exception to this rule but was seen by many Americans as a mistake. These isolationists argued during the 1930s that their country should stay out of any future European conflicts. But Japan's attack on Pearl Harbor in December 1941 brought the United States into World War II and put an end to its isolationism for good. America sent its armed forces out into the world, more than sixteen million servicemen in all, and Coca-Cola went along with them.

As the country mobilized, Robert Woodruff, president of the Coca-Cola Company, issued an order that "every man in uniform gets a bottle of Coca-Cola for five cents, wherever he is, and whatever it costs the company." The drink was already popular among soldiers and was supplied to them on exercises as a refreshing, nonintoxicating beverage. The company's well-publicized efforts to maintain the supply would, of course, have the valuable benefit of linking Coca-Cola to patriotism and support for the war effort. But it was also genuinely welcomed by the servicemen in far-flung military bases: Coca-Cola reminded them of home and helped to maintain morale.

"We sincerely hope that your Company will be able to continue supplying us during this emergency," one officer wrote to the company. "In our opinion, Coca-Cola could be classified as one of the essential morale-building products for the boys in the Service." Using dozens of similar letters as evidence, and after much lobbying in Washington with the army's explicit support, the company was even exempted from sugar rationing in 1942 on the grounds that its product was essential to the war effort. This ensured that Coca-Cola production could continue, even as rationing forced makers of rival soft drinks to reduce production by as much as half.

Shipping bottles of Coca-Cola halfway around the world to wherever troops were stationed was very inefficient, however, not least because it tied up valuable shipping capacity. So special bottling plants and soda fountains were established where possible inside military bases, which meant that only the Coca-Cola syrup had to be shipped. To many military personnel, the Coca-Cola employees who installed and ran this machinery were no less important than the mechanics who kept planes and tanks running. They were granted favored status as "technical observers" and given military ranks, so that they became known as "Coca-Cola colonels." During the war they established no fewer than sixty-four military bottling plants around the world and served around ten billion drinks. The technical observers devised a portable Coca-Cola dispenser for use in the jungle, and a slim-line dispenser that could fit through the hatch of a submarine. Coca-Cola was also made available to civilians near American bases overseas, many of whom developed a taste for the drink too. People around the world, from Polynesians to Zulus, tasted Coca-Cola for the first time.

Hundreds of letters, now preserved in the Coca-Cola archives, show how closely American servicemen identified the drink with their country and what it stood for. "To my mind, I am in this damn mess as much to help keep the custom of drinking Cokes as I am to help preserve the million other benefits our country blesses its citizens with. . . . May we all toast victory soon with a Coke," wrote one soldier. "If anyone were to ask us what we were fighting for," another soldier wrote in a letter home, "we think half of us would answer, the right to buy Coca-Cola again." Even when the drink was available in far-flung theaters of war, it was so highly prized that bottles were hoarded for special occasions or sold for vastly inflated prices. One bottle sold for five dollars in the Solomon Islands, another for ten dollars in Casablanca, and in Alaska, a bottle fetched forty dollars. Robert Scott, a pilot in the Pacific theater, was given a bottle after shooting down his fifth Japanese aircraft and becoming an "ace." But he considered it too valuable to drink and instead gave it to a surgeon who had operated on him after he sustained an injury.

The military enthusiasm for Coca-Cola was not limited to the lower ranks but went right to the top: Generals Douglas MacArthur, Omar Bradley, and George Patton also liked to drink it. The greatest enthusiast was General Dwight D. Eisenhower,

You work better
refreshed

A World War II–era Coca-Cola advertisement

supreme commander of Allied forces in Europe. In June 1943, while overseeing the Allied campaign in North Africa, he sent a detailed telegram requesting "three million bottled Coca-Cola (filled) and complete equipment for bottling, washing, capping same quantity twice monthly. Preference as to equipment is 10 separate machines for installation in different localities, each complete for bottling twenty thousand bottles per day. Also sufficient syrup and caps for 6 million refills." The production lines were running in North Africa within six months, and the next year Coca-Cola followed as Allied troops advanced into western Europe after the Normandy landings on D-Day. *Coca-Cola* was even the password used by American troops during the battle to cross the Rhine.

The Coca-Cola Company missed no opportunity to emphasize the totemic nature of the drink to America's distant servicemen. One advertisement from 1942, as fighting raged in North Africa, depicted a khaki-clad soldier encountering a sign for Coca-Cola in an otherwise inhospitable desert, above the slogan, "Howdy, friend." Another advertisement showed sailors drinking Coca-Cola on board ship. The caption beneath boasted that "wherever a U.S. battleship may be, the American way of life goes along. . . . So, naturally, Coca-Cola is there, too." It sounds like an exaggeration, but it was not.

Conversely, the Axis powers, Germany and Japan, denounced Coca-Cola as an example of everything that was wrong with the United States—despite the fact that Coca-Cola had been sold in both countries before the war and had been particularly popular in Germany. Overlooking this inconvenient fact, Nazi propagandists sneered that "America never contributed anything to world civilization except chewing gum and Coca-Cola," while their Japanese counterparts declared, "With Coca-Cola we imported the germs of the disease of American society."

After the eventual Allied victory in 1945, the military bottling operations stayed in place for three years during the ensuing period of reconstruction. Production then reverted to the civilian realm. But by this time, with the exception of Antarctica, Coca-Cola had established itself on every continent on Earth, carried on the coattails of the American military. As a company official observed, the war ensured "the almost universal acceptance of the goodness of Coca-Cola."

Cold War, Cola War

Perhaps the most unlikely convert to Coca-Cola was General Georgy Konstantinovich Zhukov, the Soviet Union's greatest military leader, who successfully defended Russia from German attack and later led his forces into Berlin to end the war in Europe. Zhukov was one of the few people who dared to disagree with Joseph Stalin, the brutal Soviet leader, who could not do away with Zhukov because of his popularity and heroic stature. During postwar negotiations over the division of Germany, Zhukov was introduced to Coca-Cola by Eisenhower and took a strong liking to the drink. But he was reluctant to be seen enjoying something so closely identified with American values, particularly as the rivalry between the two superpowers intensified. So Zhukov made an unusual request: Was it possible to make Coca-Cola without coloring, so that it resembled vodka, the traditional Russian drink? His request was passed to the Coca-Cola Company, which duly obliged and, with the endorsement of President Harry Truman, devised a colorless version. It was shipped to Zhukov in special cylindrical bottles, sealed with a white cap and labeled with a red Soviet star.

In 1948 the postwar euphoria that had attended the founding of the United Nations had evaporated, and the Soviet Union directly challenged the United States by blockading West Berlin, a tiny western toehold on the Soviet side of a now-divided Europe. The Western powers responded by airlifting supplies into West Berlin around the clock for over a year until the Soviets lifted the blockade. With the establishment in 1949 of the North Atlantic Treaty Organization (NATO), an alliance between the United States and its European allies, and the setting up of the rival Warsaw Treaty Organization by the Soviet Union, the stage was set for the decades-long military deadlock of the Cold War. During this period, in which the two blocs competed for influence and fought proxy wars in many parts of the world but never came into direct conflict, Coca-Cola came to be associated not just with America but with the broader Western values of freedom, democracy, and free-market capitalism. Among communists, conversely, Coca-Cola came to stand for everything that was deemed wrong with capitalism, particularly the notion that satisfying consumers' often trivial demands should be the organizing principle of the economy. As a placard at the Coca-Cola Company's 1948 convention put it, "When we think of Communists, we think of the Iron Curtain. But when they think of democracy, they think of Coca-Cola."

The Coca-Cola Company rapidly expanded its overseas operations during the late 1940s, so that by 1950 a third of its profits came from outside the United States. This coincided with America's growing political influence as the leading capitalist nation in the worldwide struggle against communism, and with the American-funded initiative to reconstruct Europe, the Marshall Plan. For those who objected to America's growing clout, and who regarded the Marshall Plan as imperialism by other means, Coca-Cola provided an obvious target for their anger. The term *Coca-Colonization* was first used by communist sympathizers in France, who mounted a vigorous campaign against the establishment of new bottling plants in their country. It would, they suggested, harm the domestic wine and mineral-water industries; they even tried to have Coca-Cola outlawed on the grounds that it was poisonous. This caused an outcry in America, where newspaper editorials called for the end of Marshall Plan aid to the ungrateful French. Company officials pointed out that the drink had not adversely affected the health of the American soldiers who had liberated France. The French papers responded in kind: *Le Monde* warned that "the moral landscape of France is at stake." Coca-Cola trucks were overturned by French protesters, and bottles smashed. Ultimately, however, the French campaign against Coca-Cola made little difference. Indeed, it generated huge amounts of free publicity and gave the drink an exotic, illicit cachet.

Similar campaigns were waged in other countries. Communist activists suggested that Coca-Cola had adverse health effects and that its spread would pollute European countries with American cultural values. They were often supported by brewers, bottlers of mineral water, and makers of soft drinks, who were delighted by the anti-Coca-Cola hysteria the communists were stirring up. Austrian communists claimed that their country's Coca-Cola bottling plant could be converted into an atom-bomb factory at a moment's notice. Italian communists claimed that the drink turned children's hair white overnight. The Coca-Cola Company quietly plodded on, refusing to rise to the bait, and setting up new overseas bottling franchises in the belief that direct experience of its drink would convince consumers of its merits. Robert Woodruff, the Coca-Cola Company's boss, neatly explained communist antagonism toward Coca-Cola by observing that the drink was "the essence of capitalism." But as the drink became more popular, the ridiculous claims about it—that it made drinkers impotent or led to cancer or infertility—slowly subsided.

In 1959 American vice president Richard Nixon visited Moscow, where he traded insults with the Soviet premier, Nikita Khrushchev, at a special trade fair showing off American products. In a public-relations coup for PepsiCo, Nixon and Khrushchev stopped at the Pepsi stand and were photographed drinking Pepsi together. But in 1965, when the Coca-Cola Company began to look into setting up operations in Russia, behind the Iron Curtain, where a vast potential market awaited, there was an immediate backlash. Since private companies were not allowed in communist states, the Soviet government itself would be the company's partner, and any profits would flow into the state coffers. With the Vietnam War raging, critics argued that Coca-Cola would, in effect, be helping to subsidize America's communist foes. So the company swiftly abandoned its plans.

U.S. vice president Richard Nixon and Soviet premier Nikita Khrushchev at the Pepsi stand at the U.S. Trade and Cultural Fair in Moscow in 1959

This left the way clear for Pepsi. Having been defeated in the race for the California governorship in 1962, Nixon joined Pepsi's law firm and became Pepsi's ambassador overseas. Since it was not tainted by anticommunist propaganda, Pepsi was better able to expand behind the Iron Curtain. It established operations in Romania in 1965 and with Nixon's help began selling its drink in Russia, where it was granted an exclusive license in 1972. It looked as though Coca-Cola had a foot in the door in 1980, with an agreement that it would be the official soft drink of the Olympics, to be held that year in Moscow. But President Jimmy Carter then announced an American boycott of the games in response to the Soviet Union's invasion of Afghanistan, so Coca-Cola was rebuffed once again.

Ultimately, however, Coca-Cola's failure to establish itself in the Soviet-bloc countries proved to be an advantage. The Berlin Wall fell in 1989, presaging the collapse of communist regimes across eastern Europe and the dissolution of the Soviet Union in 1991. As East Germans streamed through the cracks in the Berlin Wall, they were greeted with Coca-Cola. "We found ourselves welcoming the new arrivals with bananas, Coca-Cola, flowers, and anything else that smacked of Western consumerism," recalled one eyewitness. East Germans queued up to buy the drink by crate directly from the Coca-Cola bottling plant in West Berlin. Along with hi-fi equipment, televisions, refrigerators, and other consumer products, crates of Coca-Cola were among the consumer items most eagerly sought out by East Berliners. Pepsi's greater success behind the Iron Curtain counted against it as the communists were ousted. It was regarded by many drinkers as a local brand associated with the old regimes, whereas Coca-Cola was seen as exotic and foreign. Drinking Coca-Cola became a symbol of freedom. By the mid-1990s, Coca-Cola had overtaken Pepsi as the most popular cola in the former Soviet-bloc countries.

Coca-Cola in the Middle East

Coca-Cola's close association with American values counted against it in another part of the world: the Middle East. The problems started in 1966, when an Israeli businessman accused the Coca-Cola Company of staying out of the Israeli soft-drink market in order to protect its business in the much larger Arab market. The Arab world, with its ban on alcoholic drinks and its hot climate, was certainly a promising market for Coca-Cola; its annual profits in the region amounted to some twenty million dollars. The company argued that its attempts to open a bottling plant in Israel in 1949 had been blocked by the Israeli government; it also claimed that the Israeli market was too small to be economically viable. But if that was the case, asked its critics, why was it doing business in Cyprus, an even smaller market? Accusations of anti-Semitism mounted, and Jewish organizations in the United States, including Mount Sinai Hospital in Manhattan and Nathan's Famous Hot Dog Emporium on Coney Island, began to boycott Coca-Cola.

The company responded by announcing that it would license an Israeli bottling franchise in Tel Aviv. This, in turn, provoked the Arab League to call on its members to boycott Coca-Cola. The company refused to back down, and the Arab boycott came into force in August 1968. The company's decision was entirely pragmatic: It gave up the Arab market in order to avoid a domestic boycott by the Jewish community, which would have cost it far more. The result was that Coca-Cola once again found itself aligned with and identified with American foreign policy. Pepsi, meanwhile, took advantage of the opportunity to move into Arab markets while staying out of Israel, even though this cost it some customers in the United States, who considered its actions anti-Semitic.

Not until the late 1980s, when the Arab boycott of Coca-Cola finally crumbled, did Coca-Cola begin making inroads into Arab markets, notably in Egypt, Lebanon, and Jordan. But the real prize was Saudi Arabia, which had become Pepsi's third-largest foreign market after Canada and Mexico. During the Gulf War of 1991, Coca-Cola sent in refrigerated trucks to supply American troops stationed in Saudi Arabia, but could not compete with Pepsi, which had five factories in the country. Television viewers around the world saw General Norman Schwarzkopf, the American commander of the coalition that had evicted Iraqi forces from Kuwait, signing the cease-fire with a can of Pepsi by his side. Coca-Cola responded with a big push into the Saudi market, in order to put Pepsi on the defensive and weaken its ability to compete in other markets.

By the time of the Iraq War in 2003, the idea of expressing anti-Americanism through attacks on its soft drinks had taken several new forms. Muslim youths in Thailand poured Coca-Cola onto the ground in protest at the American-led invasion, and sales were suspended amid growing anti-American protests. Meanwhile, locally made colas started to become popular in the Middle East. Zam Zam Cola, an "Islamic" cola made in Iran by a company that used to be Pepsi's partner in the country, became popular in Iraq, Qatar, Bahrain, and Saudi Arabia, where it sold four million cans in its first week on sale. Star Cola, made in the West Bank, became popular in the United Arab Emirates. The equation of Coca-Cola with the United States persisted for both critics and supporters. When American troops occupied Saddam Hussein's palace in Baghdad in April 2003, they held a barbecue at which they consumed hamburgers, hot dogs, and, inevitably, Coca-Cola.

Globalization by the Bottle

As well as being associated with America, Coca-Cola also encapsulates the trend toward a single global marketplace: in a word, globalization. Believers in globalization argue that abolishing trade barriers, tariffs, and other obstacles to free and unfettered international commerce is the best way to improve the fortunes of rich and poor countries alike. By setting up factories in the developing world, for example, companies from rich countries can reduce their costs, while also creating jobs and boosting the economy in the poorer countries where they set up shop. Opponents of globalization complain that such practices are exploitative, since they create low-wage, low-status jobs; multinational companies are also able to exploit looser labor and environmental regulations by shifting jobs overseas. The debate rages on. But an oft-heard complaint, as companies spread their tentacles around the world and compete on a global playing field, is that globalization is merely a new form of imperialism. Antiglobalization activists argue that the world's only superpower, the United

States, is intent on invading the rest of world not with soldiers and bombs but with its culture, companies, and brands, chief among them Microsoft, McDonald's, and Coca-Cola.

Certainly no single product is more representative of globalization than Coca-Cola. The global fight with Pepsi continues around the world; the big new battleground is China. But that is just one of the more than two hundred territories where the Coca-Cola Company operates—more than the United Nations has members. Its drink is now the world's most widely known product, and "Coca-Cola" is said to be the second most commonly understood phrase in the world, after "OK." No other company can match it for global reach, visibility, or recognition. Coca-Cola consistently tops the list of the world's most valuable brands, published each year in *Business Week* magazine.

Yet even the most powerful brand in the world cannot brainwash people into buying something they do not want, despite antiglobalists' claims to the contrary. New Coke, a sweeter, more Pepsi-like drink that was introduced by the Coca-Cola Company in 1985, was a disaster. Consumers shunned the new drink, and sales plummeted, forcing the company to reintroduce the original drink as Coca-Cola Classic within weeks and sealing the fate of its attempt to meddle with an American icon.

Coca-Cola also shows how strong global brands can work in consumers' interests, not against them. Around the world, the Coca-Cola name and logo are the company's guarantee of consistent quality. With a brand worth an estimated seventy billion dollars, the company has a huge incentive to maintain its reputation and the quality of its products, or risk losing its customers. The desire to protect its global brand makes the Coca-Cola Company, like other large companies, extremely wary of bad publicity and far more accountable than it would otherwise be. Firms with national brands do not have to worry what people in other countries think about them, but firms with global brands do.

An analysis by *The Economist* magazine in 1997 found that consumption of Coca-Cola in different countries—a good proxy for those countries' degree of globalization—correlated closely with greater wealth, quality of life (measured using a scale devised by the United Nations), and social and political freedom. "Fizzy mass-market stuff—ie, capitalism—is good for you," the magazine concluded. It is not Coca-Cola that makes people wealthier, happier, or freer, of course, but as consumerism and democracy spread, the fizzy brown drink is never far behind.

Today, carbonated soft drinks are the most widely consumed beverages in the United States, accounting for around 30 percent of all liquid consumption, and the Coca-Cola Company is the biggest single supplier of such drinks. Globally, the company supplies 3 percent of humanity's total liquid intake. Coca-Cola is unquestionably the drink of the twentieth century, and all that goes with it: the rise of the United States, the triumph of capitalism over communism, and the advance of globalization. Whether you approve of that mixture or not, you cannot deny the breadth of its appeal.

Epilogue

Back to the Source

Water is a limited natural resource and a public good fundamental for life and health. The human right to water is indispensable for leading a healthy life in human dignity. It is a prerequisite for the realization of other human rights.—*the United Nations Committee on Economic, Cultural, and Social Rights, 2002*

S IX BEVERAGES HAVE defined humankind's past, but which will embody its future? One drink has already emerged as the most likely candidate. Like many of the defining drinks of history, it is highly fashionable, is the subject of conflicting medical claims, and has unseen but far-reaching geopolitical significance. Its availability will determine the path of humankind's future, on Earth and potentially beyond. Ironically, it is also the drink that first steered the course of human development: water. The history of drinking has come right back to its source.

On the face of it, this might appear to be a welcome occurrence. Much of the appeal of other beverages, starting with beer in the Neolithic period, was that they were less likely than water to be contaminated. Only when the microbiological basis of water contamination began to be unraveled in the nineteenth century did it become feasible to tackle a problem that had bedeviled humans for centuries: maintaining an adequate supply of freshwater. Where previous generations turned to other drinks as substitutes, it is now possible to address the problem of contamination directly, through water purification and other improvements in sanitation. Water's growing popularity, in other words, suggests that the danger of contamination is finally receding. But the reality is rather more complicated. Indeed, nowhere is the gulf between the developed and developing worlds more apparent than in their attitudes toward water.

Sales of bottled water are booming, with the highest levels of consumption in the developed world, where tap water is abundant and safe to drink. Italians are the world's most enthusiastic consumers of bottled water, drinking an average of 180 liters per year each; they are closely followed by the French, Belgians, Germans, and Spanish. The global bottled-water industry had revenues of around forty-six billion dollars in 2003, and consumption of bottled water is growing by 11 percent a year, faster than for any other drink. Restaurants serve expensive water in designer bottles, and the habit of carrying a small plastic bottle of drinking water at all times, pioneered by supermodels, has become widespread. Stop at a filling station in the United States, and you will find that bottled water, ounce for ounce, costs more than gasoline. Mineral waters from specific sources, from France to Fiji, are shipped to consumers around the world.

The popularity of bottled water stems from the widespread belief that it is healthier and safer than tap water. But tap water, in developed nations at least, is just as safe. While there are occasional contamination scares, they affect bottled water too. In one study, published in the *Archives of Family Medicine*, researchers compared bottled water with tap water from Cleveland, Ohio, and found that a quarter of the samples of bottled water had significantly higher levels of bacteria. The scientists concluded that "use of bottled water on the assumption of purity can be misguided." Another study carried out at the University of Geneva came to the same conclusion, as did a report from the United Nations Food and Agriculture Organization, which found that bottled water was no better from a nutritional point of view than ordinary tap water.

That is hardly surprising, since as much as 40 percent of the bottled water sold in the United States is, in fact, derived from tap water, though it is usually filtered and may have extra minerals added. America's two leading bottled-water brands, Aquafina and Dasani, are derived from municipal water supplies. And although many bottled-water labels depict glaciers, crystal streams, and ice-covered mountains, these images do not always reflect the true origins of the water within. A study by the National Resources Defense Council, an American environmental lobby group, found that one brand of bottled water, labeled as "pure glacier water," came from a municipal water supply. Another brand, claiming to be "spring water," with a label showing a lake and mountains, actually came from a well in a factory parking lot, near a hazardous waste dump. The study also noted that in both Europe and the United States, the quality of tap water is far more stringently controlled than the quality of bottled water.

There is no evidence that bottled water is any safer or healthier than the tap water available in developed nations, and in blind tasting tests, most people cannot tell the difference between the two. The differences in taste between bottled waters exceed the difference in taste between bottled water and tap water. Yet people continue to buy bottled water, even though it costs between 250 and 10,000 times as much per gallon as tap water. In short, safe water has become so abundant in the developed world that people can afford to shun the tap water under their noses and drink bottled water instead. Since both kinds are safe, the sort of water one drinks has become a lifestyle choice.

In contrast, for many people in the developing world, access to water remains a matter of life or death. A fifth of the world's population, or around 1.2 billion people, currently lack reliable access to safe drinking water. The World Health Organization estimates that 80 percent of all illness in the world is due to waterborne diseases, and that at any given time, around half of the people in the developing world are suffering from diseases associated with inadequate water or sanitation, such as diarrhea, hookworm, or trachoma. There are about four billion cases of diarrhea a year, resulting in 1.8 million deaths, 90 percent of them among children under five. Illness and death are not the only consequences of the lack of access to water; it also hinders education and economic development. Widespread illness makes countries less productive, more dependent on outside aid, and less able to lift themselves out of poverty. According to the United Nations, one of the main reasons girls do not go to school in sub-Saharan Africa is that they have to spend so much time fetching water from distant wells and carrying it home.

The United Nations has set a goal of reducing by half the proportion of people without access to freshwater and adequate sanitation by 2015. But although good progress was made during the 1980s and 1990s, the rate at which people are being connected to safe water supplies has since declined. One problem is that while access to water is still improving in rural areas, its availability in cities has declined in many parts of the developing world. This decline is worrisome, given the unstoppable trend toward urbanization. By around 2007, demographers estimate, more than half of the world's population will for the first time be living in cities; humankind will have completed the six-thousand-year transition from being a predominantly rural to a predominantly urban species. According to figures from the International Water Management Institute, it would cost an extra $1.7 billion a year beyond what is already being spent to achieve the United Nations' desired improvement in access to water, while improving sanitation would cost a further $9 billion or so a year—a small fraction of the amount spent on bottled water in rich nations. But there is more to solving the problem of access to water than money. In many cases there are political obstacles too. In recent years disputes over water rights, particularly in the Middle East and Africa, have caused political tension and even military conflict.

Water was, for example, an important unseen factor behind the Six Day War of 1967, when Israel occupied Sinai, the Golan Heights, the West Bank, and Gaza. Ariel Sharon, who was a general at the time and later became Israel's prime minister, noted in his autobiography that although people usually regard June 5,

1967, as the start of the Six Day War, "in reality, it started two and a half years earlier, on the day Israel decided to act against the diversion of the Jordan." In 1964 Syria had started building a canal to divert two of the main tributaries of the Jordan River away from Israel. Using a combination of artillery and air strikes, Israel brought work on the canal to a halt. "While the border disputes between Syria and ourselves were of great significance, the matter of water diversion was a stark issue of life and death," wrote Sharon. Israel values the territories it occupied in 1967, which granted it control of the Jordan's headwaters, as much for their water supply as for any military advantage. The Palestinians who live in the West Bank are allotted just 18 percent of the territory's water; the rest goes to Israel.

Ever since, politicians in the Middle East have cited water as a possible cause of future conflict in the region. In 1978 Egypt threatened military action against Ethiopia if it interfered with the flow of the Nile, Egypt's chief water supply. When Egypt signed a peace treaty with Israel in 1979, its president, Anwar Sadat, declared that "the only matter that could take Egypt to war again is water." And in 1985 Boutros Boutros-Ghali, then the Egyptian foreign minister and later the secretary-general of the United Nations, predicted that "the next war in the Middle East will be fought over water, not politics."

It is hardly surprising that water should be such a contentious topic; rivers and lakes mark international boundaries, and at least ten rivers flow across half a dozen or more borders, so that one country's actions affect other countries downstream. Ethiopia controls 85 percent of the waters of the Nile, upstream of Egypt; Turkey's dam on the Euphrates lets it control the flow into Syria.

Flooding has prompted Bangladesh to demand that India and Nepal build dams upstream to control the flow of the Ganges and Brahmaputra rivers.

In the arid region of central Asia, there are fears that growing water scarcity might spark conflict between the former Soviet republics of Kazakhstan, Kyrgyzstan, Tajikistan, Turkmenistan, and Uzbekistan. Another concern is that climate change will alter the distribution of water, leading to flooding in some areas and droughts in others, affecting agricultural production, and causing political instability. Many observers have, therefore, suggested that water might replace oil as the scarce commodity most likely to trigger international conflict.

Yet water can also promote international cooperation. Access to water is so fundamental that its management has often forced otherwise hostile states to work together. The Indus Basin Treaty of 1960, which dictates how India and Pakistan should share the water of the Indus and its tributaries, has remained in force despite repeated military clashes between the two nations. Similarly, Cambodia, Laos, Thailand, and Vietnam have cooperated over the management of the Mekong, even though the region through which it flows has been racked by war. And in the late 1990s the ten squabbling countries of the Nile Basin signed a cooperative water-management agreement backed by the United Nations and the World Bank. Water, it seems, has the potential to be both a cause of war and a catalyst for peace.

In the longer term, and assuming that humanity manages to avoid nuclear self-immolation, the establishment of colonies on other worlds, starting with Mars, will also depend on the availability of adequate water. The inhabitants of a Mars colony will need water to drink and wash, to grow crops, and to convert into rocket fuel, which can be made by splitting water into its component elements, hydrogen and oxygen. This, together with the search for extraterrestrial life (which is also assumed to depend on water), explains why so much effort is being put into locating and understanding the distribution of water on other bodies in the solar system. Some scientists even believe that colonizing Mars is necessary to ensure the continued survival of humanity. Only by becoming a "multiplanetary species," they argue, can we truly guard against the possibility of being wiped out by war, disease, or a mass extinction caused by an asteroid or comet crashing into the Earth. But that will depend on finding supplies of water on other worlds.

Water was the first drink to steer the course of human history; now, after ten thousand years, it seems to be back in the driving seat. To talk of colonizing other planets seems outlandish, but the idea is surely easier for us to understand than the modern world would be for a person transported through time from a Neolithic village from 5000 BCE. He would not recognize any modern language and would no doubt have difficulty comprehending aspects of modern life such as writing, plastics, airliners, and computers. But while much has changed in the intervening millennia, some things have remained the same. He would surely appreciate a glass of beer and would recognize the communal toast for good luck and the ensuing companionable atmosphere.

For our Neolithic time traveler, a drink of beer might provide a connection with the future; for us, beer is one of the beverages that can provide a window on the past. When you next raise some beer, wine, spirits, coffee, tea, or Coca-Cola to your lips, think about how it reached you across space and time, and remember that it contains more than mere alcohol or caffeine. There is history, too, amid its swirling depths.

Acknowledgments

The research for this book involved a fair amount of drinking, and it would be disingenuous to pretend that this was anything but enjoyable. For their help with my research into beer, I would like to thank Fritz Maytag at the Anchor Brewery in San Francisco, Mary Voigt at the College of William and Mary in Williamsburg, Stephan Somogyi and Iolande Bloxsom, Michael Jackson, Clint Ballinger, and Merryn Dineley. In the case of wine, I am grateful to Patrick McGovern at the University of Pennsylvania Museum and Hervé Durand and his family at the Mas des Tourelles winery in Beaucaire, France. Lance Winters at the St. George Distillery in Alameda explained the process of distillation and provided many practical examples. For assistance with the history of coffee, I am grateful to Jeremy Torz of Union Coffee Roasters and Peter Hingley at the Royal Astronomical Society. Endymion Wilkinson of Harvard University provided invaluable advice on the history of tea.

Other people helped by providing inspiration, acting as sounding boards, or pointing me in unexpected directions during my research, including George Dyson, Neal Stephenson, my

Acknowledgments

colleagues Ann Wroe, Robert Guest, Anthony Gottlieb, and Geoffrey Carr at *The Economist*, Philippe Legrain, Paul Abrahams, Phil Millo, Vasa Babic, and Henry Hobhouse. Help of various kinds was also furnished by Virginia Benz and Joe Anderer, Cristiana Marti, Oliver Morton and Nancy Hynes, Tom Moultrie and Kathryn Stinson, Daniel Illsley and Jonathan Warren at Theatre of Wine in Greenwich, Carolyn Bosworth-Davies, Roger Highfield, Maureen Stapleton and Tim Coulter, Ward van Damme, Annika McKee, and Lee McKee. George Gibson and Jackie Johnson of Walker & Company were unfailingly supportive throughout, as was Katinka Matson of Brockman, Inc. Finally, I am particularly grateful to my wife, Kirstin, and daughter, Ella, for their encouragement while I wrote this book.

Appendix

In Search of Ancient Drinks

Are you interested in tasting one of these ancient drinks? Many of them survive, in one form or another. But be warned that you may not find some of them very palatable.

Near Eastern Beer

The most important difference between ancient and modern beers is the use of hops, which is a relatively modern innovation. Hops add a refreshing bitterness to the taste of beer to balance the sweetness of the malt, and also act a preservative, making beer less liable to spoil. But from the perspective of ancient brewers, they are inauthentic. Hops became a standard ingredient of beer between the twelfth and fifteenth centuries, and initially different words were used to distinguish between hopped and unhopped drinks: in English, *beer* referred to a drink that contained hops, while *ale* was unhopped. Subsequently, *ale* came to refer to top-fermented beers, as opposed to bottom-fermented lagers, where the yeast sinks to the bottom of the barrel. I have simply used the generic term *beer* throughout this book to refer to beverages made from fermented cereal grains.

Appendix

Traditional folk beers, which survive in many parts of sub-Saharan Africa, are probably the nearest thing to Neolithic beer. They are thick, opaque drinks usually made from a mixture of sorghum and either millet or maize. A typical recipe involves soaking the sorghum in water until it starts to sprout, and then spreading it out to dry in the sun, with frequent turning to ensure it dries thoroughly and does not start to rot. Meanwhile the other, unmalted grain is put into hot water to make a thin gruel. The gruel is left overnight or until it turns sour. The malted sorghum, which has been roughly ground with a stone, is then added to the gruel, which is left to stand in a large pot until it becomes sparkling and alcoholic. Finally, the drink is filtered through a sack or sieve before drinking. (In South Africa I drank some *umqomboti*, a traditional Xhosa beverage made from a mixture of malted and unmalted sorghum. Thick, creamy, and off-white, it had a sour tang, reminiscent of yogurt. It was rather like drinking liquid bread.)

The Egyptians and Mesopotamians drank beer that was more like modern beer: It was clear or cloudy rather than opaque, since the wort—the sugary mixture created by cooking the grains in water—was strained before fermentation. During the late 1980s and early 1990s Fritz Maytag, at the Anchor Brewery in San Francisco, painstakingly recreated Mesopotamian beer using an ancient recipe dating from around 1800 BCE, the Hymn to Ninkasi. (Ninkasi was the Mesopotamian goddess of brewing.) Maytag and his team even prepared *bappir*, the traditional "beer bread" made from malted barley to enable it to be stored for long periods. When I sampled a fifteen-year-old piece of *bappir*, it tasted quite good, though it contained a lot of chaff. Those who drank the resulting beer said it tasted sweet by modern standards, due to the lack of hops.

There have also been several attempts to recreate Egyptian beer, notably the Tutankhamen Ale produced by the Scottish and Newcastle

Appendix

Breweries based on research by Delwen Samuel of Cambridge University. Her electron-microscope analysis of brewing residues led her to conclude that Egyptian beer was made from a mixture of malted barley and unmalted emmer (a kind of wheat), which makes sense since malting is a labor-intensive process. The barley was malted and ground and then mixed with cold water to liberate enzymes, and the emmer was ground and mixed with hot water to liberate starches. When the two were mixed, the enzymes broke down the starches into sugar. The wort was then sieved to remove the chaff before fermentation; depictions of this step have been wrongly interpreted, says Samuel, as loaves of bread being crumbled into the vat. Following this recipe produced a fruity, sweet beer that was golden in color and slightly cloudy. The one thousand bottles produced were sold at Harrods.

It is hard to find anything similar to Egyptian or Mesopotamian beer today since very few unhopped beers are made commercially. A rare exception is the King Cnut Ale made by St. Peter's, a British brewery, based on a recipe from the first millennium CE and named for King Canute, the eleventh-century ruler of Denmark, Norway, and England. It is made with barley, juniper, orange and lemon peel, spices, and nettles. It resembles beer, but without the bitterness of the hops it tastes sweet and fruity—and, in fact, rather like wine. Drink this beer, and you will understand why Nabonidus, the last king of the Neo-Babylonian Empire, referred to wine as "the excellent 'beer' of the mountains." Another example of an unhopped beer that is still made today is Sahti, a Finnish folk beer. Michael Jackson, a beer expert, calls it "the last primitive beer to survive in Europe." Traditionally a seasonal beer, it is available all year round at Zetor, a pub in the center of Helsinki, where it is kept in plastic kegs in a fridge. It has a bouquet of stewed chicory and the tang of a wheat beer but, of course, no hops. Instead, as with King Cnut Ale, juniper berries are used to balance the taste of the grain.

Appendix

Greek and Roman Wine

The finest ancient wines, as people of the time noted, were those that did not require adulteration or additives to conceal their faults. So they would probably have tasted similar to modern wines (though, of course, the Greeks and Romans almost always drank their wine diluted with water). Overall, though, the practice of adding things to wine, at every stage from fermentation to serving, was far more widespread. Most wine was probably of far lower quality than even the cheapest modern wine, due to the far lower standards of hygiene and the difficulty of storing wine for long periods. As a result, wines were usually blended and flavored to produce a more palatable or consistent product. Very few of these practices remain in modern wine making; a notable exception is the use of pine resin in the Greek wine, retsina. The use of resin as a flavoring and preservative has ancient origins and was not restricted to Greece in ancient times. It may have arisen from the use of resin to coat the insides of amphorae, to prevent wine from seeping out. Retsina mixed with water, then, gives a fair approximation of one style of ancient wine.

Other styles, however, involved the addition of herbs, honey, or even seawater at various stages of production. Several Roman wines have been recreated, using recipes, techniques, and equipment from the period, by Hervé Durand and his family at the Mas des Tourelles winery in the south of France, on the site of a Roman vineyard. One wine, called Mulsum, is a red wine that contains herbs and honey; it is sweet, but not overly so, with spicy notes. Diluted with water, it tastes rather like Ribena. Another wine, Turriculae, is based on a recipe recorded by the Roman writer Columella. It is a white wine made with a small quantity of seawater and herbs, chiefly fenugreek. It is straw-colored and tastes remarkably like a dry, nutty sherry; the saltiness of the seawater is well integrated and not too conspicuous, so that it tastes like a natural part of the wine, rather than an additive. The third of Durand's Roman wines, Carenum, is a dessert wine made from red wine mixed with *defrutum* (a boiled-down, spiced wine used as a cooking ingredient by the Romans) and herbs. The addition of *defrutum* raises the alcohol content and the sweetness; the result tastes quite similar to a late-harvest Zinfandel. All of these wines can be purchased at the winery.

Several winemakers produce wine using grape varieties that supposedly date back to Greek and Roman times. Particularly noteworthy is the Mastroberardino winery near Naples, which makes wines from the Greco di Tufo, Fiano di Avellino, and Aglianico grapes. The first is a white grape thought to have been introduced to Italy by the Greeks, the second is another white grape favored by the Romans, who called it Vitis Apiana, or "the vine beloved by bees," and the third is a red grape that is used in Mastroberardino's flagship wine, Taurasi. Such is the Mastroberardino family's devotion to ancient grapes that they were recently asked to replant the vineyards of Pompeii. Yet they are equally devoted to modern wine-making technologies, such as refrigerated stainless-steel tanks and rotary fermenters. This ensures that Mastroberardino wines are clean, vivid, and powerful, but also completely inauthentic; they include no herbs or seawater, for example.

To serve a modern wine in the Greek or Roman manner, the main thing to remember is to dilute it with water. Do so, and you will notice something surprising, namely, how well a wine's bouquet and taste survive dilution. André Tchernia, an expert on ancient wine, tells the story of meeting at a conference in Saint Emilion an eminent winemaker whose mother had always drunk her wine mixed with water—but who could still distinguish between different vintages. Even though the Greeks and Romans diluted their wines, in short, this did not impair their ability to recognize and appreciate various styles and vintages.

Appendix

Spirits from the Colonial Era

The process of making distilled drinks has not changed significantly since colonial times, and some distilleries dating back to that period are still operating today, making brandy, rum, and whiskey. Spirits appealed less for their taste than for their power to intoxicate, which is why they were often consumed in cocktail-like mixtures such as punch or grog, the forerunners of modern cocktails. It is a simple matter to recreate grog by mixing dark rum, water, and brown sugar with some lemon or lime juice, though modern drinkers may then wish to move swiftly on to a *mojito*, grog's more palatable descendant.

Coffee from the Seventeenth Century

The traditional Arab method for preparing coffee involves bringing a mixture of ground coffee beans and water to the boil three times in quick succession. This agitates the coffee grounds and extracts a lot of flavor, resulting in a strong, black drink. When coffee was brought to Europe, however, its preparation was rather more haphazard. In England, coffee was initially taxed liked a form of beer, namely by the gallon, which meant that London coffeehouses had to prepare their coffee in advance in order to pay duty on it. The cold coffee was then reheated for consumption. To ensure a ready supply, a pot was kept near the boil, which would have resulted in a strong, bitter drink best taken with sugar. Perhaps the nearest modern equivalent, suggests Jeremy Torz, a London-based coffee expert, is the coffee in an office percolator that has been left switched on for a day or two. He notes that seventeenth-century coffee would have been quite lightly roasted in a pan or tray; deeper, darker roasts had to await the development of elaborate roasting machines. Being transported in a damp ship, possibly alongside powerful spices, might also have affected the coffee's taste. All of this suggests that there would have been wide variations in the taste of coffee between one coffeehouse and another, and from one week to the next. The presence of caffeine, and the surroundings in which the coffee was served, would appear to have been more important than its taste. (The coffee filter was a twentieth-century invention.)

Old English Tea

The first tea to be brought to Europe in the seventeenth century was green tea made from unoxidized leaves, which was consumed without milk or sugar. Green tea from China can be readily purchased today and probably tastes very similar. Black tea became popular in the eighteenth century, partly because it was less likely to contain toxic adulterants, but its greater bitterness promoted the addition of sugar. This tea was made from semioxidized leaves and was known at the time as bohea; this style of tea became known as oolong in the 1850s, by which time even stronger teas, made from fully oxidized leaves, were also becoming popular (and which may also, confusingly, be called oolongs). So a light, semioxidized oolong gives an impression of eighteenth-century tea, but one that is inaccurate in two respects: It is not adulterated with other ingredients or blended with other teas. The nearest equivalent to the dubious blends of the eighteenth century is probably low-cost teabags. Many tea blends and styles survive unchanged from the nineteenth century, such as Earl Grey (flavored with bergamot) and English Breakfast Tea.

Cola from the Nineteenth Century

Today's Coca-Cola is still made using the original secret recipe, but that recipe has been tweaked a few times, notably to reduce the level of caffeine and replace the original trace of cocaine with flavorings extracted from coca leaves. For a cola with an entirely legal extra kick, try Jolt Cola, which contains more caffeine than Coca-Cola and was favored by programmers during the dot-com boom. Several firms also make speciality colas using old-fashioned recipes. I am partial to Fentiman's Curiosity Cola, an old-style cola that contains extracts of guarana berries and catuaba bark, both natural stimulants, as well as caffeine.

Notes

1. A Stone-Age Brew

The account of the adoption of cereal grains and the emergence of agriculture in the Near East follows Roaf, *Cultural Atlas of Mesopotamia and the Ancient Near East*; Bober, *Art, Culture and Cuisine*; and Diamond, *Guns, Germs and Steel*. The discussion of the probable origins of beer follows Katz and Voigt, "Bread and Beer"; Kavanagh, "Archaeological Parameters for the Beginnings of Beer"; Katz and Maytag, "Brewing an Ancient Beer"; Forbes, *Studies in Ancient Technology*; Hartman and Oppenheim, "On Beer and Brewing Techniques in Ancient Mesopotamia"; Ballinger, "Beer Production in the Ancient Near East"; and Braidwood et al., "Did Man Once Live by Beer Alone?" The social importance of beer, and its possible role in the emergence of complex societies, are discussed in Katz and Voigt, "Bread and Beer"; Sherratt, "Alcohol and Its Alternatives"; Schivelbusch, *Tastes of Paradise*; and Joffe, "Alcohol and Social Complexity in Ancient Western Asia."

2. Civilized Beer

The origins of the first cities in Mesopotamia and Egypt are discussed in Trigger, *Understanding Early Civilizations*; Hawkes, *The First Great*

Civilizations; Leick, *Mesopotamia*; and Kramer, *History Begins at Sumer*. The account of the use and significance of beer within Mesopotamian and Egyptian civilizations follows Darby, Ghalioungui, and Grivetti, *Food: Gift of Osiris*; Heath, *Drinking Occasions*; Michalowski, "The Drinking Gods"; Samuel, "Brewing and Baking"; Bober, *Art, Culture and Cuisine*; and Ellison, "Diet in Mesopotamia." The account of the origins of writing follows Schmandt-Besserat, *Before Writing*.

3. The Delight of Wine

The rise of wine at the expense of beer is covered by McGovern, Fleming, and Katz, eds., *The Origins and Ancient History of Wine*; Sherratt, "Alcohol and Its Alternatives"; McGovern, *Ancient Wine*; and Younger, *Gods, Men and Wine*. For Greek attitudes toward wine and drinking practices, including details of the *symposion*, see Murray, *Sympotica*; Dalby, *Siren Feasts*; and Unwin, *Wine and the Vine*. For Greek wine styles, see Younger, *Gods, Men and Wine*.

4. The Imperial Vine

For the displacement of Greek wine by Roman wine, see Fleming, *Vinum*; Unwin, *Wine and the Vine*; and Dalby, *Siren Feasts*. Roman attitudes toward wine, and the story of Marcus Antonius, are from Tchernia and Brun, *Le vin romain antique*, and Tchernia, *Le vin de l'Italie romaine*. The account of the hierarchy of Roman wines follows Fleming, *Vinum*; Allen, *A History of Wine*; and Younger, *Gods, Men and Wine*. Galenic medicine and Galen's use of wine are discussed in Porter, *The Greatest Benefit to Mankind*, and Allen, *A History of Wine*. For the rejection of wine by Muslims and its significance to Christians, see Sherratt, "Alcohol and Its Alternatives," and Unwin, *Wine and the Vine*. Alcuin's lament is quoted from Younger, *Gods, Men and Wine*.

For the ancient origins of European drinking customs, see Engs, "Do Traditional Western European Practices Have Origins in Antiquity?"

5. High Spirits, High Seas

For the Arab origins of distillation, see al-Hassan and Hill, *Islamic Technology*; Forbes, *A Short History of the Art of Distillation*; Lichine, *New Encyclopedia of Wines and Spirits*; and Kiple and Ornelas, eds., *The Cambridge World History of Food*. The story of Charles the Bad is taken from Froissart, *Chronicles of England, France, Spain and the Adjoining Countries*. The account of the spread of distilled drinks into western Europe follows Forbes, *A Short History of the Art of Distillation*; Lichine, *New Encyclopedia of Wines and Spirits*; Braudel, *Civilization and Capitalism*; and Roueché, "Alcohol in Human Culture." For the origins of the Atlantic slave trade and its relationship to sugar cultivation, see Mintz, *Sweetness and Power*; Thomas, *The Slave Trade*; Hobhouse, *Seeds of Change*; and Landes, *The Wealth and Poverty of Nations*. The role of spirits in the slave trade is discussed in Thomas, *The Slave Trade*; Mintz, *Sweetness and Power*; Harms, *The Diligent*; and Smith, "Spirits and Spirituality." The account of the origins of rum follows Ligon, *A True and Exact History of the Island of Barbadoes*; Lichine, *New Encyclopedia of Wines and Spirits*; Mintz, *Sweetness and Power*; and Kiple and Ornelas, eds., *The Cambridge World History of Food*. The significance of rum's adoption by the Royal Navy is discussed in Pack, *Nelson's Blood*, and Watt, "The Influence of Nutrition upon Achievement in Maritime History."

6. The Drinks That Built America

The mistaken belief that Virginia would have a Mediterranean climate is discussed in James, *The Rise and Fall of the British Empire*.

Notes

The account of the difficulties faced by American colonists in making beer and wine, and the adoption of rum instead, follows Unwin, *Wine and the Vine*; Baron, *Brewed in America*; and Brown, *Early American Beverages*. The role of molasses and rum in the American Revolution is discussed in Mintz, *Sweetness and Power*; Tannahill, *Food in History*; and Thompson, *Rum Punch and Revolution*. The significance of whiskey in the early United States and the Whiskey Rebellion are covered in Carson, *The Social History of Bourbon*, and Barr, *Drink*. For the use of spirits to subdue indigenous peoples, see Braudel, *Civilization and Capitalism*.

7. The Great Soberer

The sobering effect of coffee on European drinkers is discussed by Schivelbusch, *Tastes of Paradise*. For the Arab origins of coffee and coffeehouse culture and the debate over coffee's effects, see Hattox, *Coffee and Coffeehouses*; Schapira, Schapira, and Schapira, *The Book of Coffee and Tea*; and Weinberg and Bealer, *The World of Caffeine*. The account of coffee's spread into Europe and the rise of London's coffeehouses follows Ellis, *The Penny Universities*, and Jacob, *Coffee*. For the cultivation of coffee in European colonies, see Ukers, *All About Coffee*, and Weinberg and Bealer, *The World of Caffeine*.

8. The Coffeehouse Internet

For the Internet-like role of coffeehouses, see Sommerville, "Surfing the Coffeehouse," and Darnton, "An Early Information Society." For the use of coffeehouses by scientists and financiers, see Stewart, "Other Centres of Calculation"; Stewart, *The Rise of Public Science*; Ellis, *The Penny Universities*; Inwood, *The Man Who Knew Too Much*; Jacob,

Coffee; and Waller, *1700*. For coffeehouses in prerevolutionary Paris, see Darnton, "An Early Information Society"; Kors, ed., *The Encyclopedia of the Enlightenment*; and Weinberg and Bealer, *The World of Caffeine*.

9. Empires of Tea

The not-so-ancient adoption of tea in China is discussed in Wilkinson, *Chinese History*. The account of the history of tea in China follows Wilkinson, *Chinese History*; MacFarlane and MacFarlane, *Green Gold*; Lu Yu, *The Classic of Tea*; and Weinberg and Bealer, *The World of Caffeine*. Early European trade with China, and the first imports of tea into Europe, are covered in Landes, *The Wealth and Poverty of Nations*; Hobhouse, *Seeds of Change*; and Moxham, *Tea*. The account of the English embrace of tea follows Hobhouse, *Seeds of Change*; Ukers, *All About Tea*; Weinberg and Bealer, *The World of Caffeine*; Pettigrew, *A Social History of Tea*; and Forrest, *Tea for the British*.

10. Tea Power

The Industrial Revolution, and tea's helping hand in it, are discussed in Landes, *The Wealth and Poverty of Nations*, and MacFarlane and MacFarlane, *Green Gold*. For tea's influence on British foreign policy in America and China, see Scott, *The Tea Story*; Forrest, *Tea for the British*; Ukers, *All About Tea*; Bowen, "400 Years of the East India Company"; Ferguson, *Empire*; Hobhouse, *Seeds of Change*; Farrington, *Trading Places*; and Wild, *The East India Company*. The account of the introduction of tea into India follows MacFarlane and MacFarlane, *Green Gold*, and Moxham, *Tea*.

11. From Soda to Cola

For the origins of soda water, see Riley, *A History of the American Soft Drink Industry*; Gribbin, *Science*; and Hays, *Pop*. The account of the origins and history of Coca-Cola follows Weinberg and Bealer, *The World of Caffeine*; and Pendergrast, *For God, Country and Coca-Cola*, which is the definitive work on the subject.

12. Globalization in a Bottle

Coca-Cola's march to global dominance during the twentieth century is described in Pendergrast, *For God, Country and Coca-Cola*; Hays, *Pop*; Kahn, *The Big Drink*; Tedlow, *New and Improved*; and news reports from UPI, Reuters, and *The Economist*.

Sources

Allen, H. Warner. *A History of Wine*. London: Faber, 1961.

———. *Rum*. London: Faber, 1931.

Andrews, Tamra. *Nectar and Ambrosia: An Encyclopedia of Food in World Mythology*. Santa Barbara: ABC-CLIO, 2000.

Austin, Gregory. *Alcohol in Western Society from Antiquity to 1800: A Chronology*. Santa Barbara: ABC-CLIO, 1985.

Ballinger, Clint. "Beer Production in the Ancient Near East." Unpublished paper, personal communication.

Baron, Stanley. *Brewed in America: A History of Beer and Ale in the United States*. Boston: Little, Brown, 1962.

Barr, Andrew. *Drink: A Social History of America*. New York: Carroll & Graf, 1999.

Blackburn, Robin. *The Making of New World Slavery*. London: Verso, 1997.

Bober, Phyllis Pray. *Art, Culture and Cuisine: Ancient and Medieval Gastronomy*. Chicago: University of Chicago Press, 1999.

Bowen, Huw V. "400 Years of the East India Company." *History Today*, July 2000.

Braidwood, Robert, et al. "Did Man Once Live by Beer Alone?" *American Anthropologist* 55 (1953): 515–26.

Sources

Braudel, Fernand. *Civilization and Capitalism: 15th–18th Century*. London: Collins, 1981.

Brillat-Savarin, Jean Anthelme. *The Physiology of Taste*. London: Peter Davies, 1925.

Brown, John Hull. *Early American Beverages*. New York: Bonanza Books, 1966.

"Burger-Cola Treat at Saddam Palace." Reuters report, April 25, 2003.

Carson, Gerald. *The Social History of Bourbon*. New York: Dodd, Mead, 1963.

Cohen, Mark Nathan. *Health and the Rise of Civilization*. New Haven and London: Yale University Press, 1989.

Counihan, Carole, and Penny Van Esterik, eds. *Food and Culture: A Reader*. New York and London: Routledge, 1997.

Courtwright, David T. *Forces of Habit: Drugs and the Making of the Modern World*. Cambridge, Mass.: Harvard University Press, 2001.

Dalby, Andrew. *Siren Feasts: A History of Food and Gastronomy in Greece*. London: Routledge, 1996.

Darby, William J., Paul Ghalioungui, and Louis Grivetti. *Food: Gift of Osiris*. London, New York, and San Francisco: Academic Press, 1977.

Darnton, Robert. "An Early Information Society: News and Media in Eighteenth-Century Paris." *American Historical Review* 105, no.1 (February 2000): 1–35.

Diamond, Jared. *Guns, Germs and Steel*. London: Jonathan Cape, 1997.

Dunkling, Leslie. *The Guinness Drinking Companion*. Middlesex: Guinness, 1982.

Ellis, Aytoun. *The Penny Universities: A History of the Coffee-houses*. London: Secker & Warburg, 1956.

Ellison, Rosemary. "Diet in Mesopotamia: The Evidence of the Barley Ration Texts (c. 3000–1400 BC)." *Iraq* 43 (1981): 35–45.

Sources

Engs, Ruth C. "Do Traditional Western European Practices Have Origins in Antiquity?" *Addiction Research* 2, no. 3 (1995): 227–39.

Farrington, Anthony. *Trading Places: The East India Company and Asia, 1600–1834*. London: British Library, 2002.

Ferguson, Niall. *Empire: How Britain Made the Modern World*. London: Allen Lane, 2003.

Fernandez-Armesto, Felipe. *Food: A History*. London: Macmillan, 2001.

Fleming, Stuart J. *Vinum: The Story of Roman Wine*. Glenn Mills, Penn.: Art Flair, 2001.

Forbes, R. J. *A Short History of the Art of Distillation*. Leiden: E. J. Brill, 1970.

———. *Studies in Ancient Technology*. Vol. 3. Leiden: E. J. Brill, 1955.

Forrest, Denys. *Tea for the British: The Social and Economic History of a Famous Trade*. London: Chatto & Windus, 1973.

Froissart, Sir John de. *Chronicles of England, France, Spain and the Adjoining Countries*. Translated by Thomas Johnes. New York: Colonial Press, 1901.

Gaiter, Mary K., and W. A. Speck. *Colonial America*. Basingstoke, England: Palgrave, 2002.

Gleick, James. *Isaac Newton*. London: Fourth Estate, 2003.

Gribbin, John. *Science: A History, 1543–2001*. London: Allen Lane, 2001.

Harms, Robert. *The Diligent: A Voyage through the Worlds of the Slave Trade*. Reading, Mass.: Perseus Press, 2002.

Hartman, Louis F., and A. L. Oppenheim. "On Beer and Brewing Techniques in Ancient Mesopotamia." Supplement to *Journal of the American Oriental Society* 10 (December 1950).

Hassan, Ahmad Y. al-, and Donald R. Hill. *Islamic Technology: An Illustrated History*. Cambridge: Cambridge University Press, 1986.

Sources

Hattox, Ralph S. *Coffee and Coffeehouses: The Origins of a Social Beverage in the Medieval Near East*. Seattle: University of Washington Press, 1985.

Hawkes, Jacquetta. *The First Great Civilizations: Life in Mesopotamia, the Indus Valley and Egypt*. London: Hutchinson, 1973.

Hays, Constance. *Pop: Truth and Power at the Coca-Cola Company*. London: Hutchison, 2004.

Heath, Dwight B. *Drinking Occasions: Comparative Perspectives on Alcohol and Culture*. Philadelphia : Brunner/Mazel, 2000.

Hobhouse, Henry. *Seeds of Change: Six Plants That Transformed Mankind*. New York: Harper & Row, 1986.

Inwood, Stephen. *The Man Who Knew Too Much: The Strange and Inventive Life of Robert Hooke, 1635–1703*. London: Macmillan, 2002.

Jacob, Heinrich Eduard. *Coffee: The Epic of a Commodity*. New York: Viking Press, 1935.

James, Lawrence. *The Rise and Fall of the British Empire*. London: Little, Brown, 1998.

Joffe, Alexander. "Alcohol and Social Complexity in Ancient Western Asia." *Current Anthropology*, 39, pt. 3 (1998): 297–322.

Kahn, E. J. *The Big Drink*. New York: Random House, 1960.

Katz, Solomon, and Fritz Maytag. "Brewing an Ancient Beer." *Archaeology* 44, no. 4 (July–August 1991): 24–33.

Katz, Solomon, and Mary Voigt. "Bread and Beer: The Early Use of Cereals in the Human Diet." *Expedition* 28, pt. 2 (1986): 23–34.

Kavanagh, Thomas W. "Archaeological Parameters for the Beginnings of Beer." *Brewing Techniques*, September–October 1994.

Kinder, Hermann, and Werner Hilgemann. *The Penguin Atlas of World History*. London: Penguin, 1978.

Sources

Kiple, Kenneth F., and Kriemhild Coneè Ornelas, eds. *The Cambridge World History of Food*. Cambridge: Cambridge University Press, 2000.

Kors, Alan Charles, ed. *The Encyclopedia of the Enlightenment*. New York: Oxford University Press, 2003.

Kramer, Samuel Noah. *History Begins at Sumer*. London: Thames & Hudson, 1961.

Landes, David. *The Wealth and Poverty of Nations*. London: Little, Brown, 1998.

Leick, Gwendolyn. *Mesopotamia: The Invention of the City*. London: Allen Lane, 2001.

Lichine, Alexis. *New Encyclopedia of Wines and Spirits*. London: Cassell, 1982.

Ligon, Richard. *A True and Exact History of the Island of Barbadoes*. London, 1673.

Lu Yu. *The Classic of Tea*. Translated and introduced by Francis Ross Carpenter. Hopewell, New Jersey: Ecco Press, 1974.

Lucia, Salvatore Pablo, ed. *Alcohol and Civilization*. New York: McGraw Hill, 1963.

MacFarlane, Alan, and Iris MacFarlane. *Green Gold: The Empire of Tea*. London: Ebury Press, 2003.

McGovern, Patrick E. *Ancient Wine: The Search for the Origins of Viticulture*. Princeton and Oxford: Princeton University Press, 2003.

McGovern, Patrick E., Stuart J. Fleming, and Solomon H. Katz, eds. *The Origins and Ancient History of Wine*. Amsterdam: Gordon & Breach, 1996.

Michalowski, P. "The Drinking Gods." In *Drinking in Ancient Societies: History and Culture of Drinks in the Ancient Near East*, edited by Lucio Milano. Padova: Sargon, 1994.

Sources

Mintz, Sidney. *Sweetness and Power: The Place of Sugar in Modern History*. York: Viking, 1985.

Moxham, Roy. *Tea: Addiction, Exploitation and Empire*. London: Constable, 2003.

Murray, Oswyn, ed. *Sympotica: A Symposium on the Symposium*. Oxford: Clarendon Press, 1994.

"Muslims Prepare for the 'Coca-Cola War.' " UPI report, October 12, 2002.

Needham, Joseph. *Science and Civilisation in China*. Vol. 5, *Chemistry and Chemical Technology*. Cambridge: Cambridge University Press, 1999.

Needham, Joseph, and H. T. Huang. *Science and Civilisation in China*. Vol. 6, *Biology and Biological Technology*. Cambridge: Cambridge University Press, 2000.

Pack, James. *Nelson's Blood: The Story of Naval Rum*. Annapolis, Md.: Naval Institute Press, 1982.

Pendergrast, Mark. *For God, Country and Coca-Cola: The Unauthorized History of the Great American Soft Drink and the Company That Makes It*. London: Weidenfeld & Nicolson, 1993.

Pettigrew, Jane. *A Social History of Tea*. London: National Trust, 2001.

Phillips, Rod. *A Short History of Wine*. London: Allen Lane, 2000.

Porter, Roy. *Enlightenment: Britain and the Creation of the Modern World*. London: Allen Lane, 2000.

———. *The Greatest Benefit to Mankind: A Medical History of Humanity from Antiquity to the Present*. London: HarperCollins, 1997.

"A Red Line in the Sand." *The Economist*, October 1, 1994.

"Regime Change." *Economist*, October 31, 2002.

Repplier, Agnes. *To Think of Tea!* London: Cape, 1933.

Riley, John J. *A History of the American Soft Drink Industry*. Washington: American Bottlers of Carbonated Beverages, 1958.

Sources

Roaf, Michael. *Cultural Atlas of Mesopotamia and the Ancient Near East*. New York and Oxford: Facts on File, 1990.

Roueché, Berton. "Alcohol in Human Culture." In *Alcohol and Civilization,* edited by Salvatore Pablo Lucia. New York: McGraw Hill, 1963.

Ruscillo, Deborah. "When Gluttony Ruled!" *Archaeology,* November–December 2001: 20–25.

Samuel, Delwen. "Brewing and Baking." In *Ancient Egyptian Materials and Technology*, edited by Paul T. Nicholson and Ian Shaw. Cambridge: Cambridge University Press, 2000.

Schapira, Joel, David Schapira, and Karl Schapira. *The Book of Coffee and Tea*. New York: St. Martin's Griffin, 1982.

Schivelbusch, Wolfgang. *Tastes of Paradise: A Social History of Spices, Stimulants and Intoxicants*. New York: Vintage Books, 1992.

Schmandt-Besserat, Denise. *Before Writing*. Austin: University of Texas Press, 1992.

Scott, James Maurice. *The Tea Story*. London: Heinemann, 1964.

Sherratt, Andrew. "Alcohol and Its Alternatives: Symbol and Substance in Pre-industrial Cultures." In *Consuming Habits: Drugs in History and Anthropology*, edited by Jordan Goodman, Paul E. Lovejoy, and Andrew Sherratt. New York and London: Routledge, 1995.

———. *Economy and Society in Prehistoric Europe*. Edinburgh: Edinburgh University Press, 1998.

Smith, Frederick H. "Spirits and Spirituality: Alcohol in Caribbean Slave Societies." Unpublished manuscript, University of Florida, 2001.

Social and Cultural Aspects of Drinking. Oxford: Social Issues Research Centre, 2000.

Sommerville, C. John. "Surfing the Coffeehouse." *History Today* 47, no. 6 (June 1997): 8–10.

Sources

Stewart, Larry. "Other Centres of Calculation, or, Where the Royal Society Didn't Count: Commerce, Coffee-houses and Natural Philosophy in Early Modern London." *British Journal for the History of Science* 32 (1999): 133–53.

———. *The Rise of Public Science: Rhetoric, Technology and Natural Philosophy in Newtonian Britain*. Cambridge: Cambridge University Press, 1992.

Tannahill, Reay. *Food in History*. New York: Crown, 1989.

Tchernia, André. *Le vin de l'Italie romaine*. Rome: Ecole Française de Rome, 1986.

Tchernia, André, and Jean-Pierre Brun. *Le vin romain antique*. Grenoble: Glenat, 1999.

Tedlow, Robert. *New and Improved: The Story of Mass Marketing in America*. New York: Basic Books, 1990.

Thomas, Hugh. *The Slave Trade: The Story of the Atlantic Slave Trade, 1440–1870*. New York : Simon & Schuster, 1997.

Thompson, Peter. *Rum Punch and Revolution*. Philadelphia: University of Pennsylvania Press, 1999.

Toussaint-Samat, Maguelonne. *A History of Food*. Cambridge, Mass.: Blackwell, 1992.

Trager, James. *The Food Chronology*. New York: Owl Books, 1997.

Trigger, Bruce G. *Understanding Early Civilizations: A Comparative Study*. Cambridge: Cambridge University Press, 2003.

Ukers, William H. *All About Coffee*. New York: Tea and Coffee Trade Journal, 1922.

———. *All About Tea*. New York: Tea and Coffee Trade Journal, 1935.

Unwin, Tim. *Wine and the Vine: An Historical Geography of Viticulture and the Wine Trade*. London: Routledge, 1996.

Waller, Maureen. *1700: Scenes from London Life*. London: Hodder & Stoughton, 2000.

Sources

Watt, James. "The Influence of Nutrition upon Achievement in Maritime History." In *Food, Diet and Economic Change Past and Present*, edited by Catherine Geissler and Derek J. Oddy. London: Leicester University Press, 1993.

Weinberg, Alan, and Bonnie K. Bealer. *The World of Caffeine: The Science and Culture of the World's Most Popular Drug*. New York and London: Routledge, 2001.

Wells, Spencer. *The Journey of Man: A Genetic Odyssey*. London: Allen Lane, 2002.

Wild, Antony. *The East India Company: Trade and Conquest from 1600*. London: HarperCollins, 1999.

Wilkinson, Endymion. *Chinese History: A Manual*. Cambridge, Mass.: Harvard University Press, 2004.

Wilson, C. Anne, ed. *Liquid Nourishment: Potable Foods and Stimulating Drinks*. Edinburgh: Edinburgh University Press, 1993.

Younger, William. *Gods, Men and Wine*. London: Michael Joseph, 1966.

Index

Note: Page numbers in *italics* refer to illustrations.

Index

Index

Index

Index

Index

Index

Index

Index

Index

as currency, 180
earliest records of, 178–83, 185
and industry, 198–202
as medicine, 177, 178, 179, 183,
  186–87, 200–201
milk added to, 187
and opium trade, 206–12
and political power, 203–6
rituals of, 176, 178, 180–81,
  182–84, 193–95, *194*, 201
tea gardens, 194–96
Tea Act, 120, 204, 219
Temperance movement, 236–37, 238,
  239, 246–47
Theodosius I, 84
Thomas, Benjamin, 242–43
Thucydides, 52
Truman, Harry S, 256
Tufts, James, 231
Tutankhamen, King, 29, 38
Twining, Richard, 202
Twining, Thomas, 193

United States
  American century, 250
  Coca-Cola in, 5, 232–49, 251–65
  coffee in, 220
  consumerism in, 223, 224, 225
  Great Depression in, 246, 247
  independence of, 5
  industrialism in, 223–25, 232
  Prohibition in, 238, 239,
    246–47

soda water in, 228–32
as superpower, 224–25, 263–64
tea in, 219–20
*United States v. Forty Barrels and
  Twenty Kegs of Coca-Cola,*
  244–45

Vandals, 84
Vernon, Edward, 108–9
Victoria, queen of England, 236
Visigoths, 84, 85
Viticulture, 53–54, 70–71
Voltaire, François-Marie Arouet de,
  166, 168

Waller, Edmund, 190
Wallich, Nathaniel, 214–15
Washington, George, 118, 120, 125,
  125, 126–27, 229, 251
Water, 1–2, 10, 266–74
  boiling point of, 95
  bottled, 267, 269
  contaminated, 2, 21–22, 38, 59,
    135, 267–70
  irrigation systems, 31
  mineral, 227–30, 267
  on other planets, 272–73
  political rights to, 270–72
  rum diluted with, 108–9
  sparkling, 226–32
  tap, 267–69
  turned into wine, 85
  and war, 272

Index